T0351010

Kotlin

Kotlin is a free and open-source general-purpose programming language that is mostly used to create Android apps. Kotlin was developed by JetBrains initially and later picked up by Google as the language of choice for its Android platform. Over the past few years, Kotlin has become one of the most popular alternatives to Java language and is used by more than 80 percent of Android app developers.

Kotlin is a statically typed, advanced programming language that compiles Kotlin code into Java byte-code and runs on a Java Virtual Machine (JVM). It can also be compiled to native executables and JavaScript source code. It is an object-oriented programming language that includes data types, operators, I/O comments, control statements, functions, classes, object expressions, and constructors, among other features. It is not a standalone programming language; rather, is an innovative manner of coding that runs on Java.

Kotlin is a versatile language with some interesting and cool features like compatibility, low runtime, and efficient coding characteristics. The features that help distinguish Kotlin from other languages are its reliability, tool support, and interoperability. It is a simplified version of Java that is much easier to deal with.

Why Should You Learn Kotlin?

The popularity of Kotlin is growing, and it will continue to do so in the coming years. Kotlin has always been, and will continue to be, a cutting-edge programming language that best meets the needs of real professionals. Many emerging fields, including mobile, online gaming, server-side, cloud development, data science, and education, are progressively using Kotlin.

All of this indicates that there is already a high demand for Kotlin developers, and that demand will continue to grow in the future. Furthermore, if you are looking to build native Android apps, Kotlin is the language that you should be using.

Kotlin
The Ultimate Guide

Edited by
Sufyan bin Uzayr

CRC Press
Taylor & Francis Group
Boca Raton London New York

CRC Press is an imprint of the
Taylor & Francis Group, an **informa** business

First edition published 2023
by CRC Press
6000 Broken Sound Parkway NW, Suite 300, Boca Raton, FL 33487-2742

and by CRC Press
4 Park Square, Milton Park, Abingdon, Oxon, OX14 4RN

CRC Press is an imprint of Taylor & Francis Group, LLC

© 2023 Sufyan bin Uzayr

Library of Congress Cataloging-in-Publication Data

Names: Bin Uzayr, Sufyan, author.
Title: Kotlin : the ultimate guide / Sufyan bin Uzayr.
Description: First edition. | Boca Raton : CRC Press, 2023. | Includes
bibliographical references and index.
Identifiers: LCCN 2022025675 (print) | LCCN 2022025676 (ebook) | ISBN
9781032311708 (hardback) | ISBN 9781032311692 (paperback) | ISBN
9781003308447 (ebook)
Subjects: LCSH: Android (Electronic resource) | Kotlin (Computer program
language) | Application software--Development. | Mobile
apps--Development. | Java (Computer program language)
Classification: LCC QA76.73.K68 B56 2023 (print) | LCC QA76.73.K68
(ebook) | DDC 005.1/14--dc23/eng/20220917
LC record available at https://lccn.loc.gov/2022025675
LC ebook record available at https://lccn.loc.gov/2022025676

ISBN: 9781032311708 (hbk)
ISBN: 9781032311692 (pbk)
ISBN: 9781003308447 (ebk)

DOI: 10.1201/9781003308447

Typeset in Minion
by KnowledgeWorks Global Ltd.

Contents

Acknowledgments

There are many people who deserve to be on this page, for this book would not have come into existence without their support. That said, some names deserve a special mention, and I am genuinely grateful to:

- My parents, for everything they have done for me.

- My siblings, for helping with things back home.

- The Parakozm team, especially Divya Sachdeva, Jaskiran Kaur, and Vartika, for offering great amounts of help and assistance during the book-writing process.

- The CRC team, especially Sean Connelly and Danielle Zarfati, for ensuring that the book's content, layout, formatting, and everything else remain perfect throughout.

- Reviewers of this book for going through the manuscript and providing their insight and feedback.

- Typesetters, cover designers, printers, and everyone else who has helped develop this book.

- All the folks associated with Zeba Academy, either directly or indirectly, for their help and support.

- The programming community in general, and the web development community in particular, for all their hard work and efforts.

Sufyan bin Uzayr

About the Author

Sufyan bin Uzayr is a writer, coder, and entrepreneur with over a decade of experience in the industry. He has authored several books in the past, pertaining to a diverse range of topics, ranging from History to Computers/IT.

Sufyan is the Director of Parakozm, a multinational IT company specializing in EdTech solutions. He also runs Zeba Academy, an online learning and teaching vertical with a focus on STEM fields.

Sufyan specializes in a wide variety of technologies, such as JavaScript, Dart, WordPress, Drupal, Linux, and Python. He holds multiple degrees, including ones in Management, IT, Literature, and Political Science.

Sufyan is a digital nomad, dividing his time between four countries. He has lived and taught in universities and educational institutions around the globe. Sufyan takes a keen interest in technology, politics, literature, history, and sports, and in his spare time, he enjoys teaching coding and English to young students.

Learn more at sufyanism.com.

CHAPTER 1

Crash Course in Kotlin

IN THIS CHAPTER

➤ What is Kotlin?

➤ Major concepts

➤ Advantages and disadvantages

➤ Syntax and code basics

➤ Additional info

Kotlin is a basic and straightforward programming language that runs on the Java Virtual Machine (JVM). The Kotlin programming language borrows ideas from other programming languages such as Groovy, Java, Gosu, Scala, etc. Kotlin programming language is an open-source programming language that may be used everywhere Java is used; however, its syntax is not identical to that of Java programming language. Kotlin is a multi-purpose or general-purpose programming language used by developers to create Android applications. In addition to creating Android applications, the Kotlin programming language is employed in other domains such as client-server web, server-side applications, etc.

The Kotlin programming language is a high-level programming language that supports both object-oriented and functional programming styles. The Kotlin programming language supports all of the principles associated with the object-oriented programming model, such as class, inheritance, abstraction, encapsulation, and polymorphism, among others.

DOI: 10.1201/9781003308447-1

Kotlin is a statically typed programming language that provides interoperability, code safety, and clarity.

KOTLIN PROGRAMMING LANGUAGE HAS A RICH HISTORY

We're probably wondering who created the Kotlin programming language and how the language earned its name. There are some fascinating facts about the history of the Kotlin programming language. So let's go into the Kotlin programming language's history in depth.

The development of the Kotlin programming language began in 2010 and launched the project in July 2011. JetBrains, the company behind IntelliJ IDEA, invented and developed the Kotlin programming language. JetBrains established the Kotlin foundation to oversee the upkeep of the Kotlin programming language.

The former launch of the Kotlin programming language was in 2016, and the most recent version is Kotlin 1.5.0. JetBrains called Kotlin after "Kotlin Island," located near St. Petersburg.

FEATURES OF THE KOTLIN PROGRAMMING LANGUAGE

The Kotlin programming language has several qualities that make it a popular and fast programming language. So let's go through the primary features of the Kotlin programming language in depth.

1. **General aim:** Kotlin programming language is a multipurpose or general-purpose programming language, which implies that programmers may use it to create various apps and programs for Android and other operating systems. Pinterest, Uber, Corda, Gradle, Square, and other well-known apps that use the Kotlin programming language are examples.

2. **Object-oriented programming:** The Kotlin programming language supports several paradigms, including functional, imperative, and object-oriented programming. Because it supports all of the elements of the object-oriented programming method, the Kotlin programming language is considered an object-oriented programming language. And Kotlin programming language adheres to all object-oriented programming concepts such as class, inheritance, abstraction, polymorphism, and encapsulation. The characteristics of the object-oriented programming method make development and maintenance easier.

3. **Open source:** Since its inception, the Kotlin programming language has been an open-source language. It implies that anybody may get it from its official website and use and change it for free to meet the needs of their project. Kotlin is a computer language created under the Apache 2 license.

4. **Quick compilation:** Compiling code written in the Kotlin programming language takes relatively little time. Compared to other programming languages, the performance of programs created in the Kotlin programming language is better and faster.

5. **Interoperability:** The Kotlin programming language likewise supports the interoperability capability. Interoperability is the ability to utilize codes from one programming language to another or vice versa. Kotlin programming language can utilize Java programming language code, and Java programming language can use Kotlin programming language code.

6. **Simple to learn:** The Kotlin programming language is contemporary, straightforward, and simple. After learning the Java programming language, novice programmers may quickly learn the Kotlin programming language. The Kotlin programming language is simple to read and write a programming language.

7. **Platform independent:** The Kotlin programming language is a platform-independent and cross-platform programming language. The Kotlin programming language was designed primarily for the production of Android applications. However, developers may also utilize Kotlin codes on other platforms such as Windows, iOS, macOS, Linux, etc.

The following are some different characteristics of the Kotlin programming language:

- Kotlin is a programming language that is statically typed.

- The Kotlin programming language also supports the extension function.

- In the Kotlin programming language, semicolons are not necessary.

- The Kotlin programming language has a short execution time.

- Kotlin code is straightforward and simple to read.

- The Kotlin programming language supports several paradigms such as imperative, functional, etc.

- The Kotlin programming language also has null safety.

KOTLIN PROGRAMMING LANGUAGE APPLICATIONS

Kotlin is a contemporary, easy-to-learn, and powerful programming language. The Kotlin programming language is an open-source programming language, which means that anybody may download it from its official website and use or change it for free. The Kotlin programming language is a general-purpose, platform-independent programming language. The Kotlin programming language is commonly utilized in developing many Android applications. Still, it is used on other platforms such as Windows, Linux, macOS, iOS, watchOS, etc. Pinterest, Coursera, Trello, Basecamp 3, Evernote, and other well-known applications that use the Kotlin programming language are examples.

WHY SHOULD WE STUDY THE KOTLIN PROGRAMMING LANGUAGE? WHAT ARE THE BENEFITS OF LEARNING THE KOTLIN PROGRAMMING LANGUAGE?

We're probably thinking about why we should learn Kotlin programming language or the benefits of studying Kotlin programming language are. So, let's go through the primary benefits of the Kotlin programming language in depth.

- Kotlin is an introductory programming language that is easy to read, learn, and write.

- The Kotlin programming language's performance and code compilation are speedy.

- The Kotlin programming language is a general-purpose programming language.

- The Kotlin programming language is a platform-agnostic or cross-platform programming language.

- Null safety is a characteristic of Kotlin programming languages.

- The Kotlin programming language also supports extension functions.

- The Kotlin programming language also offers its users interoperability.
- Since its creation, the Kotlin programming language has been open-source.
- The Kotlin programming language is a strong and statically typed programming language.
- Code created in the Kotlin programming language is easier to maintain.

DISADVANTAGES OF KOTLIN

- **Kotlin learning opportunities are limited:** While most developers are transitioning to Kotlin, a tiny number of developers are accessible globally. It provides basic tools for learning programming languages and answering numerous queries during the software development process.

- **Compilation time is longer:** In several cases, Kotlin outperforms Java, particularly during incremental constructions. Keep in mind that when it comes to tidy building, Java will always create growth.

- **Distinct from Java:** While Kotlin and Java have certain similarities, they also differ significantly. Mobile app developers who have spent a considerable amount of time learning Kotlin cannot switch to another programming language.

- **Fewer Kotlin professionals to recruit:** Despite Kotlin's importance, only a few programmers are now accessible in this industry. Any mobile application developer who wants to work with Kotlin must be well-versed in the language.

WHAT IS THE PURPOSE OF KOTLIN?

Kotlin is intended to operate on a JVM and can coexist alongside Java. Although Kotlin began as a language for Android development, its features soon expanded beyond the Java community, and it is now utilized for a wide range of applications.

Android Development

Kotlin is the recommended language for Android development because it allows developers to produce more concise, expressive, and secure code. Android Studio, the official IDE for Android development, fully supports it, so we can receive the same sort of code completion and type checking to assist us in creating Kotlin code as we can with Java.

Because more people now access the Internet via mobile phones, most companies must have a mobile presence. Because Android accounts for more than 70% of the mobile phone market, Kotlin developers would be in great demand even if they use Kotlin alone for Android development. It may, however, be used for much more.

Back-End Web Development

Back-end web development in Java is common, with popular frameworks such as Spring. However, since it was simpler to work with, Kotlin made inroads into server-side web development.

The language's contemporary capabilities enable Web Developers to create apps that expand fast on commodity hardware. Because Kotlin and Java are compatible, we may gradually migrate an application to use Kotlin one file at a time while the remainder of the program continues to use Java.

Kotlin also works with Spring and other frameworks, so migrating to Kotlin does not need a complete overhaul of our existing code. Google, Amazon, and many more organizations have already replaced Java in their server-side code with Kotlin.

Full-Stack Web Development

Kotlin makes sense for server-side web development. After all, Java has been around since the beginning. We may still use Kotlin for front-end programming using Kotlin/JS.

Kotlin/JS gives developers type-safe access to sophisticated browsers and online APIs. Full-Stack Developers need to be familiar with Kotlin. They can create front-end code in the same language as back-end code, and it will be compiled to JavaScript to execute in the browser.

Data Science

Data Scientists have long used Java to crunch information, discover patterns, and make predictions, so it seems to reason that Kotlin will find a home in the field as well.

Data Scientists can utilize all of the normal Java libraries that they are accustomed to using in Java projects, but they must develop their code in Kotlin. Jupyter and Zeppelin, two tools that many Data Scientists regularly utilize for data visualization and exploratory study, both support Kotlin.

Mobile Development for Several Platforms

Kotlin Multiplatform Mobile is a software development kit for building cross-platform mobile applications. This implies that we'll be able to generate apps that operate not only on Android phones but also on iPhones and the Apple Watch from a single Kotlin codebase. Even at its initial stage, this project has a lot of potential.

KOTLIN'S ARCHITECTURE

A well-designed architecture is required for an application to grow its features and meet the expectations of its end-user base. Kotlin has its own proprietary architecture for allocating memory and generating high-quality outcomes for developers and end-users.

Coroutines and classes in Kotlin build the core, resulting in reduced boilerplate code, improved speed, and enhanced efficiency. The Kotlin compiler can respond differently in various contexts, most notably when distinguishing between multiple types of languages.

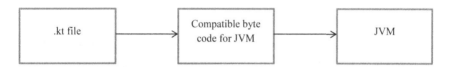

Architecture in Kotlin.

The architectural design demonstrates that code execution is divided into the following three easy phases:

- The first step is to include a ".kt" or kotlin file in the compiler's path.

- In the second stage, the Kotlin compiler converts the code to byte-code.

- In the third stage, the byte-code is loaded into the JVM and executed by the JVM itself.

When two byte-code files execute on the JVM, they commence mutual communication. This is how interoperability for Java, the feature of Kotlin, was created.

When Kotlin targets JavaScript, it undergoes Kotlin to JavaScript transformation.

When JavaScript is chosen as the target, any Kotlin code component of the library that contains Kotlin is subsequently splattered with JavaScript. However, the Java Development Kit (JDK) or any java library used is not included.

This procedure does not take into account non-Kotlin files while attempting to achieve JavaScript. To generate consistent JavaScript code, the Kotlin compiler translates the kt file to ES5.1. The Kotlin compiler aims for the smallest possible output size, compatibility with existing modules, standard library functionality, and JavaScript readable output.

The debate has demonstrated that Kotlin compilers may generate more efficient, competent, and independent code, leading to a high-performing software product.

KOTLIN FRAMEWORKS FOR SERVER-SIDE DEVELOPMENT

- Spring starts with version 5.0, which uses Kotlin language features to deliver more concise APIs. We can quickly build a new Kotlin project using the online project generator.

- Vert.x, a framework for constructing reactive Web apps on the JVM, provides substantial documentation and Kotlin support.

- Ktor is a JetBrains framework for creating Kotlin Web applications that employ coroutines for excellent scalability and have an easy-to-use and idiomatic API.

- kotlinx.html is a DSL used to generate HTML in a Web application. It's a fantastic alternative to traditional templating technologies like JSP and FreeMarker.

- Micronaut is a modern, full-stack JVM-based framework for creating modular, testable microservice and serverless applications. It includes a wealth of handy built-in features.

- http4k is a functional toolkit with a tiny footprint for Kotlin HTTP applications written exclusively in Kotlin. Based on Twitter's "Our Server as a Function," the module portrays HTTP Servers and Clients as simple Kotlin functions together.

- Javalin is a web framework written in Kotlin and Java that supports WebSockets, HTTP2, and async requests.

- Persistence options include direct JDBC access, JPA, and the usage of NoSQL databases via Java drivers. The kotlin-jpa JPA compiler plugin conforms Kotlin-compiled classes to the framework's requirements.

KOTLIN ENVIRONMENT FOR COMMAND LINE SETUP

We'll look at how to set up a Kotlin environment using a command-line compiler.

- **The following conditions must be met before installing Kotlin:**

  - We must install JDK and put the path in the local system environment variable since Kotlin runs on the JVM.

- **You may get the Kotlin compiler here:**

  - Github Releases has the most recent version of the Kotlin standalone compiler. Version 1.3.31 is the most recent.

- **Configure Kotlin compiler for command line use:**

  - First and foremost, extract the downloaded file to a write-accessible area.

  - Navigate to the kotlinc bin directory.

  - Now navigate to my computer's settings ->Advanced System Settings -> Environment Variables.

  - In system variables, click the route, then click the edit button.

  - Paste the copied path to the bin directory into this field and press OK -> OK -> OK.

To confirm the installation, run kotlinc in the command prompt.

Intellij IDEA IS USED TO BUILD UP A KOTLIN ENVIRONMENT

JetBrains' Kotlin is a statically typed, general-purpose programming language that has been used to create world-class IDEs such as IntelliJ IDEA, PhpStorm, Appcode, and others. JetBrains initially offered it in 2011. Kotlin is an object-oriented language superior to Java while remaining completely compatible with Java code.

Let's create a Kotlin environment with Intellij IDEA and run our first Kotlin code.

- Install the most recent version of IntelliJ IDEA to get started. JetBrains' free Community Edition is available for download, https://www.jetbrains.com/idea/download/#section=windows.

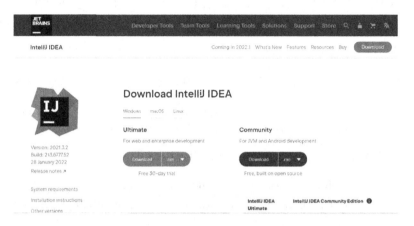

Downloading IntelliJ IDEA

- Create a Kotlin application after installing Intellij IDEA.

- Creating a new project by selecting File -> New -> Project.

- Then choose Kotlin -> JVM | IDEA.

- Give our project a name and choose an SDK version. HelloEveryone is the project's name in this case.

- HelloEveryone is our new project. Make a new Kotlin file in the source(src) folder and call it firstpro.kt.

- After we've created the file, write the main function. IntelliJ IDEA has a template for doing this quickly. Simply write main and press the tab key. Insert a line of code to print "Hello Everyone."

- Start the application. The program is now available to use. The simplest method is to pick Run "FirstproKt" from the sidebar's green Run button. By hitting Ctrl + Shift + F10, we may run directly.

- The results will be displayed in the Run Tool Window if our program compiles appropriately.

THE FIRST PROGRAM IS WRITTEN IN KOTLIN

The first fundamental program in every programming language is Hello, Everyone. Let's start with writing the first program in the Kotlin programming language.

The Kotlin program "Hello, Everyone":

Open our chosen editor, notepad or notepad++, and create a file called firstpro.kt containing the code below.

```
// Kotlin Hello Everyone Program
fun main(args: Array<String>) {
    println("Hello, Everyone")
}
```

We can use a command-line compiler to compile the program.

```
$ kotlinc firstpro.kt
```

Run the program now to view the output in the command-line compiler.

```
$kotlin firstpro.kt
Hello, Everyone
```

The details of the "Hello Everyone" program are as follows:

- **Line 1:** The first line is a comment that the compiler disregards. Comments are added to programs to help readers comprehend the source code.
  Kotlin accepts two types of comments:

  - Single line comment:

    ```
    // This is a single-line comment
    ```

  - Mulitple line comment:

    ```
    /*   This is
    Multiple-line
      comment
            */
    ```

- **Line 2:** In the second line, the main function is defined.

  ```
  fun main(args: Array<String>) {
      // .....
  }
  ```

The main() function is at the heart of any program. All Kotlin functions begin with the fun keyword, then the function name (here main), a list of parameters, an optional return type, then the function body ({.......}).

The parameter – an array of strings and return units – is included in the main function in this case. The unit type, equivalent to void in Java, indicates that the function returns no value.

- **Line 3:** The third line is a statement that prints "Hello Everyone" to the program's standard output.

```
println("Hello Everyone")
```

Semicolons are optional in Kotlin, as they are in most other programming languages.

KOTLIN DATA TYPES

A Kotlin data type is a form of data categorization that tells the compiler how the programmer intends to utilize the data. Kotlin data can be numeric, string, boolean, and so on.

Because Kotlin interprets everything as an object, we may invoke member functions and properties on any variable.

Because Kotlin is a statically typed language, one should know the data type of each expression at build time.

Kotlin's built-in data types are classified as follows:

- Number

- Character

- String

- Boolean

- Array

Number Data Types in Kotlin

Number data types in Kotlin are used to construct variables that contain numeric values and are classified into two categories: (a) Integer types are used to hold entire integers, whether positive or negative. (b) Floating-point numbers contain one or more decimals and have a fractional portion.

The following table lists all of the Kotlin number data types, the keywords used to define their variable types, the amount of memory used by the variables, and the value range stored in those variables.

Data Type	Size (bits)	Data Range
Byte	8	−128 to 127
Short	16	−32768 to 32767
Int	32	−2,147,483,648 to 2,147,483,647
Long	64	−9,223,372,036,854,775,808 to +9,223,372,036,854,775,807
Float	32	1.40129846432481707e-45 to 3.40282346638528860e+38
Double	64	4.94065645841246544e-324 to 1.79769313486231570e+308

Example:

```
fun main(args: Array<String>) {
    val x: Int = 1000
    val y: Double = 110.00
    val fz Float = 110.00f
    val a: Long = 1100000004
    val b: Short = 100
    val c: Byte = 1
    println("Int Value is " + x)
    println("Double  Value is " + y)
    println("Float Value is " + z)
    println("Long Value is " + a )
    println("Short Value is " + b)
    println("Byte Value is " + c)
}
```

Character Data Type in Kotlin

The type Char keyword represents the Kotlin character data type, which holds a single character. A Char value, such as 'X' or '1', must be enclosed by single quotes.

Below given example demonstrates how to define and use a Kotlin Char data type:

```
fun main(args: Array<String>) {
    val letters: Char      // defining Char variable
    letters = 'X'          // Assigning value to it
    println("$letters")
}
```

Kotlin supports a variety of character escape sequences. When a character is preceded by a backslash (), it is referred to as an escape sequence, and the compiler interprets it differently. For example, in the following sentence, n is a legitimate character known as a new line character.

```
println('\n') //prints newline character
println('\$') //prints dollar $ character
println('\\') //prints backslash \ character
```

String Data Type in Kotlin

String data types are used to hold a string of characters. String values must be enclosed in double-quotes (" ") or triple quotations ("""" """"").

Kotlin supports two types of strings: Escaped String and Raw String.

Escaped strings are stated within double quotes (" ") and may contain escape characters such as '\n','\t', '\b', and so on.

Raw strings are specified within triple quotes ("""" """"") and can include numerous lines of text without any escape characters.

Example:

```
fun main(args: Array<String>) {
   val escapedStrings : String  = "I'm escaped
String!\n"
   var rawStrings :String  = """This is going to
be a
   multiline string and will not have escape
sequence""";
   print(escapedStrings)
   println(rawStrings)
}
```

Boolean Data Type in Kotlin

Boolean, like other programming languages, is fairly simple. The Boolean data type has two values: true or false.

```
fun main(args: Array<String>) {
   val X: Boolean = true    // defining variable with
true value
   val Y: Boolean = false   // defining variable with
false value
```

```
   println("Value of variable X "+ X )
   println("Value of variable Y "+ Y )
}
```

Array Data Type in Kotlin

Arrays in Kotlin are collections of homogenous data. Instead of defining distinct variables for each item, arrays hold multiple values in a single variable.

Let's look at one example of how to build an array of integers and then access one of its elements.

```
fun main(args: Array<String>) {
   val numbers: IntArray = intArrayOf(11, 22, 33, 44, 55)
   println("The Value at third position : " + numbers[2])
}
```

DATA TYPE CONVERSION IN KOTLIN

Data type conversion is converting the value of one data type to another. Kotlin does not enable direct conversion of one numeric data type to another; for example, you cannot convert an Int type to a Long type:

```
fun main(args: Array<String>) {
   val a: Int = 110
   val b: Long = a  // Not valid assignment
   println(b)
}
```

Kotlin provides a collection of methods for converting a numeric data type to another type:

- toByte()

- toShort()

- toInt()

- toLong()

- toFloat()

- toDouble()

- toChar()

Let's change the previous example and test it again:

```
fun main(args: Array<String>) {
    val a: Int = 110
    val b: Long = a.toLong()
    println(b)
}
```

OPERATORS IN KOTLIN

An operator is a symbol that instructs the compiler to do particular mathematical or logical operations. Kotlin has a plethora of built-in operators, including the following:

- Arithmetic Operators

- Relational Operators

- Assignment Operators

- Unary Operators

- Logical Operators

- Bitwise Operations

Let's take a look at these Kotlin Operators one by one.

Arithmetic Operators in Kotlin

Arithmetic operators in Kotlin are used to execute simple mathematical operations such as addition, subtraction, multiplication, and division.

Operator	Name	Description	Example
+	Addition	Adds the together two values	a + b
−	Subtraction	Subtracts the one value from another	a − b
*	Multiplication	Multiplies the two values	a * b
/	Division	Divides one value by another	a / b
%	Modulus	Returns division remainder	a % b

Example:

```
fun main(args: Array<String>) {
    val a: Int = 50
    val b: Int = 10
```

```
    println("a + b = " +   (a + b))
    println("a - b = " +   (a - b))
    println("a / b = " +   (a / b))
    println("a * b = " +   (a * b))
    println("a % b = " +   (a % b))
}
```

Relational Operators in Kotlin

Relational (comparison) operators in Kotlin are used to compare two values and return a Boolean value: true or false.

Operator	Name	Example
>	greater than	a > b
<	less than	a < b
>=	greater than or equal to	a >= b
<=	less than or equal to	a <= b
==	is equal to	a == b
!=	not equal to	a != b

Example:

```
fun main(args: Array<String>) {
    val a: Int = 50
    val b: Int = 10
    println("a > b = " +   (a > b))
    println("a < b = " +   (a < b))
    println("a >= b = " +   (a >= b))
    println("a <= b = " +   (a <= b))
    println("a == b = " +   (a == b))
    println("a != b = " +   (a != b))
}
```

Assignment Operators in Kotlin

Assignment operators in Kotlin are used to assign values to variables.

Below is an example of how we used the assignment operator = to assign values to two variables:

```
fun main(args: Array<String>) {
    val a: Int = 50
    val b: Int = 10
    println("a = " +   a)
    println("b = " +   b)
}
```

Below is a complete list of all assignment operators:

Operator	Example	Expanded Form
=	a = 10	a = 10
+=	a += 10	a = a - 10
-=	a -= 10	a = a - 10
*=	a *= 10	a = a * 10
/=	a /= 10	a = a / 10
%=	a %= 10	a = a % 10

Example:

```kotlin
fun main(args: Array<String>) {
    var a: Int = 50
    a += 5
    println("a += 5 = " + a )
    a = 50;
    a -= 5
    println("a -= 5 = " +  a)
    a = 50
    a *= 5
    println("a *= 5 = " +  a)
    a = 50
    a /= 5
    println("a /= 5 = " +  a)
    a = 53
    a %= 5
    println("a %= 5 = " + a)
}
```

Unary Operators in Kotlin

The unary operators require just one operand to execute operations like incrementing/decrementing a value by one, negating an expression, or inverting a boolean value.

The following are the Kotlin Unary Operators:

Operator	Name	Example
+	unary plus	+a
−	unary minus	−a
++	increment by 1	++a
—	decrement by 1	—a
!	inverts the value of a boolean	!

Example:

```
fun main(args: Array<String>) {
   var a: Int = 50
   var b:Boolean = true
   println("+a = " +  (+a))
   println("-a = " +  (-a))
   println("++a = " +  (++a))
   println("--a = " +  (--a))
   println("!a = " +  (!y))
}
```

Logical Operators in Kotlin

The logical operators in Kotlin are used to identify the logic between two variables or values.

The following are the Kotlin Logical Operators:

Operator	Name	Description	Example
&&	Logical and	Returns true if both the operands are true	a && b
||	Logical or	Returns true if either of the operands is true	a || b
!	Logical not	Reverse result returns false if the operand is true	!a

Example:

```
fun main(args: Array<String>) {
   var a: Boolean = true
   var b:Boolean = false
   println("a && b = " +  (a && b))
   println("a || b = " +  (a || b))
   println("!b = " +  (!b))
}
```

Bitwise Operations in Kotlin

Although Kotlin lacks bitwise operators, it does provide many assistance functions for doing bitwise operations.

Here is a list of Kotlin Bitwise Functions:

Function	Description	Example
shl (bits)	signed shift left	a.shl(b)
shr (bits)	signed shift right	a.shr(b)
ushr (bits)	unsigned shift right	a.ushr(b)
and (bits)	bitwise and	a.and(b)
or (bits)	bitwise or	a.or(b)
xor (bits)	bitwise xor	a.xor(b)
inv()	bitwise inverse	a.inv()

Example:

```
fun main(args: Array<String>) {
    var a:Int = 70
    var b:Int = 15
    var c:Int
    c = a.shl(2)
    println("a.shl(2) = " +  c)
    c = a.shr(2)
    println("a.shr(2) = " +  c)
    c = a.and(b)
    println("a.and(b)  = " +  c)
    c = a.or(b)
    println("a.or(b)   = " +  c)
    c = a.xor(b)
    println("a.xor(b)  = " +  c)
    c = a.inv()
   println("a.inv()  = " +  c)
}
```

BOOLEANS IN KOTLIN

We are often faced with a circumstance in which we must decide whether to answer Yes or No, or whether to declare True or False. Kotlin features a Boolean data type that can accept the values true or false to handle such situations.

Create Boolean Variables

The Boolean keyword can be used to construct a boolean variable, which can only accept the values true or false:

Example:

```kotlin
fun main(args: Array<String>) {
    val isCold: Boolean = true
    val isSummer: Boolean = false
println(isCold)
println(isSummer)
}
```

Boolean Operators in Kotlin

For boolean variables, Kotlin includes the following built-in operators. These are also known as Logical Operators:

Operator	Name	Description	Example
&&	Logical and	Returns true if both the operands are true	a && b
||	Logical or	Returns true if either of the operands is true	a || b
!	Logical not	Reverse result returns false if the operand is true	!a

Example:

```kotlin
fun main(args: Array<String>) {
    var a: Boolean = true
    var b:Boolean = false
    println("a && b = " +  (a && b))
    println("a || b = " +  (a || b))
    println("!b = " +  (!b))
}
```

Boolean Expression in Kotlin

A boolean expression yields either a true or false value and is commonly used in condition checking with if...else expressions. A boolean expression employs relational operators such as >,<, >=, and so on.

Example:

```kotlin
fun main(args: Array<String>) {
    val a: Int = 50
    val b: Int = 10
    println("a > b = " +  (a > b))
    println("a < b = " +  (a < b))
    println("a >= b = " +  (a >= b))
    println("a <= b = " +  (a <= b))
```

```
    println("a == b = " +  (a == b))
    println("a != b = " +  (a != b))
}
```

and() and or() Functions in Kotlin

The and() and or() functions in Kotlin are used to conduct logical AND and logical OR operations between two boolean operands.

These functions vary from the && and || operators in that they do not conduct short-circuit evaluation and always evaluate both operands.

```
fun main(args: Array<String>) {
    val a: Boolean = true
    val b: Boolean = false
    val c: Boolean = true

    println("a.and(b) = " +  a.and(b))
    println("a.or(b) = " +  a.or(b))
    println("a.and(c) = " +  a.and(c))
}
```

Boolean to String

To convert a Boolean object into its string form, use the toString() method.

This translation is required when assigning a true or false value to a String variable.

```
fun main(args: Array<String>) {
    val a: Boolean = true
    var c: String
    c = a.toString()
    println("a.toString() = " +  a.toString())
    println("c = " +  c)
}
```

STRINGS IN KOTLIN

In the Kotlin programming language, the string data type is used to hold a string of characters. String values must be enclosed in double-quotes (" ") or triple quotations ("""" """"").

Kotlin supports two types of strings: Escaped String and Raw String.

- Escaped strings are stated within double quotes (" ") and may contain escape characters such as '\n', '\t', '\b', and so on.

- Raw strings are specified within triple quotes ("""" """") and can include numerous lines of text without any escape characters.

Example:

```
fun main(args: Array<String>) {
    val escapedStrings : String  = "I escaped
String!\n"
    var rawStrings :String  = """This is going to
be a multiline
  string and will
  not have any escape sequence""";
    print(escapedStrings)
    println(rawStrings)
}
```

String Templates in Kotlin

String templates in Kotlin are blocks of code evaluated, and the results are interpolated into the string. A template expression begins with a dollar symbol ($) and can be a name or an expression.

Example:

```
fun main(args: Array<String>) {
    val name : String = "Sara AliKhan"
    println("Name  - $name")  // Using the template
with variable name
    println("Name length - ${name.length}")  // Using
the template with expression.
}
```

String Object in Kotlin

A Kotlin String is an object with various attributes and methods that may conduct multiple actions on strings by appending a dot character (.) after the relevant String variable.

String Indexes in Kotlin

String in Kotlin can be thought of as a sequence of characters or an array of characters. We can access its element by using square brackets to define the element's index.

String indices begin with 0; thus, if we want to access the fourth element of a string, we need to provide an index as 3.

Example:

```
fun main(args: Array<String>) {
    val name : String = "Sara AliKhan"
    println(name[3])
    println(name[5])
}
```

String Length in Kotlin

To determine the length of a Kotlin string, we may utilize its length attribute.

The Kotlin method count() returns the length of a given string.

Example:

```
fun main(args: Array<String>) {
    val name : String = "Sara AliKhan"
    println("Length of name :" + name.length)
    println("Length of name :" + name.count())
}
```

String Kotlin Last Index

To obtain the index of the final character in the char sequence, we may utilize the lastIndex attribute of a Kotlin string. If a string is empty, the function returns −1.

Example:

```
fun main(args: Array<String>) {
    val name : String = "Sara AliKhan"
    println("Index of last character in name :"
+ name.lastIndex)
}
```

String Case Changing

To transform a string into upper or lower case, Kotlin offers the toUpperCase() and toLowerCase() methods.

Example:

```
fun main(args: Array<String>) {
    val name : String = "Sara AliKhan"
    println("The Upper case of name :" + name.
toUpperCase())
    println("The Lower case of name :" + name.
toLowerCase())
}
```

String Concatenation in Kotlin

We may use either the + operator or the plus() function to concatenate two strings.

Example:

```
fun main(args: Array<String>) {
    var firstName : String = "Sara "
    var lastName : String = "AliKhan"
    println("The Full Name is :" + firstName +
lastName)
    println("The Full Name is :" + firstName.
plus(lastName) )
}
```

Trim Characters from the String

Using the drop() and dropLast() methods, we may eliminate a string's beginning and final characters.

Example:

```
fun main(args: Array<String>) {
    var name : String = "Sara AliKhan"
    println("Remove the first two characters from
name : " + name.drop(2))
    println("Remove the last two characters from
name : " + name.dropLast(2))
}
```

Quotes Inside a String

To use quotes within a string, use single quote ('):

Example:

```
fun main(args: Array<String>) {
    var strg1 : String = "That's Ok"
    var strg2 : String = "It's Alright"
    println("strg1 : " + strg1)
    println("strg2 : " + strg2)
}
```

Finding a String Inside a String

Kotlin includes the indexOf() method for finding text inside a string. This method returns index of the first occurrence of a string's provided text.

Example:

```
fun main(args: Array<String>) {
    var strg : String = "Meditation & Yoga are
synonymous with India"
    println("The Index of Yoga in the string - " +
strg.indexOf("Yoga"))
}
```

Comparing Two Strings

To compare two strings, Kotlin provides the compareTo() method. If two strings are equal, this method returns 0. Else it returns 1.

Example:

```
fun main(args: Array<String>) {
    var strg1 : String = "Apple"
    var strg2 : String = "Apple"
    println(strg1.compareTo(strg2))
}
```

getOrNull() Function in Kotlin

The getOrNull() method in Kotlin returns a character at the specified index or null if the index is out of the bound of this char sequence.

Example:

```
fun main(args: Array<String>) {
    var names : String = "Sara"
    println(names.getOrNull(0))
    println(names.getOrNull(2))
    println(names.getOrNull(100))
}
```

toString() Function in Kotlin

The function toString() method in Kotlin returns the object's string representation.

Example:

```
fun main(args: Array<String>) {
    var names : String = "Sara AliKhan"
    println(names.toString())
}
```

ARRAYS IN KOTLIN

Arrays are used to store multiple items of the same data type, such as an integer or string, in a single variable with a single variable name.

For example, if we need to hold the names of 1000 workers, rather than establishing 1000 individual String variables, we may simply build a string array with a size of 1000.

Kotlin, like any other modern programming language, supports arrays and offers a comprehensive set of array characteristics and support methods for manipulating arrays.

Creating Arrays

In Kotlin, we use the arrayOf() method to build an array and insert the values in a comma-separated list into it:

```
val fruits = arrayOf("Grapes", " Apple ", "Mango",
"Kiwi")
```

We can optionally provide the following data type:

```
val fruits = arrayOf<String>("Grapes", " Apple ",
"Mango", "Kiwi")
```

Alternatively, the arrayOfNulls() method may generate an array of null entries of a specific size.

Arrays of the Primitive Type

Kotlin also includes factory methods for creating arrays of primitive data types. The factory method for creating an integer array, for example, is:

```
val num = intArrayOf(1, 2, 3, 4)
```

Other factory methods for creating arrays include:

- byteArrayOf()

- charArrayOf()

- shortArrayOf()

- longArrayOf()

Elements of an Array Can Be Get and Set

Use the index number inside square brackets to retrieve an array element. The index of a Kotlin array begins with zero (0). So, if we want to retrieve the 4th element of the array, enter 3 as the index.

Example:

```
fun main(args: Array<String>) {
    val fruits = arrayOf<String>("Grapes",
"Orange", "Kiwi", " Apple")
    println( fruits [0])
    println( fruits [3])
}
```

Array Length in Kotlin

Kotlin has an array property called size that returns the array's size, i.e., length.

Example:

```
fun main(args: Array<String>) {
    val fruits = arrayOf<String>("Grapes", "Orange",
"Kiwi", " Apple")
```

```
    println( "The Size of fruits array " + fruits.
size )
}
```

Loop through an Array

We may use the for loop to loop through an array.

Example:

```
fun main(args: Array<String>) {
    val fruits = arrayOf<String>("Grapes",
"Orange", "Kiwi", " Apple")
    for( item in fruits ){
        println( item )
    }
}
```

Check if an Element Exists

To check if an element in an array exists, we may use the in operator in along with if…else.

Example:

```
fun main(args: Array<String>) {
    val fruits = arrayOf<String>("Orange", " Apple
", "Grapes", "Banana")

    if ("Apple" in fruits){
        println( "The Apple exists in fruits" )
    }else{
        println( "The Apple does not exist in
fruits" )
    }
}
```

Distinct Values from the Array

Kotlin enables us to store duplicate values in an array, but we can also use the distinct() member function to get a set of different values stored in the array.

Example:
```kotlin
fun main(args: Array<String>) {
    val fruits = arrayOf<String>("Grapes",
"Orange", "Kiwi", " Apple ", "Grapes")
    val distinct = fruits.distinct()
    for( item in distinct ){
        println( item )
    }
}
```

Dropping Elements from the Array

We may utilize the drop() or dropLast() member methods to drop elements from the beginning or the end.

Example:
```kotlin
fun main(args: Array<String>) {
    val fruits = arrayOf<String>("Grapes",
"Orange", "Kiwi", " Apple ", "Grapes")

    val result = fruits.drop(2) // drops the first
two elements.
    for( item in result ){
        println( item )
    }
}
```

Checking an Empty Array

We may utilize the isEmpty() member function to determine whether or not an array is empty. If the array is empty, this method returns true.

Example:
```kotlin
fun main(args: Array<String>) {
    val fruits = arrayOf<String>()
    println( "The Array is empty : " + fruits
.isEmpty())
}
```

RANGES IN KOTLIN

The range in Kotlin is defined by the two endpoint values included in the range. Ranges in Kotlin are constructed with the rangeTo() method or by utilizing the downTo or (..) operators. The main range operation is contained, which is often used in the form of in and !in operators.

Example:

```
1..10  // The Range of integers starting from 1 to 10
a..z   // The Range of characters starting from
the a to z
A..Z   // The Range of capital characters
beginning from the A to Z
```

Because both ends of the range are always included, the 1..4 expression corresponds to the numbers 1,2,3, and 4.

Creating Ranges Using the rangeTo() Function

To create a Kotlin range, we use the rangeTo() method with the range start value as an argument and the range end value as an argument.

Example:

```
fun main(args: Array<String>) {
    for ( numb in 1.rangeTo(4) ) {
      println(numb)
    }
}
```

Creating the Ranges Using the .. Operator

rangeTo() is frequently used in its operator form … As a result, the above code may be rewritten using the .. operator as follows:

Example:

```
fun main(args: Array<String>) {
    for ( numb in 1..4 ) {
      println(numb)
    }
}
```

Creating the Ranges Using downTo() Operator

We may use the downTo operator to define a backward range:

Example:

```
fun main(args: Array<String>) {
    for ( numb in 4 downTo 1 ) {
        println(numb)
    }
}
```

step() Function in Kotlin

To specify the distance between the range's values, we may utilize the step() method. Take a look at the following example:

```
fun main(args: Array<String>) {
    for ( numb in 1..10 step 2 ) {
        println(numb)
    }
}
```

Range of Characters in Kotlin

Generate range for the character in the same way for integer values.

Example:

```
fun main(args: Array<String>) {
    for ( chr in 'a'..'d' ) {
        println(chr)
    }
}
```

reversed() Function in Kotlin

To reverse the range values, use the reversed() method.

Example:

```
fun main(args: Array<String>) {
    for ( numb in (1..5).reversed() ) {
        println(numb)
    }
}
```

until() Function in Kotlin

The method until() generates a range, but it skips the last element given.

Example:

```
fun main(args: Array<String>) {
    for ( numb in 1 until 5 ) {
        println(numb)
    }
}
```

The last, first, and step Elements

We can utilize the first, last, and step attributes of a range to get the range's first, last, or step value.

Example:

```
fun main(args: Array<String>) {
    println((6..10).first)
    println((6..10 step 2).step)
    println((6..10).reversed().last)
}
```

Filtering Ranges

The filter() method returns a list of elements that match a specified predicate:

Example:

```
fun main(args: Array<String>) {
    val x = 1..10
    val y = x.filter { T -> T % 2 == 0 }
    println(y)
}
```

Distinct Values in Range

The distinct() method will provide a list of different values from a range of values that contain repeated values:

Example:

```
fun main(args: Array<String>) {
    val x = listOf(11, 11, 22, 44,4 4, 66, 10)
    println(x.distinct())
}
```

Range Utility Functions

We can apply many other valuable functions to our range such as min, max, sum, average, and count:

Example:

```
fun main(args: Array<String>) {
    val x = 1..10
    println(x.min())
    println(x.max())
    println(x.sum())
    println(x.average())
    println(x.count())
}
```

FUNCTIONS IN KOTLIN

Kotlin is a statically typed language; functions play an essential part. We are somewhat familiar with function. A function is a piece of code written to execute a particular purpose. All current programming languages provide functions, sometimes known as methods or subroutines.

A function, in general, receives particular inputs called parameters, performs specific actions on these inputs, and eventually returns a value.

Built-in Functions in Kotlin

Kotlin has a lot of built-in functions, and we've utilized a few of them in our examples. For example, the most widely used built-in functions for printing output to the screen are print() and println().

Example:

```
fun main(args: Array<String>) {
    println("Hello, Everyone")
}
```

User-Defined Functions

Using the term fun, we can define our own function in Kotlin. A user-defined function accepts one or more parameters, performs an action, and returns the outcome as a value.

Syntax:

```
fun functionName(){
    // body of the function
}
```

Once we've defined a function, we may call it as many times as we need to. The following is a basic syntax for calling a Kotlin function:

```
functionName()
```

Here's an example of how to define and call a user-defined function that prints a basic "Hello, Everyone."

```
fun main(args: Array<String>) {

    printHello()
}
fun printHello(){
    println("Hello, Everyone")
}
```

Function Parameters

A user-defined function can accept Zero or more arguments. Parameters are options that can use based on the situation. For example, the above-defined function made no use of a parameter.

Below is an example of how to construct a user-defined function that adds two numbers and prints their sum:

```
fun main(args: Array<String>) {
    val x = 20
    val y = 10
    printSum(x, y)
}
fun printSum(x:Int, y:Int){
    println(x + y)
}
```

Return Values

A Kotlin function returns a value based on its parameters. Returning a value is, once again, entirely voluntary.

Use the return keyword and provide the return type after the function's parentheses to return a value.

Here's an example of a user-defined function that will add two numbers and return the sum:

```
fun main(args: Array<String>) {
    val x = 20
    val y = 10
    val result = sumTwo(x, y)
    println( result )
}
fun sumTwo(x:Int, y:Int):Int{
    val a = x + y
    return a
}
```

Unit-Returning Functions

If a function does not return useful value, its return type is Unit. Unit is a type that has only one value which is Unit.

```
fun sumTwo(x:Int, y:Int):Unit{
    val a = x + y
    println( a )
}
```

The declaration of the Unit return type is also optional. The preceding code is equivalent to:

```
fun sumTwo(x:Int, x:Int){
    val a = x + y
    println( a )
}
```

Recursive Function in Kotlin

Recursion functions are helpful in various situations, such as computing the factorial of a number or producing the Fibonacci series. Recursion is supported in Kotlin, which means that a Kotlin function can call itself.

Syntax:

```
fun functionName(){
    .....
```

```
functionName()
    .....
}
```

Example:

```
fun main(args: Array<String>) {
    val x = 4
        val result = factorial(x)
    println( result )
}
fun factorial(x:Int):Int{
    val result:Int
    if( x <= 1){
        result = x
    }else{
        result = x*factorial(x-1)
    }
        return result
}
```

Tail Recursion in Kotlin

A recursive function is suitable for tail recursion if the last operation is a function call to itself.

The following Kotlin program uses tail recursion to determine the factorial of number 10. In this situation, we must guarantee that the multiplication occurs before the recursive call, not after.

```
fun main(args: Array<String>) {
    val x = 4
    val result = factorial(x)
    println( result )
}
fun factorial(x: Int, accum: Int = 1): Int {
    val result = x * accum
    return if (x <= 1) {
        result
    } else {
        factorial(x - 1, result)
    }
}
```

Higher-Order Functions

A higher-order function in Kotlin accepts another function as a parameter and/or returns another function.

The following example is a function that accepts two integer arguments, x and y, as well as another function operation as a parameter:

```
fun main(args: Array<String>) {
    val result = calculate(14, 3, ::sum)
    println( result )
}
fun sum(x: Int, y: Int) = x + y
fun calculate(x: Int, y: Int, operation:(Int, Int) ->
Int): Int {
    return operation(x, y)
}
```

Lambda Function in Kotlin

Kotlin lambda is a function with no name defined with curly braces and accepts zero or more parameters and the body of the function.

The body of the function is written after the variable (if any) and the -> operator.

Syntax:

```
{variable with type -> body of function}
```

Example:

```
fun main(args: Array<String>) {
    val upperCase = { str: String -> str.
toUpperCase() }
    println( upperCase("hello, everyone") )
}
```

Inline Function in Kotlin

The inline keyword is used to declare an inline function. Using inline functions improves the efficiency of higher-order functions. The inline function tells the compiler to copy arguments and functions to the call site.

Example:

```kotlin
fun main(args: Array<String>) {
    myFunction({println("The Inline function
parameter")})
}
inline fun myFunction(function: ()-> Unit){
    println("I'm inline function - A")
    function()
        println("I'm inline function - B")
}
```

If-else EXPRESSION IN KOTLIN

Decision-making in programming is analogous to decision-making in real life. A particular code block must be executed when a specific condition is satisfied in programming. In programming languages, regulated statements control program execution flow depending on particular criteria. The program enters the conditional block and executes the instructions if the condition is fulfilled.

In Kotlin, there are several forms of if-else expressions:

- if expression
- if-else expression
- if-else-if ladder expression
- nested if expression

if Statement

If-statement is used to specify whether or not a block of statements should be executed, i.e., if a specific condition is true, the statement or block of statements should execute; else, the statement or block of statements should not run.

Syntax:

```kotlin
if(condition) {
        // code to run if condition is true
}
```

Flowchart:

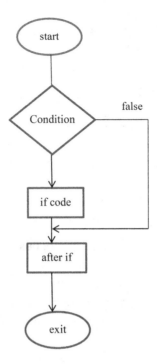

Statement of if.

Example:

```
fun main(args: Array<String>) {
    var c = 8
    if(c > 0){
        print("True, the number is positive")
    }
}
```

if-else Statement

The if-else statement is comprised of two statements blocks. When the condition is true, the 'if' statement is used to execute the code block; when the condition is false, 'else' statement is used.

Syntax:

```
if(condition) {
        // code to run if condition is true
}
```

```
else {
        // code to run if condition is false
}
```

Flowchart:

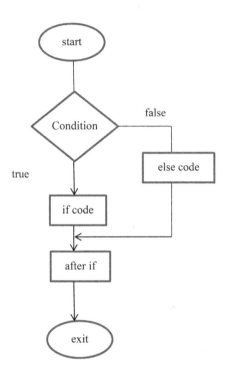

Statement of if-else.

Example:

```
fun main(args: Array<String>) {
        var a = 9
        var b = 15
        if(a > b){
            print("Number 9 is larger than 15")
        }
        else{
            println("Number 15 is larger than 9")
        }
    }
```

if-else Expression in Kotlin as the Ternary Operator

If-else may be used as an expression in Kotlin since it returns a result. In Kotlin, there is no ternary operator, unlike in Java, because if-else returns the value based on the situation.

The Kotlin program for determining the greater of two numbers using an if-else condition is presented below:

```kotlin
fun main(args: Array<String>) {
    var y = 90
    var z = 40
    // if-else returns value which is to be stored in
the max-variable
    var maxi = if(y > z){
        print("The Greater number: ")
        y
    }
    else{
        print("The Greater number:")
        z
    }
    print(maxi)
}
```

if-else-if Ladder Expression

A user can input a variety of criteria here. All 'if' statements are executed. All the conditions are checked one by one. If any of them is true, the code associated with the if statement is executed. Otherwise, all other statements are skipped until the block is completed. If none of the requirements are satisfied, the final else expression is executed.

Syntax:

```kotlin
if(first-condition)
{
    // code to run if the condition is true
}
else if(second-condition)
{
    // the code to run if the condition is true
}
```

```
else
{
}
```

Flowchart:

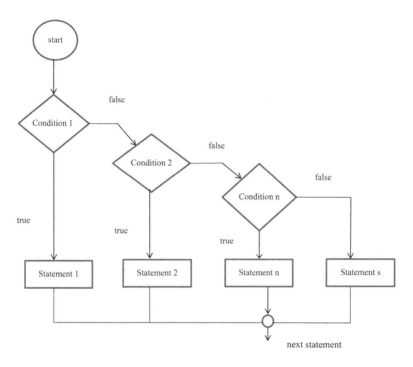

Statement of if-else-if.

Example:

```
import java.util.Scanner
fun main(args: Array<String>) {
    // to create object for scanner-class
    val reader = Scanner(System.'in')
    print("Enter number: ")
    // to read next Integer-value
    var numb = reader.nextInt()
    var results  = if ( numb > 0){
        "$numb is a positive number"
    }
    else if( numb < 0){
        "$numb is negative number"
    }
```

```
    else{
        "$numb is equal to zero"
    }
    println(results)
}
```

nested if Expression

If statements nestled inside another if statement is referred to as nested if statements. If the first condition is true, execute the associated block. Then check for the if condition nested in the first block, and if it is also true, execute the related block. It will keep going till the last condition is satisfied.

Syntax:

```
if(condition1)
{
            // code1
        if(condition2)
{
                    // code2
        }
}
```

Flowchart:

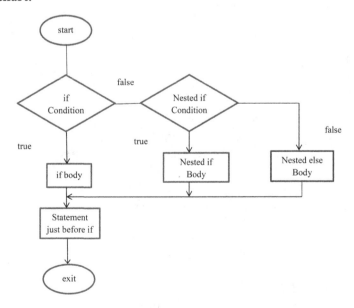

Statement of nested-if.

Example:

```kotlin
import java.util.Scanner
fun main(args: Array<String>) {
    // to create object for the scanner class
    val reader = Scanner(System.'in')
    print("Enter three numbers: ")
    var numb1 = reader.nextInt()
    var numb2 = reader.nextInt()
    var numb3 = reader.nextInt()
    var maxi  = if ( numb1 > numb2) {
        if (numb1 > numb3) {
            "$numb1 is the largest number"
        }
        else {
            "$numsb is the largest number"
        }
    }
    else if( numb2 > numb3){
        "$numb2 is the largest number"
    }
    else{
        "$numb3 is the largest number"
    }
    println(maxi)
}
```

while loop IN KOTLIN

A loop is a programming construct used to repeatedly execute a particular code block until a condition is met. If we wish to print a count from 1 to 100, use the print command 100 times. On the other hand, using a loop may save time and result in only two lines.

While loops are made up of a code block and a condition, the condition is tested first, and, if true, the code within the block is executed. Because the condition is tested before entering the block each time, it is repeated until the condition becomes false. The while loop may be thought of as a sequence of repeated if statements.

Syntax:

```kotlin
while(condition) {
            // code to run
}
```

Flowchart:

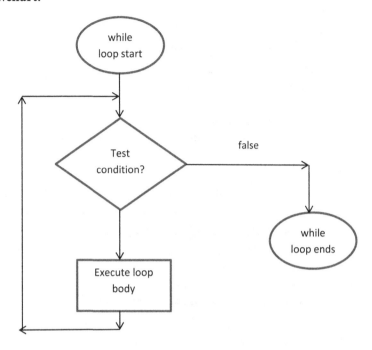

Statement of while-loop.

Using while loop, this Kotlin program prints integers from 1 to 20: We use a while loop to show the numbers in the following code. To begin, assign the variable numb to 1. Check whether the expression (number = 20) is true or false in a while loop. If true, it enters the block, runs the print statement, and adds one to the number. This step is continued until the condition is no longer true.

```kotlin
fun main(args: Array<String>) {
    var numbr = 1
    while(numbr <= 20) {
        println(numbr)
        numbr++;
    }
}
```

Using a while loop, this Kotlin program prints the elements of an array: In the following code, we create an array (names), populate it with a random number of strings, and set a variable index to 0. arrayName.size is used to determine the size of an array. Provide the condition (index < names.size) in the while loop.

If index value is less than or equal to the array size, it enters the block and prints the name stored at the associated index after each iteration. It increments the index value after each iteration. This step is continued until the condition is no longer true.

```kotlin
fun main(args: Array<String>) {
    var names = arrayOf("Prithvi","Karan","Abhay","Rid
hi","Anmol","Manas")
    var index = 0
    while(index < names.size) {
        println(names[index])
        index++
    }
}
```

do-while loop IN KOTLIN

The do-while loops are control flow statements that run the block of code at least once without validating the condition and then execute the block repeatedly, or not, based entirely on a Boolean condition after the do-while block. Unlike the while loop, which executes the block only when the condition is true, the do-while loop executes the code first and then evaluates the expression or test condition.

Method of do-while loop

After all of the statements in the block have been performed, the condition is assessed. The code block is re-executed if the condition is satisfied. As long as expression evaluates to true, the code block execution operation is repeated. If the expression becomes false, the loop is terminated, and control is passed to the sentence after the do-while loop.

It checks the condition after the block has been run. It is also known as a post-test loop.

Syntax:

```kotlin
do {
        //code to run
    {
while(condition)
```

Flowchart:

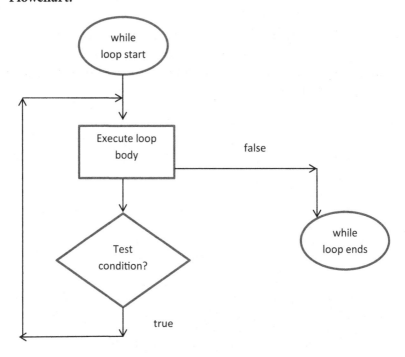

Statement of do-while-loop.

Example:

```kotlin
fun main(args: Array<String>) {
    var numbr = 9
    var factorial = 1
    do {
        factorial *= numbr
        numbr--
    }while(numbr > 0)
    println("The Factorial of 9 is $factorial")
}
```

for loop IN KOTLIN

In Kotlin, the for loop is analogous to the foreach loop in other languages such as C#. The for loop is used here to iterate through any data structure using an iterator. In other programming languages, such as Java or C, it is not utilized in the same way as the for a loop.

Syntax:

```
for(item in collection) {
        // code to execute
}
```

The for loop in Kotlin is used to iterate across the following because they all provide an iterator:

- Range

- Array

- String

- Collection

Iterate across the Range Using a for loop

The range provides an iterator, allowing us to traverse it. There are various methods for iterating through Range. In the for loop, the in operator is used to determine whether or not the value is within the Range.

The following programs demonstrate several methods of traversing the range, where in is the operator to validate the value in the range. If the value falls inside one of the ranges, it returns true and prints the value.

- **Print the values when we iterate over the range:**

```
fun main(args: Array<String>)
{
    for (d in 1..8) {
        print("$d ")
    }
}
```

- **Using step-3, iterate over the range to jump:**

```
fun main(args: Array<String>)
{
    for (d in 1..20 step 3) {
        print("$d ")
    }
}
```

- **We can't iterate across Range from top to down unless we use DownTo:**

```kotlin
fun main(args: Array<String>)
{
    for (d in 6..1) {
        print("$d ")
    }
    println("Print nothing")
}
```

- **Iterate over the Range from top to down using downTo:**

```kotlin
fun main(args: Array<String>)
{
    for (d in 6 downTo 1) {
        print("$d")
    }
}
```

- **Iterate over the Range from top to down using downTo, and then step 3:**

```kotlin
fun main(args: Array<String>)
{
    for (d in 20 downTo 1 step 3) {
        print("$d ")
    }
}
```

Using a for loop, Iterate over the Array

A data structure that stores data of the same kind, such as an integer or a string, is known as an array. An array may be browsed using a for a loop since it has an iterator. Each array has a starting index, which is always 0.

Traverse the array in the following ways:

- Without using the Index property

- With using the Index property

- Using the withIndex library function

- **Without utilizing the index property, traverse an array:**

```kotlin
fun main(args: Array<String>) {
    var numbs = arrayOf(110,220,330,440,550,660,
770,880,990,1000)
```

```
        for (numr in numbs){
            if(numr%2 == 0){
                print("$numr ")
            }
        }
    }
```

- **Using the Index property, traverse an array:**

```
fun main(args: Array<String>) {
    var colors = arrayOf("Grey", "Pink", "Black",
"Red", "White")
    for (c in colors.indices) {
        println(planets[c])
    }
}
```

- **Using the withIndex() library function, we may traverse an array:**

```
fun main(args: Array<String>) {
    var colors = arrayOf("Grey", "Pink", "Black",
"Red", "White")
    for ((index,value) in colors.withIndex()) {
        println("Element at $index th index is
$value")
    }
}
```

Iterate through a String Using the for loop

Because the for loop includes an iterator, it can traverse a string.

The string may be traversed using the following methods:

- Without using the Index property

- With using the Index property

- Using the withIndex library function

```
fun main(args: Array<String>) {
    var name = "TheHub"
    var name2 = "oftutorials"
    // traversing the string without using index
property
```

```
    for (alphabets in name)    print("$alphabets ")
    // traversing string with using the index property
    for (c in name2.indices) print(name2[c]+" ")
    println(" ")
    // traversing the string using withIndex() library
function
    for ((index,value) in name.withIndex())
    println("The Element at $index th index is
$value")
}
```

Iterate over the Collection Using the for loop

Use the for loop to iterate through the collection. There are three sorts of collections: list, map, and set.

We may use the listOf() function to send many data types simultaneously.

The program to traverse the list using a for loop is shown below:

```
fun main(args: Array<String>) {
    // to read only, fix-size
    var collection = listOf(1,2,3,"listOf", "mapOf",
"setOf")
    for (elements in the collection) {
        println(elements)
    }
}
```

KOTLIN when expression

In Kotlin, expression substitutes the switch operator in other languages such as Java. When a particular condition is satisfied, a specific block of code must be executed. When using the when expression option, each branch is compared one by one until a match is discovered. When the first match is found, the program proceeds to the end of the when block and runs the code that follows the when block. Unlike a switch case in Java or any other programming language, we do not require a break statement after each case.

In Kotlin, when may be used in two ways:

• when as a statement

• when as an expression

when to Use as a Statement with else

When is a statement that may use with or without the else branch? When used as a statement, the values of all individual branches are sequentially compared with the argument. The appropriate branch is performed when the condition is met. If none of the branches meet the criteria, the else branch is performed.

```
import java.util.Scanner;
fun main(args: Array<String>) {
    var reader = Scanner(System.'in')
    print("Enter the largebody:")
    var lbt = reader.next()
    when(lbt) {
        "Sun" -> println("The Sun is Star")
        "Moon" -> println("The Moon is Satellite")
        "Earth" -> println("The Earth is planet")
         else -> println("We don't know anything")
    }
}
```

Using when as a Statement in the Absence of an else Branch

In the lack of an otherwise branch, we can use when as a statement. When used as a statement, the values of all individual branches are compared sequentially with the argument. The relevant branch is performed when the condition is met. If none of the branches meet the criteria, the block exits without publishing anything to the system output.

```
import java.util.Scanner;
fun main(args: Array<String>) {
    var reader = Scanner(System.'in')
    print("Enterthename:")
    var lbt = reader.next()
    when(lbt) {
        "Sun" -> println("The Sun is Star")
        "Moon" -> println("The Moon is Satellite")
        "Earth" -> println("The Earth is planet")
    }
}
```

when Used as an Expression

When used as an expression, the value of the branch that satisfies the condition becomes the value of the overall expression. When we use an expression, we get a result that matches the argument, which we may keep in a variable or simply display.

```
import java.util.Scanner;
fun main(args: Array<String>) {
    var reader = Scanner(System.'in')
    print("Enter month of the number:")
    var monthyear = reader.nextInt()
    var months = when(monthyear)
{
        1->"Jan"
        2->"Feb"
        3->"March"
        4->"April"
        5->"May"
        6->"June"
        7->"July"
        8->"Aug"
        9->"Sept"
        10->"Oct"
        11->"Nov"
        12->"Dec"
        else -> {
            println("Not month of the year")
        }
    }
println(months)
}
```

If the argument fails to meet any branch conditions, the other branch is executed. Unless the compiler can demonstrate that branch conditions handle all potential cases, the else branch is required as an expression. A compiler error is raised if we cannot use the other branch.

Error:(7, 16) Kotlin: 'when' expression must be exhaustive, add the necessary 'else' branch.

In Kotlin, Different Ways to Use a when Block

A comma is used to divide numerous branches within one: a comma can be used to divide many branches within one. When two or more branches have the same logic, we can combine them into a single branch. In the example below, we need to decide whether the input largebody is a planet or not; thus, we combined all planet names into a single branch. Anything other than the planet name will result in the else branch is performed.

```kotlin
import java.util.Scanner;
fun main(args: Array<String>) {
    var reader = Scanner(System.'in')
    print("Enter name of the planet: ")
    var names = reader.next()
    when(names) {
        "Mercury", "Mars","Jupiter",
            "Earth","Neptune","Saturn","Venus",
"Uranus" -> println("Planet")
        else -> println("Neither the planet nor the star")
    }
}
```

- **Check whether the input value is inside the range:** By using the in or !in operator, we can check the range of arguments given in the when block. The 'in' operator in Kotlin is used to check for the existence of a specific variable or attribute inside a range. The in operator returns true if argument is within a given range; the !in operator returns true if the argument is not within a specific range.

```kotlin
import java.util.Scanner;
fun main(args: Array<String>) {
    var reader = Scanner(System.'in')
    print("Enter the month number of the year: ")
    var numbr = reader.nextInt()
    when(numbr) {
        in 1..3 -> println("It is the spring
season")
        in 4..6 -> println("It is the summer
season")
        in 7..8 ->println("It is the rainy
season")
        in 9..10 -> println("It is the autumn
season")
        in 11..12 -> println("It is the winter
season")
        !in 1..12 ->println("Enter the valid month
of the year")
    }
}
```

- **Check whether a provided variable is of a specific type:** Using the is or !is operator, we can check the type of variable supplied as an input in the when block. Is Int returns true if the variable is of the integer type; otherwise, it returns false.

```kotlin
fun main(args: Array<String>) {
    var numbr: Any = "TheHuboftutors"
    when(numbr) {
        is Int -> println("it's an Integer")
        is String -> println("it's a String")
        is Double -> println("it's a Double")
    }
}
```

- **Using when as a replacement for if-else-if chain:** When might be used instead of if-else-if. If no arguments are given, the branch conditions are boolean expressions, and the branch is only executed when its condition is true:

```kotlin
fun isOdd(d: Int) = d % 2 != 0
fun isEven(d: Int) = d % 2 == 0
fun main(args: Array<String>) {
    var numbr = 8
    when{
        isOdd(numbr) ->println("Odd")
        isEven(numbr) -> println("Even")
        else -> println("neither even or odd")
    }
}
```

- **Verify if a string includes a specific prefix or suffix:** The method below is used to look for a prefix or suffix in a string. It will return true if the string has the prefix or suffix; otherwise, it will return false.

```kotlin
fun hasPrefix(compani: Any) = when (compani) {
    is String -> compani.
startsWith("TheHuboftutors")
    else -> false
}

fun main(args: Array<String>) {
    var compani = "TheHuboftutors a computer
science portal"
```

```
        var result = hasPrefix(compani)
        if(result) {
            println("Yes, the string started with
TheHuboftutors")
        }
        else {
            println("No, the String does not start
with TheHuboftutors")
        }
    }
```

UNLABELED BREAKS IN KOTLIN

When working with loops, we may use either a break or a return expression to exit the loop if we want to immediately halt the loop's execution if a particular condition is fulfilled.

Here we will demonstrate how to use break expression to exit a loop. When a program encounters the break statement, it returns to the nearest enclosing loop.

There are two kinds of break expressions in Kotlin: unlabeled break expressions and labeled break expressions. We'll look at how to use unlabeled break expressions in a while, do-while, and for loops.

In a while loop, Use of an Unlabeled Break

An unlabeled break is used to exit the loop without examining the test expression when a condition is met. The control is subsequently transferred to the following while block statement.

Syntax:

```
while(test expression) {
        // code to run
            if(break condition) {
                break
            }
        // another code to run
}
```

Example:

```
fun main(args: Array<String>) {
    var sum = 0
```

```
var d = 1
while(i <= Int.MAX_VALUE) {
    sum += d
    d++
    if(d == 11) {
        break
    }
}
print("The sum of integers from 1 to 11: $sum")
}
```

To compute the sum of numbers from 1 to 10, we utilize a while loop and a break statement in the above program. Make a variable sum with a value of 0 as its initial value. Iterate through the loop once more, this time setting variable I to 1.

Iterator now proceeds from d = 1 and runs the sum statement. When iterator value d reaches 11, the break expression is performed, and the loop is terminated without checking the test expression d = Int.MAX_VALUE. The control is then transferred to the while block's print() instruction, which outputs the total number of integers = 55.

In a do-while loop, Use of an Unlabeled Break

We can also use the break expression to exit the loop without checking the test expression in a do-while loop.

Syntax:

```
do {
    //code to run
        if(break-condition) {
            break
        }
}
while(test-expression)
```

Example:

```
fun main(args: Array<String>) {
    var name = arrayOf("Earth","Venus","Jupiter","
Mars","Saturn","Uranus")
    var d = 0
    do{
```

```
        println("The name of $c th planet: "+name[d])
        if(name[d]=="Jupiter") {
            break
        }
        d++
    }while(d<=name.size)
}
```

In the above program, we traverse the array to display the names of planets. First, populate the array names with planet names, and d is the test statement's iterator. We use name.size to compute the size of an array.

The do block first prints the array's element, then compares the array's value at any index to "Jupiter" every time. If it matches, increase the iterator and run one more time. If the expressions match, the break expression is performed, and the do-while loop ends without checking for the test expression.

Use of an Unlabeled Break in a for loop

We may utilize a break expression when traversing a for loop within an array or string.

Syntax:

```
for(iteration through iterator) {
                // code to run
        if(break-condition){
            break
        }
}
```

- **Kotlin program for printing a string up to a specific character:**
  In the program below, we traverse the string by comparing the char value to break at a specific location. First, make an array with the name "TheHubsoftutors" and the value "TheHubsoftutors" in it. Then a for loop using iterator d to investigate. It outputs the char value and compares it to the char 's' at each stage. The loop is terminated if a match is discovered, and control is passed to the following line.

  ```
  fun main(args: Array<String>) {
      var name = "TheHubsoftutors"
      for (d in name){
  ```

```
        print("$d")
            if(d == 's') {
                break
            }
    }
}
```

LABELED BREAKS IN KOTLIN

Suppose we want to immediately halt the loop's execution when engaging with loops if a specified condition is satisfied. In this case, we may leave the loop by using either a break or a return expression.

In this lesson, we'll look at quitting a loop using a break expression. When a program encounters the break statement, it returns to the nearest enclosing loop.

In Kotlin, there are two sorts of break expressions:

- Unlabeled break, as we all know, is used to terminate to the nearest enclosing loop when a particular condition is fulfilled.

- On the other hand, a named break returns to the intended loop when a stated condition is fulfilled. It is feasible to do this through the use of labels. An identifier followed by a @ sign, such as inner@, outer@, first@, second@, and so on, is referred to as a label. Use any phrase with a label, but it must be written before. We'll look at using labeled break expressions in a while, do-while, and for loops.

In a while loop, Using a Labeled Break

A marked break is used to exit the target block without checking the condition in the while loop when a condition is fulfilled. The control is subsequently passed to the following while block statement.

If we use the label outer@ to identify the outer loop, we can simply break it in the break condition block with break@outer.

Syntax:

```
outer@ while(condition) {
    // code
    inner@ while(condition) {
        // code
        if(breakcondition) {
```

```
            break @outer
        }
    }
}
```

Example:

```
fun main(args: Array<String>) {
    var numbr1 = 6
    outer@ while (numb1 > 0) {
        var numbr2 = 6
        inner@ while (numb2 > 0) {
            if (numbr1==2)
                break@outer
            println("numbr1 = $numbr1, numbr2 =
$numbr2")
            numbr2--
        }
        numbr1--
    }
}
```

In a do-while loop, Using a Labeled Break

The designated break is also executed in the do-while loop to complete the intended loop. In this example, we've used outer@ for the outer do-while loop and inner@ for the inside do-while loop.

Syntax:

```
outer@ do {
        // code
        inner@ do {
            // code
            if(breakcondition) {
                break@outer
            }
        } while(condition)
} while(condition)
```

Example:

```
fun main(args: Array<String>) {
    var numbr1 = 4
```

```
    outer@ do {
        var numbr2 = 4
        inner@ do {
            if (numbr1 == 2)
                break@outer
            println("numbr1 = $numbr1; numbr2 =
$numbr2")
            numbr2--
        } while (numbr2 > 0)
        numbr1--
    } while (numbr1 > 0)
}
```

Here, we print the same output as in the while loop. When the (numbr1 == 2) condition is true, the break@outer command is executed, which terminates the desired outer@ loop.

Using a Labeled Break in a for loop

A labeled break may also end the desired loop if a particular condition in the for loop is fulfilled. The outer for loop is labeled as outer@, and the inside for loop is labeled as inner@. An iterator is used to perform iteration in a for loop.

Syntax:

```
outer@ for(iteration through iterator) {
    // code
        inner@ for(iteration through iterator)
            // code
            if(breakcondition) {
            break@outer
            }
        }
}
```

Example:

```
fun main(args: Array<String>) {
    outer@ for (numbr1 in 4 downTo 1) {
        inner@ for (numbr2 in 4 downTo 1) {
            if (numbr1 == 2)
                break@outer
```

```
            println("numbr1 = $numbr1; numbr2 =
$numbr2")
        }
    }
}
```

KOTLIN UNLABELED CONTINUE

In the following section, we will enlighten on how to utilize continue in Kotlin. When programming with loops, it is occasionally beneficial to skip the current iteration of the loop. In such a situation, we may utilize the program's continue statement. Continue is essentially used to repeat the loop for a given condition. It skips the following statements and moves on to the next loop iteration.

Use of Unlabeled Continues in the while loop

The unlabeled continue to function in Kotlin is used to skip the current iteration of the nearest enclosing while loop. If the condition for continue is true, it skips the instructions following continue and returns to the while loop's commencement. It will check for the condition again, and the loop will continue until the condition is false.

Syntax:

```
while(condition) {
    //code
        if(condition for continue) {
        continue
        }
    //code
}
```

Example:

```
fun main(args: Array<String>) {
    var numbr = 0
    while (numbr <= 15) {
        if (numbr % 3 == 0) {
            numbr++
            continue
        }
        println(numbr)
```

```
        numbr++
    }
}
```

We display the numbers and skip all multiples of 3 in the prior program. If a number is divisible by three, the statement (numbr % 3 == 0) is used to determine if it is divisible by three. Increase the number without publishing it to standard output if it is a multiple of three.

In a do-while loop, Use an Unlabeled Continue

We may also skip the iteration of the nearest closed loop by using the unmarked continue in do-while. In this scenario, we must include the continue condition in the do block. If the condition becomes false, it will skip the next instruction and transfer the control to the while condition.

Syntax:

```
do{
    // code
    if(condition for continue) {
    continue
    }
}
while(condition)
```

Example:

```
fun main(args: Array<String>) {
    var numbr = 1
    do {
        if (numbr <= 5 || numbr >=25) {
            numbr++
            continue
        }
        println("$numbr")
        numb++
    } while (numbr < 10)
}
```

Use of Unlabeled Continues in a for loop

We can also use unlabeled continue in for loop to skip the current iteration and go straight to the closing loop. In the following program, we traversed the array planets utilizing an array of letters and an iterator. The equation (c < 2) skips iterating over array indices less than two; therefore, the text stored at indexes 0 and 1 is not shown.

Syntax:

```
for(iteration through iterator)
{
    //code
    if(condition for continue)
{
    continue
    }
}
```

Example:

```
fun main(args: Array<String>) {
    var colors = arrayOf("Pink", "Green", "Black",
"White", "Grey")
    for (c in colors.indices) {
        if(c < 2){
            continue
        }
        println(colors [c])
    }
}
```

KOTLIN LABELED CONTINUES

In this topic, we'll look at how to use continue in Kotlin. It is sometimes advantageous to skip the current loop iteration when dealing with a loop in programming. In this case, we may use the program's continue statement. Continue is used to continue the loop for a given condition effectively. It goes on to the next loop iteration after skipping the following statements.

Use of Labeled Continues in a while loop

Labeled continue is used in the while loop to skip the iteration of the desired block when it fulfills a defined condition without examining the condition in the while loop. We may simply skip for the provided condition in the conditional block by using continue@outer if we mark the outside loop with outer@ and the inside loop with inner@.

Syntax:

```
outer@ while(firstcondition) {
    // code
    inner@ while(secondcondition) {
        //code
        if(condition for continue) {
            continue@outer
        }
    }
}
```

Example:

```
fun main(args: Array<String>) {
    var numbr1 = 6
    outer@ while (numb1 > 0) {
        numbr1--
        var numbr2 = 6
        inner@ while (numbr2 > 0) {
            if (numbr1 <= 2)
                continue@outer
            println("numbr1 = $numbr1, numbr2 =
$numbr2")
            numbr2--
        }
    }
}
```

Use of Labeled Continues in a do-while loop

We may also use the specified continue in the do-while loop. In the following program, we used a nested do-while loop, labeling the outside loop with outer@ and the inner loop with inner@. Within an inner do-while loop, the continue condition is executed. If the condition is true, continue@outer skips the following lines or expressions and returns control to the outer do-while loop for repetition.

Syntax:

```
outer@ do {
    // code
    inner@ do {
```

```
        // code
        if(condition for continue) {
            continue@outer
        }
    } while(firstcondition)
} while(secondcondition)
```

Example:

```
fun main(args: Array<String>) {
    var numbr1 = 6
    outer@ do {
        numbr1--
        var numbr2 = 6
        inner@ do {
            if (numbr1 <= 2)
                continue@outer
            println("numbr1 = $numbr1; numbr2 =
$numbr2")
            numbr2--
        } while (numbr2 > 0)

    } while (numbr1 > 0)
}
```

Use of Labeled Continues in a for loop

We may use labeled continue in a for loop. We used nested for loops in the following program, labeling the outside loop with outer@ and the inner loop with inner@. Within the inner for-loop, the continue condition is executed. If the condition is fulfilled, the subsequent sentences are skipped, and control is given to the outer for-loop for iteration.

Syntax:

```
outer@ for(iteration through iterator) {
    // code
        inner@ for(iteration through iterator) {
            // code
            if(condition for continue) {
            continue@outer
            }
        }
}
```

Example:

```
fun main(args: Array<String>) {
    outer@ for (numbr1 in 4 downTo 1) {
        inner@ for (numbr2 in 4 downTo 1) {
            if (numbr1 <= 3)
                continue@outer
            println("numbr1 = $numbr1; numbr2 =
$numbr2")
        }
    }
}
```

EXCEPTIONAL HANDLING

An exception is an undesirable or unexpected occurrence that occurs during program execution, i.e., during run time, and disrupts normal flow of the program's instructions. Exception handling is an approach for dealing with errors and avoiding run-time crashes, which might cause our program to crash.

Exceptions are classified into two types:

- **Checked Exception:** IOException, FileNotFoundException, and other exceptions are often added to functions and examined at build time.

- **Unchecked Exception:** Exceptions, such as NullPointerException and ArrayIndexOutOfBoundException, are frequently produced by logical errors and are examined at run time.

Exceptions in Kotlin

Exceptions in Kotlin are only unchecked and may be detected only at run time. The Throwable class is the origin of all exception classes.

To throw an exception object, we frequently use the throw-expression:

```
throw Exception("Throwmeexception")
```

Among the most common exceptions are:

- **NullPointerException:** We receive a NullPointerException when executing a property or method on a null object.

- **Arithmetic Exception:** This exception is raised when numbers are exposed to incorrect arithmetic operations. Divide by zero, for example.

- **SecurityException:** This exception is raised to indicate a security breach.

- **ArrayIndexOutOfBoundsException:** This error is generated when we attempt to obtain the incorrect index value of an array.

Example:

```kotlin
fun main(args : Array<String>){
    var numb = 30 / 0       // throw an exception
    println(numb)
}
```

Exception Handling in Kotlin

In the example below, we divide an integer by 0 (zero), which results in an ArithmeticException. The catch block will be performed because this code is in the try block.

The ArithmeticException occurred in this case. Therefore, the ArithmeticException catch block was executed, and "Arithmetic Exception" was printed in the output.

When an exception occurs, everything beyond that point is disregarded, and control is sent to the catch block, if one exists. The final block is always run, regardless of whether or not an exception occurs.

```kotlin
fun main(args: Array<String>) {
    try {
        var numb = 50/0
        println("Beginners ")
        println(numb)
    } catch (c: ArithmeticException) {
        println("Arithmetic Exception")
    } catch (c: Exception) {
        println(c)
    } finally {
        println("in any case it'll print")
    }
}
```

Avoiding NullPointerException

Avoid the NullPointerException by using the following checks and protections:

- Including a null check before using an object's methods or properties to ensure that it is properly initialized.

- Using Apache Commons StringUtils for String operations, such as StringUtils.isNotEmpty() to ensure that a string is not empty before using it.

- Use primitives rather than objects wherever possible since they cannot have null references, such as int instead of Integer and boolean instead of Boolean.

What If We Fail to Deal with Exceptions?

Assume that the application will fail if we do not handle the exception in the preceding example.

The program terminated with an error in this scenario because we did not handle exceptions.

How to Throw an Exception

The term throw is used to throw an exception. In the following example, the throw keyword is used to throw an exception. The statement preceding the exception is executed, but the statement after the exception is not performed because control is transferred to the catch block.

```kotlin
fun main(args: Array<String>) {
    try{
        println("Before the exception")
        throw Exception("Something went wrong ")
        println("After the exception")
    }
    catch(c: Exception){
        println(c)
    }
    finally{
        println("can't-ignore ")
    }
}
```

NullPointerException Example:

```
public class ExceptionExp {
    private static void printLength(String strg) {
        System.out.println(strg.length());
    }
    public static void main(String args[]) {
        String myString = null;
        printLength(myString);
    }
}
```

The printLength() function in this example utilizes the length() method of a String without first performing a null check. Because the string returned by the main() method has no value, the preceding code throws a NullPointerException:

```
Exception in thread "main" java.lang.
NullPointerException
    at ExceptionExp.printLength(ExceptionExample.java:3)
    at ExceptionExp.main(ExceptionExample.java:8)
```

KOTLIN try-catch block

To manage exceptions in the program, we use the try-catch block in Kotlin. The try block contains the code that throws an exception, whereas the catch block handles the exception. This block must include either the main or other methods. There should be a catch block, a final block, or both after the try block.

Syntax:

```
try {
    // the code that can throw an exception
} catch(c: ExceptionName) {
    // catch-exception and handle it
}
```

Example:

```
import kotlin.ArithmeticException
fun main(args : Array<String>){
    try{
```

```
        var numb = 30 / 0
    }
    catch(c: ArithmeticException){
        // caught, handles it
        println("It not allowed divide by zero")
    }
}
```

The try-catch block as an Expression in Kotlin

As previously stated, expressions always return a value. We may use the Kotlin try-catch block as an expression in our program. The return result of the expression will be either the last expression of the try block or the final expression of the catch block. If an exception occurs in the function, the catch block returns the value.

Example:

```
fun test(x: Int, y: Int) : Any {
    return try {
        x/y
        //println("The Result is: "+ x / y)
    }
    catch(e:Exception){
        println(e)
        "The Divide by zero is not allowed"
    }
}
//the main function
fun main(args: Array<String>) {
    // invoke test-function
    var results1 = test(30,2  ) //execute
try-block
    println(results1)
    var results = test(30,0  )    // execute
catch-block
    println(results)
}
```

The final block in Kotlin

Whether or not the catch block handles an exception, the final block is always run in Kotlin. As a result, it is used to carry out crucial code statements.

We may unite the finally and try blocks and eliminate the catch block.

Syntax:

```
try {
    //the code that can throw an exception
} finally {
    // the code of finally block
}
```

Example:

```
fun main(args : Array<String>){
    try{
        var ar = arrayOf(101,202,303,404,505)
        var int = ar[6]
        println(int)
    }
    finally {
        println("This will always executes")
    }
}
```

Syntax of Finally block with try-catch block:

```
try {
    // the code that can throw an exception
} catch(c: ExceptionName) {
    // catch the exception, handle it.
} finally {
    //the code of finally block
}
```

Example:

```
fun main (args: Array<String>){
    try {
        var int = 30 / 0
        println(int)
    } catch (c: ArithmeticException) {
        println(c)
    } finally {
```

```
        println("This will always executes")
    }
}
```

Kotlin throw keyword

In Kotlin, we use the throw keyword to throw an explicit exception. It also can throw a custom exception.

Example:

```
fun main(args: Array<String>) {
    test("xyzde")
    println("executes after the validation")
}
fun test(password: String) {
    // it calculate the length of entered password
and compare
    if (password.length < 6)
        throw ArithmeticException("Password is too
short")
    else
        println("Password is strong ")
}
```

NESTED try block AND MULTIPLE catch block

Nested try block

This section will teach us about nested try-catch blocks and multiple catch blocks. A nested try block has one try catch block within another.

When an exception occurs in the inner try-catch block that is not handled by the inner catch blocks, the outer try-catch blocks are inspected for that exception.

Syntax:

```
// the outer try-block
try
{
    //the inner try-block
    try
    {
        //the code that can throw an exception
    }
```

```
    catch(c: SomeException)
    {
     //it catch the exception, handle it
    }
}
catch(c: SomeException)
{
// it catch the exception, handle it
}
```

Example:

```
fun main(args: Array<String>) {
    val numbers = arrayOf(101,202,303,404)
    try {
        for (x in numbers.indices) {
            try {
                var nm = (0..4).random()
                println(numbers[x+1]/nm)
            } catch (c: ArithmeticException) {
                println(c)
            }
        }
    } catch (c: ArrayIndexOutOfBoundsException) {
        println(e)
    }
}
```

Multiple catch block

A try block may include several catch blocks. When we are unclear what type of exception may occur inside the try block, we may insert several catch blocks for the various exceptions. The parent exception class in the last catch block handles all the remaining exceptions in the program that are not described by catch blocks.

Syntax:

```
try {
    // the code may throw an exception
} catch(c: ExceptionNameOne) {
    // catch the exception one, handle it
} catch(c: ExceptionNameTwo) {
    // it catch the exception two, handle it
}
```

Example:

```
import java.util.Scanner
object Tests {
    @JvmStatic
    fun main(args: Array<String>) {
        val scn = Scanner(System.'in')
        try {
            val n = Integer.parseInt(scn.
nextLine())
            if (812% n == 0)
                println("$n is a factor of 812")
        } catch (c: ArithmeticException) {
            println(c)
        } catch (c: NumberFormatException) {
            println(c)
        }
    }
}
```

- **Expression in catch block use:** In Kotlin, an expression in a catch block can be used to replace several catch blocks. In the part that follows, we will show us how to use when expression.

```
import java.lang.NumberFormatException
import java.util.Scanner
object Tests {
    @JvmStatic
    fun main(args: Array<String>) {
        val scn = Scanner(System.'in')
        try {
            val n = Integer.parseInt(scn.
nextLine())
            if (812% n == 0)
                println("$n is a factor of 812")
        } catch (c: Exception ) {
            when(c) {
                is ArithmeticException -> {
println("Arithmetic-Exception: Divide by zero") }
                is NumberFormatException -> {
println("Number Format-Exception ") }
            }
        }
    }
}
```

NULL SAFETY

Kotlin's type system aims to eliminate the possibility of null references in code, which is a billion-dollar mistake. The program throws NullPointerExceptions at run-time, resulting in the application or system failure.

If we've ever written code in Java or another language that has the concept of a null reference, we've almost certainly seen a NullPointerException. If the Kotlin compiler encounters a null reference without executing any additional instructions, a NullPointerException is thrown.

The following are some possible sources of NullPointerExceptions:

- The !! Operator is used.

- NullPointerException() is thrown explicitly.

- Attempting to access a member on a null reference and generics types with erroneous nullability are examples of Java interoperations.

- Some data inconsistency in terms of initialization, such as using an uninitialized this as an input.

Nullable and Non-Nullable Sorts in Kotlin

The Kotlin type system differentiates between two sorts of references: those that may hold null (nullable references) and those that cannot (non-nullable references).

You cannot assign value null to a String variable. We get a compiler error when we attempt to assign a null value to the variable.

```
var str1: String = "Hub"
str1 = null // compilation-error
```

To allow it to retain null, we define a variable as a nullable string, typed String:

```
var str2: String? = "TheHuboftutors"
str2 = null // ok
print(str2)
```

Now, if we want to acquire the length of the string str1, we can be assured that it will not throw an NPE; hence, we can confidently say:

```
val l = str1.length
```

Accessing the length of the string str2 is not safe, and the compiler reports an error:

```
val l = str2.length          // error: variable 'str2'
can be null
```

non-nullable program:

```
fun main(args: Array<String>){
    // the variable is declared as non nullable
    var str1 : String = "Hubs"
    //str1 = null  // gives compiler error
    print("length of the string str1 is: "+str1.
length)
}
```

In this example, assigning a null value to a non-nullable variable result in a compiler time error. However, trying to read the length of the string will result in a NullPointerException.

Nullable type program:

```
fun main(args: Array<String>) {
    // the variable is declared as nullable
    var str2: String? = "TheHuboftutors"
    str2 = null    // no compile-error
    println(str2.length)  // the compile error because
string can be null
}
```

Checking for the null in Conditions

The most common method for checking for null references is to utilize an if-else expression. We may explicitly verify if the variable is null and handle the two alternatives independently.

Example:

```
fun main(args: Array<String>) {
    // variable declared as nullable
    var str: String? = "TheHuboftutors"
    println(str)
    if (str != null) {
```

```
        println("String of length ${str.length}")
    } else {
        println("The Null string")
    }
    // assign null
    str = null
    println(str)
    if (str != null) {
        println("String of length ${str.length}")
    } else {
        println("The Null String")
    }
}
```

Safe Call operator(?.)

Null comparisons are simple, but the number of nested if-else phrases may be challenging. As a solution, Kotlin has a Safe call operator ?., which removes this complexity by only executing an action when the specified reference has a non-null value. It allows us to employ a null-check and a method call in the same expression.

The following expression:

```
firstname?.toUpperCase()
```

is equivalent to:

```
if(firstname != null)
    firstname.toUpperCase()
else
    null
```

Example:

```
fun main(args: Array<String>) {
    // variable declared as nullable
    var firstname: String? = "Reena"
    var lastname: String? = null
    println(firstname?.toUpperCase())
    println(firstname?.length)
    println(lastname?.toUpperCase())
}
```

Elvis Operator(?:)

When the original variable is null, the Elvis operator returns a value that is not null or a default value. In other words, the Elvis operator returns the left expression if it is not null; else, the right expression is returned. If it is determined that the left-hand side expression is null, the right-hand side expression is evaluated.

The following expression:

```
val name = firstname ?: "Unknown"
```

is equivalent to:

```
val name1 = if(firstname != null)
        firstname
    else
        "Unknown"
```

Furthermore, we may use throw and return expressions on the right side of the Elvis operator, which is particularly handy in functions. As a result, we can throw an exception instead of returning the default value on the Elvis operator's right side.

```
val name1 = firstname ?: throw
IllegalArgumentException("Enter the valid name")
```

Example:

```
fun main(args: Array<String>) {
    var str : String?  = "TheHuboftutors"
    println(str?.length)
    str = null
    println(str?.length ?: "-1")
}
```

Not null assertion: !! Operator

If the value is null, the not null assertion operator (!!) converts it to a non-null type and throws an exception.

If someone needs a NullPointerException, they can use this operator to obtain one.

```
fun main(args: Array<String>) {
    var str : String?  = "TheHuboftutors"
```

```
    println(str!!.length)
    str = null
    str!!.length
}
```

TYPE CHECKING AND SMART CASTING

Type Checking

In Kotlin, we may use this operator to identify the type of a variable at run-time. It is a way of separating the flow of multiple objects at run-time by checking the type of a variable.

Program of Type checking in Kotlin with if-else blocks:

```
fun main(args: Array<String>) {
    var names = "Rishi"
    var ages = 36
    var salary = 7100.24
    val employeeDetails: List<Any> =
listOf(names,ages,salary)
    for(attribute in employeeDetails) {
        if (attribute is String) {
            println("Name is: $attribute")
        } else if (attribute is Int) {
            println("Age is: $attribute")
        } else if (attribute is Double) {
            println("Salary is: $attribute")
        } else {
            println("Not an attribute")
        }
    }
}
```

Using when expression:

- When expressions may easily replace if-else blocks.

Kotlin type checking program is used when:

```
fun main(args: Array<String>) {
    var names = "Ridhi"
    var ages = 30
    var salary = 6200.55
    var emp_id = 11275f
```

```kotlin
val employeeDetails: List<Any> = listOf(names,
ages, salary, emp_id)
    for (attribute in employeeDetails) {
        when (attribute) {
            is String -> println("The Name is:
$attribute ")
            is Int -> println("The Age is:
$attribute")
            is Double -> println("The Salary is:
$attribute")
            else -> println("Not an attribute")
        }
    }
}
```

Smart Casting

Before accessing a variable's properties in Java or other programming languages, explicit type casting is necessary, but Kotlin employs smart casting. When you send a variable through a conditional operator, the Kotlin compiler automatically converts it to a particular class reference.

Consider the following Java example. We first use the instanceOf operator to discover the variable's type, and then we cast it to the target type, as seen below:

```java
Object obj = "TheHuboftutors";
if(obj instanceof String) {
    // the Explicit type casting
    String str = (String) obj;
    System.out.println("length of String " + str.
length());
}
```

One of the most fascinating features of Kotlin is smart type casting. We use the is or !is operator to validate the type of a variable, and the compiler automatically casts the variable to the required type, as seen below:

```kotlin
fun main(args: Array<String>) {
    val str1: String? = "TheHuboftutors"
    var str2: String? = null    // prints String is null
    if(str1 is String) {
        // No Explicit-type Casting needed.
```

```
        println("length of String ${str1.length}")
    }
    else {
        println("String is null")
    }
}
```

Use of !is Operator

Similarly, we may use the !is operator to verify the variable.

```
fun main(args: Array<String>) {
    val str1: String? = "thehuboftutors"
    var str2: String? = null  // prints String is null
    if(str1 !is String) {
        println("String is null")
    }
    else {
        println("The length of String ${str1.length}")
    }
}
```

Smart casts are ineffective if the compiler cannot guarantee that the variable will not change between the check and the usage. The following guidelines determine the usage of smart casts:

- val local variables, except local delegated properties, always work.

- val properties are only helpful if the property is private or internal or if the check is performed in the same module as the property is defined. Smart casts do not support open properties and properties with custom getters.

- var local variables work only if the variable has not been modified between the check and usage, is not captured in the lambda that modifies it, and is not a local delegated property.

- var properties never work since the variable can change at any time.

EXPLICIT TYPE CASTING

In smart casting, we usually use the is or!is the operator to verify the type of a variable, and the compiler automatically converts the variable to the target type. Still, in explicit typecasting, we use the as operator.

Explicit type casting can be accomplished by employing:

- **Unsafe cast operator:** as

- **Safe cast operator:** as?

Unsafe Cast Operator: as

To manually convert a variable to the target type, we use the type cast operator.

In the following code, variable str1 of string type is cast to target type using as operator.

```
fun main(args: Array<String>) {
    val str1: String = "work's okay"
    val str2: String = str1 as String        // Works
    println(str1)
}
```

It is conceivable that we may be unable to cast a variable to the target type, resulting in an exception at run-time, which is why it is referred to as an unsafe casting.

A ClassCastException is thrown when an Integer type is used to cast to a String type.

```
fun main(args: Array<String>) {
    val str1: Any = 22
    val str2: String = str1 as String
// throw-exception
    println(str1)
}
```

We are unable to convert a nullable string to a non-nullabe string, and an error is thrown as TypeCastException.

```
fun main(args: Array<String>) {
    val str1: String? = null
    val str2: String = str1 as String
// throw-exception
    println(str1)
}
```

As a result, we must also use the target type as a nullable string to prevent type casting from throwing an exception.

```
fun main(args: Array<String>){
    val str1: String? = null
    val str2: String? = str1 as String?      // throw
exception
    println(str1)
}
```

Safe Cast Operator: as?

Kotlin also supports type casting using the safe cast operator, as? If casting is not feasible, the function returns a null value instead of raising a ClassCastException.

Here's an example: it works beautifully when we try to cast any string value known to the programmer into a nullable string. When we initialize the Any with an integer value and convert it into a nullable string, the typecasting fails, and str3 returns null.

```
fun main(args: Array<String>){
    var str1: Any = "Safe casting"
    val str2: String? = str1 as? String      // it works
    str1 = 22
    // the type casting not possible so returns null
to st3
    val str3: String? = str1 as? String
    val str4: Int? = str1 as? Int             // it works
    println(str2)
    println(str3)
    println(str4)
}
```

REGEX AND RANGES

Regular Expressions in Kotlin

Regular Expressions are a fundamental element of nearly every programming language, including Kotlin. In Kotlin, regular expressions are supported through the Regex class. The objects in this class represent regular expressions used for string matching.

```
class Regex
```

Regular expressions may be found in various software, from the most simple to the most complex.

Constructors:

- **<init>(pattern: String):** Based on the pattern string, this constructor generates a regular expression.

- **<init>(pattern: String, option: RegexOption):** Based on the pattern and option supplied, this constructor creates a regular expression. The option is an enum constant from the RegexOption class.

- **<init>(pattern: String, options: Set<RegexOption>):** This constructor generates a regular expression from the specified string pattern and arguments.

Properties:

- **val options: Set<RegexOption>:** It contains the settings that must be used while constructing a regex.

- **val pattern: String:** It contains the descriptive string for the pattern.

Regex Functions

- **containsMatchIn():** This method returns a boolean indicating whether or not it found our pattern in the input.

  ```
  fun containsMatchIn(input: CharSequence): Boolean
  ```

This example will demonstrate how to utilize Kotlin's containsMatchIn() method:

```
fun main()
{
    // A regex that matches any text that begins with
the letter 'b'
    val pattern = Regex("^b")
    println(pattern.containsMatchIn("acbd"))
    println(pattern.containsMatchIn("bcad"))
}
```

- **find():** This function returns the first matched substring corresponding to our pattern in the input starting at the specified beginning index.

```
fun find(input: CharSequence, start_Index: Int):
MatchResult?
```

This example will demonstrate how to utilize Kotlin's find() method:

```
fun main()
{
    // Regex to match "ol" in a string
    val pattern1 = Regex("ol")
    val ans : MatchResult? = pattern1.
find("HlloooHllooo", 6)
    println(ans ?.value)
}
```

- **findAll():** This function retrieves all matchings of the provided pattern in the input, starting at the specified start index.

```
fun findAll(
    input: CharSequence,
    start_Index: Int
): Sequence
```

This example will demonstrate how to utilize Kotlin's findAll method:

```
fun main()
{
    // A regex to match a 3 pattern starting with ab
    val pattern2 = Regex("ab.")
    val ans1 : Sequence<MatchResult> = pattern2.
findAll("absgffhdbabc", 0)
    // forEach loop used to display all the matches
    ans1.forEach()
    {
            matchResult -> println(matchResult.value)
    }
    println()
}
```

- **matches():** This function returns a boolean indicating whether the input string matches the pattern completely.

```
infix fun matches(input: Char_Sequence): Boolean
```

This example will demonstrate how to utilize Kotlin's matches() method:

```kotlin
fun main()
{
    //to tests the demonstrating entire string match
    val patterns = Regex("p([ee]+)ks?")
    println(patterns.matches("peeks"))
    println(patterns.matches("peeeeeeeeeks"))
    println(patterns.matches("peeksforpeeks"))
}
```

- **matchEntire():** This function tries to match the entire input string to the specified pattern string and returns the string if it succeeds. If it does not match the string, return null.

  ```kotlin
  fun matchEntire(input: Char_Sequence):
  MatchResult?
  ```

This example will demonstrate how to utilize Kotlin's matchEntire() method:

```kotlin
fun main()
{
    // Tests demonstrating entire string match
    var patterns = Regex("peeks?")
    println(patterns.matchEntire("peeks")?.value)
    println(patterns.matchEntire("peeeeeeks")?.value)
    patterns = Regex("""\D+""")
    println(patterns.matchEntire("peeks")?.value)
    println(patterns.matchEntire("peeks13245")?.value)
}
```

- **replace():** This function replaces all occurrences of the given pattern in the input string with the replacement string.

  ```kotlin
  fun replace(input: Char_Sequence, replacement:
  String): String
  ```

- **replaceFirst():** The first regular expression match in the input replaces the replacement string.

  ```kotlin
  fun replaceFirst(
      input: Char_Sequence,
      replacement: String
  ): String
  ```

Here's an example of the replace() and replaceFirst() work methods in Kotlin:

```
fun main()
{
    // Experiments to demonstrate replacement
functions
    val pattern4 = Regex("abzz")
    // replace all abzz with xycd in the string
    println(pattern4.replace("abzzabzzzzzzzz",
"abcd"))
    // replace only first xyz with abc not all
    println(pattern4.replaceFirst("abzzddddddabzz",
"abcd"))
    println()
}
```

- **split():** This function separates the input text into tokens based on the given value.

    ```
    fun split(input: Char_Sequence, limit: Int): List
    ```

This example will demonstrate how to utilize Kotlin's split() method:

```
fun main()
{
    // Tests demonstrating split function
    val patterns = Regex("\\s+")  // separate for the
white-spaces
    val ans : List<String> = patterns.split("This is
the class")
    ans.forEach { word -> println(word) }
}
```

RANGES IN KOTLIN

In Kotlin, a range is a collection of finite values defined by endpoints. A range in Kotlin is made of a start, a stop, and a step. The Range's start and endpoints are inclusive, and the step value is set to 1 by default.

The range is given to comparable types.

Range may create in three ways in Kotlin:

- Using the (..) operator

- Using downTo() function

- Using rangeTo() function

(..) operator

It is the most fundamental way to interact with range. It will construct a beginning to end range containing both the beginning and ending values. It is the operator form of the rangeTo() function. Using the (..) operator, we can build ranges for integers and characters.

To create an integer range program in Kotlin, use the (..) operator:

```kotlin
fun main(args : Array<String>){
    println("Integer-range:")
    // creation of integer range
    for(numb in 1..6){
        println(numb)
    }
}
```

Kotlin character range program with the (..) operator:

```kotlin
fun main(args : Array<String>){
    println("Character-range:")
    // creation of the character range
    for(xh in 'a'..'e'){
        println(xh)
    }
}
```

rangeTo() Function

It is comparable to the (..) operator. It will produce a range up to the provided value. It's also used to make a range of numbers and characters.

In Kotlin, use the rangeTo() function to build an integer range:

```kotlin
fun main(args : Array<String>){
    println("Integer-range:")
    // creation of the integer range
    for(numbs in 1.rangeTo(6)){
        println(numbs)
    }
}
```

In Kotlin, use the rangeTo() function to build a character range:

```
fun main(args : Array<String>){
    println("Character -range:")
    // creation of the character range
    for(xh in 'a'.rangeTo('f')){
        println(xh)
    }
}
```

downTo() Function

It is the reverse of the rangeTo() or (..). It produces a range from larger to smaller numbers in decreasing order. This section will define ranges for integers and characters in reverse order.

Kotlin code with an integer range and the downTo() function:

```
fun main(args : Array<String>){
    println("The Integer range in descending order:")
    // creation of the integer range
    for(numbs in 6.downTo(1)){
        println(numbs)
    }
}
```

In Kotlin, use the downTo() method to program a character range:

```
fun main(args : Array<String>){
    println("The Character range in the reverse order:")
    // creation of the character range
    for(xh in 'f'.downTo('a')){
        println(xh)
    }
}
```

Range Using the forEach loop

The forEach loop may also use to iterate through the range.

```
fun main(args : Array<String>){
    println("Integer-range:")
    // creation integer-range
    (3..6).forEach(::println)
}
```

step()

To create a step between values, use the keyword step. It is mainly used in rangeTo(), downTo(), and the (..) operator to provide the space between two numbers. Because the step has a default value of 1, the step function cannot have a value of zero.

A step-by-step Kotlin program is provided below:

```
fun  main(args: Array<String>) {
    //for iterating over range
    var x = 2
    // for loop with the step keyword
    for (x in 3..10 step 2)
        print("$x ")
    println()
    // print first value of the range
    println((11..20 step 2).first)
    // print the last value of the range
    println((11..20 step 4).last)
    // print the step used in the range
    println((11..20 step 5).step)
}
```

reverse() Function

It is used to reverse the range type specified. To print the range in descending order, we may use the reverse() function instead of downTo().

```
fun main(args: Array<String>) {
    var range = 2..8
    for (z in range.reversed()){
        print("$z ")
    }
}
```

Various Predefined Functions in the Range

In Kotlin Range, the following functions are predefined: min(), max(), sum(), and average ().

```
fun main() {
    val predefined = (13..20)
    println("The minimum value of the range is:
"+predefined.min())
```

```
    println("The maximum value of the range is:
"+predefined.max())
    println("The sum of all values of the range is:
"+predefined.sum())
    println("The average value of the range is:
"+predefined.average())
}
```

Check to see whether the value is inside a range:

```
fun  main(args: Array<String>)
{
    var x = 3
    //to check whether value lies in the range
    if( x in 6..10)
        println("$x is lie within range")
    else
        println("$x does not lie within range")
}
```

In this chapter, we covered what is Kotlin, its central concepts, installations, advantages and disadvantages of Kotlin. Moreover, we also covered syntax, control flow statements, exception handling, null safety, and regex & ranges.

CHAPTER 2

OOP in Kotlin

IN THIS CHAPTER

➢ Objects and classes

➢ Inheritance

➢ Composition

➢ Polymorphism

➢ Encapsulation

➢ Abstraction

In the previous chapter, we covered the crash course in Kotlin, where we covered installation, advantages, disadvantages, control flow statement, and exceptional handling. In this chapter, we will cover the OOPs concept.

OBJECTS AND CLASSES

Kotlin supports both functional and object-oriented programming (OOP). We spoke about functions, higher-order functions, and lambdas in the last section, and we mentioned Kotlin as an accessible language. This section will cover the essential OOPs concepts that characterize Kotlin as an OOP language.

Object-Oriented Programming Language

Class and object are the essential concepts of an OOP language. These support OOP ideas like inheritance, abstraction, and so forth.

DOI: 10.1201/9781003308447-2

Class

Class, like Java, is a blueprint for objects with similar characteristics. We must first declare a class before creating an object, and the class keyword is used to do so.

The class declaration comprises the class name, the class header, and the class body, which are all separated by curly brackets.

Syntax:

```
class className
{       // the class header
   // property
   // the member-function
}
```

- **Class name:** Each class has a unique name.

- **Class header:** Class headers are composed of the arguments and constructors of a class.

- **Class body:** Curly brackets surround the class body, containing member functions and other properties.

The header and class body are optional; the class body can be deleted if there is nothing between the curly braces.

```
class blankClass
```

We must use the term immediately after the class name if we want to include a constructor.

Creating a constructor:

```
class className constructor(parameters) {
   // property
   // the member-function
}
```

Example:

```
class employe
   {
```

```
   // properties
   var names: String = ""
   var ages: Int = 0
   var gender: Char = 'D'
   var salary: Double = 0.toDouble()
   //the member functions
   fun names(){
   }
   fun ages() {
   }
   fun salary(){
   }
}
```

Object

It is a key unit of OOP that represents real-world entities with state and behavior. Objects are used to access the properties and member functions of a class. In Kotlin, several instances of the same class can create. An item is made up of the following components:

- **State:** It is represented by the properties of an item. It also reflects an object's attributes.

- **Behavior:** It is expressed by the methods of an object. It also illustrates the interaction of a thing with other objects.

- **Identity:** It gives an object a unique name and enables one object to connect with other things.

- **Create an object:** We may build an object by using the class reference.

  ```
  var objt = className()
  ```

- **Accessing class's properties:** We may use an object to access the properties of a class. First, construct an object using the class reference and access the property.

  ```
  objt.nameOfProperty
  ```

- **Access to a class member function:** The object can use to access a class member function.

  ```
  objt.funtionName(parameters)
  ```

Example:

```
class employees
{// Constructor Declaration of Class
    var names: String = ""
    var ages: Int = 0
    var gender: Char = 'F'
    var salary: Double = 0.toDouble()
    fun insertValues(n: String, a: Int, g: Char, s:
Double) {
        names = n
        ages = a
        gender = g
        salary = s
        println("The Name of the employees: $name")
        println("The Age of the employees: $age")
        println("The Gender: $gender")
        println("The Salary of the employees:
$salary")
    }
    fun insertName(n: String) {
        this.name = n
    }
}
fun main(args: Array<String>) {
    // creating the multiple objects
    var objt = employees()
    // object 2 of class employees
    var objt2 = employees()
    //accessing the member function
    objt.insertValues("Raveen", 8, 'F', 40000.00)
    // accessing the member function
    objt2.insertName("Jlie")
    // accessing the name property of class
    println("Name of the new employees: ${objt2
.name}")

}
```

NESTED CLASS AND INNER CLASS IN KOTLIN

Nested Class

A class is referred to as nested when declared within another class. Because nested classes are static by default, we may use dot(.) notation to access their attributes or variables without creating an instance of the class.

Syntax:

```
class out_Class {
        . . . . . . . . . . . . .
        // the properties of the outer class or a
member function
        class nest_Class {
            . . . . . . . . . . .
            // the properties of the inner class
or member function
        }
}
```

It is important to note that nested classes cannot access the members of the outer class, but we may access nested class properties from the outer class without creating an object for the nested class.

In Kotlin, use the following program to access nested class attributes:

```
// the outer class declaration
class outer_Class {
    var strg = "Outer class"
    // the nested class declaration
    class nested_Class {
        val firstName  = "Ravi"
        val lastName = "Ridhi"
    }
}
fun main(args: Array<String>) {
    // accessing the member of Nested class
    print(outer_Class.nested_Class().firstName)
    print(" ")
    println(outer_Class.nested_Class().lastName)
}
```

In Kotlin, we must first create the nested class's object and then invoke the member function from it.

In Kotlin, the following program is used to access nested class member functions:

```
// the outer class declaration
class outer_Class {
    var strg = "Outer class"
    // the nested class declaration
    class nested_Class {
        var str1 = "Nested class"
        // nested class member function
        fun nestfunc(strg2: String): String {
            var str2 = st1.plus(strg2)
            return str2
        }
    }
}
fun main(args: Array<String>) {
    // the creating object of Nested class
    val nested = outer_Class.nested_Class()
    //invoking the nested member function by passing
the string
    var result = nested.nestfunc(" Member function-
call successful")
    println(result)
}
```

In comparison to Java: When it comes to functionality and use cases, Kotlin classes are similar to but not identical to Java classes. The Nested class in Kotlin corresponds to a static nested class in Java, but the Inner class corresponds to a non-static nested class in Java.

Kotlin	Java
Nested class	Static Nested class
Inner class	Non-Static class

Inner Class in Kotlin

An "inner class" is a class that may be defined within another class using the keyword inner. We may access the outer class property from within the inner class by using the inner class.

```
class outer_Class {
    . . . . . . . . . . . . .
        // properties of the outer class or member-function
```

```
    inner class inner_Class {
        . . . . . . . . . . .
        // properties of the inner class or
member-function
    }
}
```

We try to access strg from the inner class member function in the following program. It does not, however, work and creates a compile-time error.

Inner-Class Kotlin Program

```
// the outer class declaration
class outer_Class {
    var strg = "Outer class"
    // the inner_Class declaration without using inner
keyword
    class inner_Class {
        var st1 = "Inner class"
        fun nestfunc(): String {
            // it can not access the outer class
property strg
            var st2 = strg
            return st2
        }
    }
}
//the main function
fun main(args: Array<String>) {
    // creating the object for inner class
    val inner= outer_Class().inner_Class()
    // inner function call using the object
    println(inner.nestfunc())
}
```

To begin, place the inner keyword before the inner class. Then, create an instance of outer class; otherwise, we will be unable to use inner classes.

```
// the outer class declaration
class outer_Class {
    var strg = "Outer class"
    // inner_Class declaration with using inner keyword
```

```
    inner class inner_Class {
        var st1 = "Inner class"
        fun nestfunc(): String {
            // can access the outer class property
strg
            var st2 = strg
            return st2
        }
    }
}
// the main function
fun main(args: Array<String>) {
    // for inner class creating the object
    val inner= outer_Class().inner_Class()
    // using object inner function call
    println(inner.nestfunc()+" property accessed
successfully from inner class ")
}
```

SETTERS AND GETTERS

Every programming language requires the use of properties. In Kotlin, properties may declare in the same manner that variables can. In Kotlin, properties may be designated as changeable or immutable by using the var keyword.

Syntax:

```
var <propertyName>[: <PropertyType>]
[= <property_initializer>]
    [<getter>]
    [<setter>]
```

The property initializer, getter, and setter are all optional in this scenario. We may also omit the property type if we can infer it from the initializer. A read-only or immutable property declaration differs from a mutable property declaration in two ways:

- It begins with the val rather than var.

- It does not permit a setter.

```
fun main(args : Array) {
    var a: Int = 0
```

```
    val b: Int = 1
    a = 2 // It can be allocated unlimited number
of times
    b = 0 // It'll never be allocated again
    }
```

Setters and Getters

In Kotlin, the setter is used to set the value of a variable, whilst the getter is used to get the discount. The code generates Getters and Setters automatically. In the 'company' class, let us define a 'names' property. 'names' is of the data type String and will be set to a default value.

```
class companie
{
var names: String = "Defaultvalues"
}
```

The previous code relates to the following code:

```
class companie
{
    var names: String = "defaultvalues"
        get() = field                      // getter
        set(value) { field = value }       // setter
}
```

We make a 'y' object of the type 'companie.' We provide the setter's parameter value when we initialize the 'names' property, which sets the 'field' to value. When we try to access the object's names property, we receive a field since the code gets () = field. We can acquire or set the properties of a class object using the dot(.) syntax.

```
val y = companie()
y.names = "TheHuboftutor"   // access setter
println(y.names)            // access getter
```

Program of Default Setter and Getter in Kotlin

```
class companie
{
    var names: String = ""
```

```
        get() = field          // getter
        set(value) {           // setter
            field = value
        }
}
fun main(args: Array<String>) {
    val y = Companie()
    y.name = "TheHuboftutor"  // access setter
    println(y.names)           // access getter
}
```

Identifiers for Values and Fields

We have discovered these two Identifiers.

- **Value:** We usually use the name of the setter parameter as the value, but we may use whatever name we choose. The value argument contains the value that has been assigned to a property. In the above program, we set the property name to y.name = "TheHuboftutor" and we set the value parameter to "TheHuboftutor."

- **Backing Field (field):** It allows us to save the property value in memory. When we initialize property with value, the value is written to the property's backing field. In the preceding program, the value is assigned to the field, and then the field is assigned to obtain ().

Private Modifier

If we want the public to be allowed to utilize the get function, we may use the following code:

```
var names: String = ""
    private set
```

We can only set the name in a method within the class due to the private modifier near the set accessor. In a Kotlin program, a method within a class is used to set the value.

```
class companie () {
    var names: String = "cde"
        private set

    fun myfunc(x: String) {
```

```
          names = x               // here, we set the name
      }
}
fun main(args: Array<String>) {
    var d = company()
    println("The Name of the company is: ${d.names}")
    d.myfunc("TheHuboftutor")
    println("The Name of the new company is: ${d.
names}")
}
```

Explanation: We used the private modifier in combination with the set in this situation. To begin, create an object of type companie() and access the property name. The name "TheHuboftutor" is then sent as a parameter to the method defined within the class. Once again, access is given when the name property is changed with the new name.

Setter and Getter with Custom Parameters

```
class registrations( email: String, pwd: String, age:
Int,  gender: Char) {
    var email_id: String = email
        // the Custom Getter
        get() {
            return field.toLowerCase()
        }
    var password: String = pwd
        // the Custom Setter
        set(values){
            field = if(values.length > 7) value else
throw IllegalArgumentException("Password is small")
        }

    var age: Int = age
        // the Custom Setter
        set(values) {
            field = if(values > 19 ) value else throw
IllegalArgumentException("Age must be 19+")
        }
    var gender : Char = gender
        // the Custom Setter
        set (values){
```

```
            field = if(values == 'F') value else throw
IllegalArgumentException("User should be male")
        }
}
}

fun main(args: Array<String>) {

    val peek = registrations("ruhi1998@GMAIL.
COM","Hub@123",29,'F')
    println("${hub.email_id}")
    peek.email_id = "HUBTUTOR@CAREERS.ORG"
    println("${hub.email_id}")
    println("${hub.password}")
    println("${hub.age}")
    println("${hub.gender}")

    // throw IllegalArgumentException("Passwords is
small")
    peek.password = "abc"
    // throw IllegalArgumentException("Age should be
19+")
    peek.age= 5
    // throw IllegalArgumentException("User should be
male")
    peek.gender = 'M'
}
```

CLASS PROPERTIES AND CUSTOM ACCESSORS

Encapsulation is the most fundamental and important idea in a class. It's a feature that lets us merge code and data into a single object. Data in Java is saved in fields, which are usually private. Consequently, accessor methods – a getter and a setter – are provided to allow users of the given class to access the data. In the setter, additional logic is included for providing change alerts and validating the passed value.

Property

It is a combination of accessories and fields in the case of Java. In Kotlin, properties are meant to be first-class language features. These features have replaced fields and accessor methods. The val and var keywords are used to specify class properties in the same manner as variables are. A var-declared property is mutable, which means it may change.

Creating a class:

```
class Cbad(
    val names: String,
    val ispassed: Boolean
)
```

- **Readable Property:** Generates field and trivial getter

- **Writable Property:** A getter, setter, and field

The property declaration essentially declares the linked accessors (both setter and getter for writable and getter for the readable property). A field is used to hold the value.

Let's have a look at how the class is implemented:

```
class Cbad(
    val names: String,
    val ispassed: Boolean
)
fun main(args: Array<String>) {
    val abcd = Cbad("Bobbin",true)
    println(abcd.names)
    println(abcd.ispassed)
    /*
    In Java
    Cbad abcd = new Cbad("Bobi",true);
    System.out.println(person.getName());
    System.out.println(person.isMarried());
    */
}
```

In Kotlin, the constructor can be called without the requirement for a new keyword. Instead of utilizing a getter, the property is addressed directly. The logic is the same, but the code is much shorter. Setters of mutable properties work in the same way.

Customer Accessors

Implementation of property accessors on a specific instance basis:

```
class Rect(val height: Int, val width: Int)
{
    val isSquare: Boolean
```

```
            get() {
                return height == width
            }
}
fun main(args: Array<String>) {
    val rect = Rect(22, 14)
    println(rect.isSquare)
}
```

KOTLIN CONSTRUCTOR

Constructor is a member function that is invoked when a class object is created to initialize variables or properties. Every class must have a constructor, and if we don't define one, the compiler will create one for us.

There are kinds of constructors in Kotlin:

- Primary Constructor
- Secondary Constructor

A class in Kotlin can have one primary constructor and one or more subsidiary constructors. The primary constructor is responsible for initializing the class, whereas the secondary constructor is in charge of initializing the class and introducing some extra logic.

Primary Constructor

After the class name, the constructor keyword is used to initialize the primary in the class header. The main constructor's parameters are optional.

```
class Addconstructor(val x: Int, val y: Int) {
    // code..
}
```

The constructor keyword can omit if no annotations or access modifiers are supplied.

```
class Add(val x: Int, val y: Int) {
    // code..
}
```

Example:

```
//the main function
fun main(args: Array<String>)
{
    val add = Add(10, 2)
    println("The Sum of numbers 10 and 2 is:
${add.a}")
}
//the primary constructor
class Add constructor(x: Int,y:Int)
{
    var a = x+y;
}
```

Primary Constructor with Initializer Block
The primary constructor may not include any code; however, the initialization code may include in a separate initializer block headed by the init keyword.

Example:

```
fun main(args: Array<String>) {
    val empy = employees(27117, "Rani")
}
class employees(empy_id : Int,  empy_name: String)
{
    val id: Int
    var names: String
    // initializer block
    init {
        id = empy_id
        names = empy_names
        println("Employees id is: $id")
        println("Employees name: $names")
    }
}
```

The Default Value in the Primary Constructor
We can initialize the function constructor parameters with some default values, similar to how we establish the default values of functions.

Example:

```
fun main(args: Array<String>) {
    val empy = employees(27117, "Rani")
    // the default value for empy_name will be
used here
    val empy2 = employees(10011)
    //default values for the both parameters
because no arguments passed
    val empy3 = employees()
}
class employees(empy_id : Int = 110,  empy_name:
String = "cbad") {
    val id: Int
    var name: String
    // initializer block
    init {
        id = empy_id
        name = empy_name
         print("Employee id is: $id, ")
        println("Employee name: $name")
        println()
    }
}
```

Secondary Constructor

Kotlin, as previously noted, may have one or more secondary constructors. Secondary constructors enable variable initialization and the inclusion of logic to the class. The keyword constructor precedes them.

Example:

```
//the main function
fun main(args: Array<String>)
{
    Add(10, 3)
}
//class with the one secondary constructor
class Add
{
    constructor(x: Int, y:Int)
    {
```

```
         var a = x + y
         println("The sum of numbers 10 and 3 is:
${a}")
      }
}
```

The compiler determines which secondary constructor will be executed based on the arguments provided. The above program does not specify which constructor should be called, and the compiler decides.

Example:

```
fun main(args: Array<String>) {
    employee(17117, "Rani")
    employee(12011,"Prithwi",52000.5)
}
class employee {
      constructor (empy_id : Int, empy_name:
String ) {
           var id: Int = empy_id
           var name: String = empy_name
           print("Employee id is: $id, ")
           println("Employee name: $name")
           println()
      }
       constructor (empy_id : Int, empy_name:
String, empy_salary : Double) {
           var id: Int = empy_id
           var name: String = empy_name
           var salary : Double = empy_salary
           print("The Employee id is: $id, ")
           print("The Employee name: $name, ")
           println("The Employee name: $salary")
      }
}
```

In a Kotlin program, there are three secondary constructors in a class:

```
//the main function
fun main(args: Array<String>)
{
    Add(31, 51)
```

```
    Add(31, 51, 61)
    Add(31, 51, 61, 71)
}
//class with the three secondary constructors
class Add
{
    constructor(x: Int, y: Int)
    {
        var a = x + y
        println("Sum of 31, 51 = ${a}")
    }
    constructor(x: Int, y: Int, a: Int)
    {
        var b = x + y + a
        println("Sum of 31, 51, 61 = ${b}")
    }
    constructor(x: Int, y: Int, a: Int, b: Int)
    {
        var e = x + y + a + b
        println("Sum of 31, 51, 61, 71 = ${e}")
    }
}
```

VISIBILITY MODIFIERS IN KOTLIN

In Kotlin, visibility modifiers are used to restrict access to classes, objects, interfaces, constructors, methods, properties, and their setters. There is no need to make getters visible because they are visible in the same way as the property.

In Kotlin, there are four visibility modifiers:

Modifier	Description
Public	The Visible everywhere
Private	The Visible inside same class only
Internal	The Visible inside the same module
Protected	The Visible inside the same class and its subclasses

If no modifier is specified, the value is set to public by default. Let's go through the modifiers listed above one by one.

Public Modifier

The public modifier is the default in Kotlin. It is the most commonly used modifier in the language, and there are additional restrictions on who may access the component being modified. Unlike Java, there is no need to specify anything as public in Kotlin; it is the default modifier; if no other modifier is specified, public works the same in Kotlin as it does in Java. When the public modifier is added to top-level elements, classes, methods, or variables written directly within a package, any other code can access them. If the public modifier is added to a nested element an inner class or function within a class, then any code that can access the container may also access this element.

```
// by default public
class X {
    var int = 40
}

// specified with the public modifier
public class Y {
    var int2 = 20
    fun display() {
    println("Accessible-everywhere")
    }
}
```

Classes X and Y access from anywhere in the code, and the variables int and int2 and the function display() can access from anything that can access classes X and Y.

Private Modifier

In Kotlin, private modifiers limit access to code specified inside the same scope, which makes it impossible to access the modifier variable or function outside the scope. In contrast to Java, Kotlin allows several top-level declarations in the same file – a private top-level element in the same file can be accessed by everything else in the same file.

```
// class X is accessible from the same source file
private class X {
    private val int = 30
    fun display()
    {
        // we can access int in same-class
        println(int)
```

```
        println("Accessing int successful")
    }
}
fun main(args: Array<String>){
    var x = X()
    x.display()
    // can not access 'int': it is private in class X
    println(x.int)
}
```

In this situation, Class X can only access the int variable from inside the same source file, and Class X can only access the int variable from within Class X. We encountered a compile-time error when attempting to access int from outside the class.

Internal Modifier

The internal modifier is a new Kotlin modifier that Java does not support. Internal means that it will only be accessible inside the same module; attempting to access the declaration from another module will result in an error. A module is a group of files that have been assembled.

```
internal class X {
}
public class Y {
    internal val int = 30
    internal fun display() {
    }
}
```

Class X is only accessible from inside the same module in this situation. Even though class Y may be accessible from everywhere, the variable int and function display() are only available within the same module.

Protected Modifier

In Kotlin, the protected modifier restricts access to the declaring class and its subclasses. The protected modifier cannot be shown at the top level. In the following example, we utilized the getvalue() function of the derived class to obtain the int variable.

```
// base class
open class X {
```

```
        // protected variable
    protected val int = 30
}
// derived class
class Y: X() {
    fun getvalue(): Int {
            // accessed from the subclass
        return int
    }
}

fun main(args: Array<String>) {
    var c = Y()
    println("The value of integer is: "+c.getvalue())
}
```

Overriding the Protected Modifier

We must use the open keyword to override the protected variable or function in the derived class. In the following program, we override the int variable.

```
// base class
open class X {
      // protected variable
    open protected val int = 30
}
// derived class
class Y: X() {
    override val int = 40
    fun getvalue():Int {
            // accessed from the subclass
        return int
    }
}
fun main(args: Array<String>) {
    var c = Y()
    println("The overridden value of integer is: "+c.
getvalue())
}
```

Constructor Visibility

Constructors are always public by default, although modifiers can change that.

```
class X (name : String) {
    // other-code
}
```

When changing the visibility, we must indicate this clearly by using the constructor keyword.

```
class X private constructor (name : String) {
    // other-code
}
```

INTERFACES IN KOTLIN

Interfaces are Kotlin-provided custom types that cannot be directly instantiated. These, on the other hand, indicate a style of behavior that the implementing types must exhibit. The interface enables us to define a set of traits and methods that concrete types must comply and implement.

Creating Interfaces

In Kotlin, the interface declaration begins with the interface keyword, followed by the interface's name, and lastly by the curly brackets containing the interface's members. The members, on the other hand, will not have their definition. The conforming types will provide these definitions.

Example:

```
interface Machine()
{
    fun start()
    fun stop()
}
```

Implementing Interfaces

A class or an object can implement an interface. When we implement an interface, we must define all of its members in the conforming type.

To implement an interface, the name of the custom-type is followed by a colon and the name of the interface to be implemented.

```
class Bus: Machine
```

An example of an interface in Kotlin:

```
interface Machine {
    fun start()
    fun stop()
}

class Bus : Machine {
    override fun start()
    {
        println("The Bus is started")
    }

    override fun stop()
    {
        println("The Bus is stopped")
    }
}

fun main()
{
    val obj = Bus()
    obj.start()
    obj.stop()
}
```

Explanation: The user interface in this application, Vehicle defines two methods, start() and stop(), which must be overridden. Bus implements the interface with class-literal syntax and uses the override keyword to override the two methods. Finally, the main function constructs a Bus object and invokes the two functions.

Default Methods and Default Values

Methods of an interface can have default values for their parameters. If a parameter's value is not supplied at the function call, the default value is used. The methods may also have default implementations. They are used when the method is not overridden.

Example:

```kotlin
interface FirstInterface {
    fun add(x: Int, y: Int = 9)
    fun print()
    {
        println("This is a default-method defined
in the interface")
    }
}
class InterfaceDemo : FirstInterface {
    override fun add(x: Int, y: Int)
    {
        val c = x + y
        println("Sum is $c")
    }

    override fun print()
    {
        super.print()
        println("It has overridden")
    }
}

fun main()
{
    val objt = InterfaceDemo()
    println(objt.add(9))
    objt.print()
}
```

Explanation: In the above program, the FirstInterface exposes two methods: add() and print(). The add() method takes two parameters, one set to 9 by default. The print() method also has a default implementation. As a result, when the class InterfaceDemo implements the interface, it employs the super keyword to override both methods and invoke the default implementation of print (). Furthermore, only one parameter is required because the second argument is assigned to a default value when utilizing the add method in the primary function.

Interface Properties

Attributes can be included in interfaces, just as they can in methods. However, because the interface lacks a state, they cannot be generated, and hence no underlying fields to store their values exist. As a result, the interface fields are either left abstract or provided an implementation.

Example:

```
interface InterfaceProperties {
    val x : Int
    val y : String
        get() = "Heyyyy"
}

class PropertiesDemo : InterfaceProperties {
    override val x : Int = 5000
    override val y : String = "Property-Overridden"
}

fun main()
{
    val x = PropertiesDemo()
    println(a.x)
    println(a.y)
}
```

Explanation: In the above program, InterfaceProperties provide two properties: (a) an integer and (b) a String with a getter. PropertiesDemo is a class that implements InterfaceProperties and adds value to the two properties. The method main creates a class object and accesses its attributes through dot-syntax.

Interface Inheritance

Interfaces in Kotlin can inherit from other interfaces. When one interface extends another, it may add its own properties and methods, but the implementing type must specify all of the properties and methods in both interfaces. An interface can inherit many interfaces.

Example:

```
interface Dimension {
    val len : Double
    val br : Double
}
```

```kotlin
interface CalculateParameters : Dimension {
    fun area()
    fun perimeter()
}
class CDE : CalculateParameters {
    override val len : Double
        get() = 30.0
    override val br : Double
        get()= 19.0
    override fun area()
    {
        println("Area is ${len * br}")
    }

    override fun perimeter()
    {
        println("Perimeter is ${2*(len+br)}")
    }
}
fun main()
{
    val obj = CDE()
    objt.area()
    objt.perimeter()
}
```

Implementation of Multiple Interfaces

Because Kotlin classes adhere to the concept of single inheritance, which means that each class may inherit just one class, interfaces permit multiple inheritances, referred to as multiple conformance in Kotlin. A class can implement several interfaces as long as it defines all of the members of each interface.

Example:

```kotlin
interface InterfaceProperties {
    val x : Int
    val y : String
        get() = "Heyyyy"
}
interface InterfaceMethods {
    fun description()
}
```

```kotlin
class MultipleInterface : InterfaceProperties,
InterfaceMethods {
    override val x : Int
        get() = 80
    override fun description()
    {
        println("Multiple-Interfaces implemented")
    }
}
fun main()
{
    val objt = MultipleInterface()
    objt.description()
}
```

DATA CLASSES

We often create classes to store data in them. Few standard functions may frequently be derived from the data in such classes. In Kotlin, this class is a data class and is labeled as such.

Example:

```kotlin
data class Stud(val name: String, val roll_no: Int)
```

The compiler automatically produces the following functions:

- hashCode()
- toString()
- copy()
- equals()

Rules for Creating Data Classes

To ensure consistency, data classes must fulfill the following criteria:

- The primary constructor requires at least one parameter.
- All parameters to the main constructor must be denoted with val or var.

- Data classes cannot be abstract, open, sealed, or inner.

- Data classes may implement only interfaces.

toString()

This function returns a string containing all of the parameters to the data class.

Example:

```
fun main(args: Array<String>)
{
    //the declarion of data-class
    data class woman(val roll: Int,val name:
String,val height:Int)
    //declarion of variable of the above data
class and initializing values to all parameters
    val woman1=woman(1,"woman",40)
    //print all details of the data class
    println(woman1.toString());
}
```

The compiler only utilizes the characteristics specified inside the primary constructor for the automatically produced functions.

It excludes the properties declared in the class's body.

Example:

```
fun main(args: Array<String>)
{
    //declarion of data-class
    data class woman(val name: String)
    {
        //the property declared in class-body
        var height: Int = 0;
    }
    //declarion of variable of the above data
class and initializing values to all parameters
    val woman1=woman("Rhiana")
    //class body properties must be assigned
uniquely
    woman1.height = 50
```

```
    //this method print the details of class that
are declared in primary constructor
    println(woman1.toString());
    //printing the height of woman1
    println(woman1.height);
}
```

copy()

We may need to copy an object and update its characteristics while leaving others unchanged.

In this case, the copy() function is used.

- **copy() properties:**

  All of the arguments or members defined in the main constructor are duplicated.

  When two objects are defined, they may have the same main parameter values but different class body values.

- **copy() declaration:**

```
fun copy(name: String = this.x, age: Int = this.y)
= user(x, y)
```

  where user is a data class: user(String, Int).

Example:

```
fun main(args: Array<String>)
{
    //declarion of a data class
    data class woman(val name: String, val age:
Int)
    {
        //property declared in class-body
        var height: Int = 0;
    }
    val woman1 = woman("Damini",16)
    //copying details of man1 with change in name
of man
    val woman2 = woman1.copy(name="Pari")

    //copying all details of woman1 to woman3
```

```
    val woman3 = woman1.copy();

    //declaring heights of individual men
    woman1.height=110
    woman2.height=92
    woman3.height=130

    //woman1 & woman3 have different class body
values, but same parameter values
    //printing info all 3 men
    println("${woman1} has ${woman1.height} cm
height")
    println("${woman2} has ${woman2.height} cm
height")
    println("${woman3} has ${woman3.height} cm
height")
}
```

hashCode() and equals()

- The hashCode() function returns the hash code value of the object.

- The equals() method returns true if two objects have the same contents and work in the same way as "==", but with Float and Double values.

hashCode() declaration:

```
open fun hashCode(): Int
```

hashCode() properties:

- Two hash codes that are specified twice on the same item are equal.

- The hash codes will be the same if two objects are equal according to the equals() method.

```
fun main(args: Array<String>)
{
    //declaring a data-class
    data class woman(val name: String, val age: Int)
```

```
val woman1 = woman("ridhi",19)
val woman2 = woman1.copy(name="rahi")
val woman3 = woman1.copy();
val hash1=woman1.hashCode();
val hash2=woman2.hashCode();
val hash3=woman3.hashCode();
println(hash1)
println(hash2)
println(hash3)
//checking equality of  these hash-codes
println("hash1 == hash 2 ${hash1.equals
(hash2)}")
println("hash2 == hash 3 ${hash2.equals
(hash3)}")
println("hash1 == hash 3 ${hash1.equals
(hash3)}")

}
```

SEALED CLASSES

Kotlin provides a new class type that is not found in Java. These are known as sealed classes. As the name indicates, Sealed classes adhere to confined or bounded class hierarchies. A collection of subclasses is specified within a sealed class. It is used when it is known in advance that a type will conform to one of the subclass types. Sealed classes ensure type safety by restricting the types that can match at compile time rather than at runtime.

Declaration of sealed class:

```
sealed class Demo1
```

To define a sealed class, just use the sealed keyword before the class modifier. Another feature that distinguishes sealed classes is that their constructors are, by default, private.

A sealed class cannot instantiate since it is inherently abstract.

```
sealed class Demoo1
fun main(args: Array)
{
    var x = Demoo1()      //compiler error
}
```

Example:

```
sealed class Demo1 {
    class X : Demo1() {
        fun display()
        {
            println("Subclass X of sealed class
Demo")
        }
    }
    class Y : Demo1() {
        fun display()
        {
            println("Subclass Y of sealed class
Demo")
        }
    }
}
fun main()
{
    val objt = Demo1.Y()
    objt.display()
    val objt1 = Demo1.X()
    objt1.display()
}
```

It should note that all sealed class subclasses must specify in the same Kotlin file. However, they do not have to be declared within the sealed class; instead, they can be defined anywhere the sealed class is accessible.

Example:

```
//sealed class with the single subclass defined
inside
sealed class CDEF {
 class X: CDEF(){...}
}
// Another subclass of the sealed class defined
class Y: CDEF() {
  class Z: CDEF()    // This will result in an
error. The sealed class is not visible in this
case.
}
```

Sealed class with when: Because the types to which a sealed class reference can conform are limited, it is usually used in combination with a when clause. This completely eliminates the requirement for the otherwise clause.

Example:

```
// A sealed class with string-property
sealed class Fruit
    (val a: String)
{
    // Two subclasses of sealed-class defined
within
    class Banana : Fruit("Banana")
    class Grapes : Fruit("Grapes")
}

// A subclass defined outside the sealed-class
class Apple: Fruits("Apple")
// A function to take in an object of type Fruit
// And to display an appropriate message depending
on the type of Fruit
fun display(fruits: Fruits){
    when(fruits)
    {
        is Fruits.Banana -> println("${fruits.a}
is good for iron")
        is Fruits.Grapes -> println("${fruits.a}
is yummy")
        is Apple -> println("${fruits.a} is good
for vitamin d")
    }
}
fun main()
{
    // Objects of different subclasses created
    val objt = Fruits.Banana()
    val objt1 = Fruits.Grapes()
    val objt2 = Apple()
    // Function called with the different objects
    display(objt)
    display(objt1)
    display(objt2)
}
```

KOTLIN ABSTRACT CLASS

In Kotlin, the abstract keyword is used in front of class to declare an abstract class. We cannot create objects because an abstract class cannot instantiate.

Declaration of an abstract class:

```
abstract class className {
    ...........
}
```

Keep the following in mind:

- We can't create an object for the abstract class.

- By default, all variables (properties) and member functions of an abstract class are non-abstract. As a result, we must use the open keyword to override these members in the child class.

- Because member functions are open by default, we don't need to annotate them with the open keyword when we designate them as abstract.

- Because it lacks a body, a derived class must implement an abstract member function.

Abstract class can have both the abstract and non-abstract members, as seen below:

```
abstract class class_Name(val c: String) {    //
Non-Abstract-Property
    abstract var y: Int        // Abstract-Property
    abstract fun method1()     // Abstract-Methods
    fun method2() {            // Non-Abstract-Method
        println("Non-abstract-function")
    }
}
```

Example:

```
//abstract-class
abstract class Emp(val name: String,val
experience: Int) {    // Non-Abstract-Property
```

```kotlin
    // Abstract-Property (Must be overridden by
Subclasses)
    abstract var salary: Double
    // Abstract-Methods (Must be implemented by
Subclasses)
    abstract fun dateOfBirth(date:String)
    // Non-Abstract-Method
    fun empDetails() {
        println("Name of the employee: $name")
        println("Experience in years:
$experience")
        println("Annual Salary: $salary")
    }
}
// derived-class
class Engineer(name: String,experience: Int) :
Emp(name,experience) {
    override var salary = 610000.00
    override fun dateOfBirth(date:String){
        println("Date of Birth is: $date")
    }
}
fun main(args: Array<String>) {
    val eng = Engineer("Praniti",3)
    eng.empDetails()
    eng.dateOfBirth("02 Jan 1993")
}
```

Explanation: The previous computer's Engineer class is developed from the Employee class. Object eng is generated for the Engineer class. We sent two arguments to the primary constructor while building it. This sets the non-abstract properties name and experience of the Emp class.

The empDetails() method is then called using the eng object. The name, experience, and override wage of the emp will print.

Finally, we call dateOfBirth() on the eng object and provide the parameter date to the primary. It overrides the Emp class's abstract fun and writes the value to standard output.

Use of an abstract open member in place of a non-abstract open member: To override the non-abstract open member function of the open class in Kotlin, use the override keyword followed by an abstract in the abstract class. This will accomplish in the following program.

Example:

```kotlin
open class Livebeing {
    open fun breathe() {
        println("All live being breathe")
    }
}
abstract class Creature : Livebeing() {
    override abstract fun breathe()
}
class Cat: Creature(){
    override fun breathe() {
        println("Cat breathe")
    }
}
fun main(args: Array<String>){
    val lb = Livebeing()
    lb.breathe()
    val c = Cat()
    c.breathe()
}
```

Multiple Derived Classes

All derived classes can override an abstract member of an abstract class. In the program, we override the cal function in three derived classes of calculators.

Example:

```kotlin
// abstract-class
abstract class Calculation {
    abstract fun cal(e: Int, f: Int) : Int
}
// addition of two-numbers
class Add : Calculation() {
    override fun cal(e: Int, f: Int): Int {
        return e + f
    }
}
// subtraction of two-numbers
class Sub : Calculation() {
```

```
        override fun cal(e: Int, f: Int): Int {
            return e - f
        }
}
// multiplication of two-numbers
class Mul : Calculation() {
        override fun cal(e: Int, f: Int): Int {
            return e * f
        }
}
fun main(args: Array<String>) {
        var add: Calculation = Add()
        var e1 = add.cal(15, 26)
        println("Addition of two numbers $e1")
        var sub: Calculation = Sub()
        var e2 = sub.cal(21,36)
        println("Subtraction of two numbers $e2")
        var mul: Calculation = Mul()
        var e3 = mul.cal(32,61)
        println("Multiplication of two numbers $e3")
}
```

INHERITANCE IN KOTLIN

Inheritance is a major concept in OOP. Inheritance enables code reuse by allowing a new class to inherit (derived-class) all of the characteristics of an existing class (base-class). The derived class can add its own features.

Syntax:

```
open class baseClass (x:Int ) {
        . . . . . . . . . . .
}
class derivedClass(x:Int) : baseClass(x) {
        . . . . . . . . . . .
}
```

All Kotlin classes are final by default. To allow the derived class to inherit from the base class, we must use the open keyword in front of it.

The following properties and methods are inherited from the base class:

- We inherit all of its attributes and functionalities when we inherit a class. Variables and functions from the base class can use in the derived class, and functions from the derived class object can call.

```
//base-class
open class baseClass{
    val name = "TheHubtutor"
    fun X(){
        println("BaseClass")
    }
}
//derived class
class derivedClass: baseClass() {
    fun Y() {
        println(name)            //inherit name
property
        println("Derivedclass")
    }
}
fun main(args: Array<String>) {
    val derived = derived-Class()
    derived.X()            // inheriting base-class
function
    derived.Y()            // calling derived-class
function
}
```

Explanation: There is a base class and a derived class in this situation. When we instantiate the derived class, we create an object that is then used to invoke the functions of the base and derived classes. The derived.X() function is used to call the X() method, which returns the string "Base Class." The derived.Y() method calls the Y() function, which outputs the variable name inherited from the base class and the "Derived class."

Inheritance Use

Assume a company employs three people: a webDeveloper, an iOSDeveloper, and an androidDeveloper. They all share some traits, such as a name, an age, and specific special skills.

First, we split the individuals into three classes, each with its own set of standard and unique talents.

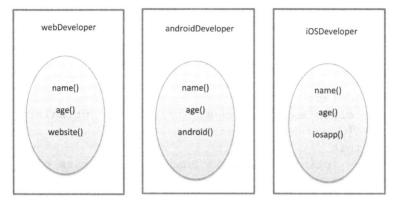

Use of Inheritance with example.

Although all three developers have the same name and age, their programming abilities are vastly different. We would use the same code for each character's name and age in each class.

If we want to add a salary() method, we must replicate the code in each of the three classes. This results in multiple duplicate copies of code in our program, which nearly always leads to more intricate and chaotic code.

The use of inheritance makes the work more approachable. We could create a new base class Employee with the same characteristics as the three original kinds. These three classes can then inherit the base class's shared attributes while adding their own. Without duplicating, we can easily add salary functionality to the Employee class.

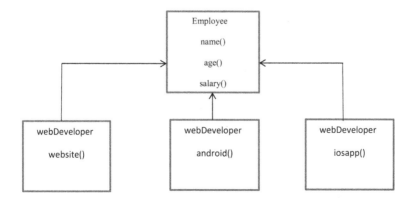

Inherit class.

In this scenario, webDeveloper inherits all of the base class's features and its feature website(). The same is true for the two other classes, iOS-Developer and androidDeveloper. It increases our code's readability and extensibility.

Example:

```
//baseclass
open class Employ( names: String,age: Int,salary :
Int) {
    init {
        println("Name is $names, $age years old
and earning $salary per month. ")
    }
}
//derivedclass
class web_Developers( names: String,age:
Int,salary : Int): Employ(names, age,salary) {
    fun website() {
        println("website-developer")
        println()
    }
}
//derived-class
class android_Developer( names: String,age:
Int,salary : Int): Employ(names, age,salary) {
    fun android() {
        println("android-app-developer")
        println()
    }
}
//derived class
class ios_Developers( names: String,age:
Int,salary : Int): Employ(names, age,salary) {
    fun iosapp() {
        println("iOS-app-developer")
        println()
    }
}
//the main method
fun main(args: Array<String>) {
    val wd = web_Developers("Rheinna", 21, 13000)
    wd.website()
```

```
        val ad = android_Developers("Payal", 24,15000)
        ad.android()
        val iosd = ios_Developers("Pranav", 27,19000)
        iosd.iosapp()
}
```

Explanation: In this scenario, we have a base class called Employ, which is prefixed with the open keyword and contains the common properties of the derived classes. Employ has a primary constructor that accepts three parameters: 'name, age, and salary.' There are three derived classes: web-Developers, androidDevelopers, and iOSDevelopers, each with three variables and a primary constructor.

First, we construct an object for the webDevelopers class and pass the name, age, and salary as parameters to the derived class. It will set the local variables' values and transmit them to the base class. Then, with the object 'wd,' we call the member function website(), which prints the string to standard output.

Similarly, we create objects for the last two classes and call their member functions.

Primary Constructor for an Inheritance
If derived class has a primary constructor, we must use the parameters from the derived class to initialize the base class constructor. In the following program, we have two parameters in the primary constructor of the base class and three parameters in the derived class.

```
//baseclass
open class Employ(names: String,age: Int) {
    init{
        println("Name of Employee is $names")
        println("Age of an Employee is $age")
    }
}
// derivedclass
class CEO( names: String, age: Int, salary: Double):
Employ(names,age) {
    init {
        println("Salary per annum is $salary crore
rupees")
    }
}
```

```
fun main(args: Array<String>) {
    CEO("Damini Rai", 33, 120.00)
}
```

Explanation: In this scenario, we instantiate the derived class CEO using the parameters names, age, and salary. The local variables of the derived class are initialized with the proper values, and the variable name and age are sent as arguments to the Employee class.

Before passing control to the derived class, the employ class prints the variable names and values to standard output. Following the execution of the println() command, the derived class ends.

Secondary Constructor for an Inheritance
If the derived class lacks the main constructor, we must use the super keyword to invoke the secondary constructor of the base class from the secondary constructor of the derived class. We must also use the inputs from the derived class to initialize the base class's secondary constructor.

```
//baseclass
open class Employ {
    constructor(names: String,age: Int){
            println("Name of Employee is $names")
            println("Age of Employee is $age")
    }
}
// derived class
class CEO : Employ{
    constructor( names: String,age: Int, salary:
Double): super(names,age) {
        println("Salary per annum is $salary million
dollars")
    }
}
fun main(args: Array<String>) {
    CEO("Raniti Dela", 59, 320.00)
}
```

Explanation: In this scenario, we instantiate the class CEO and provide the parameter values to the secondary constructor. It will initialize the local variables and give them to the base class Employees through super (names,ages).

Overriding Member Functions and Attributes

If member function with the same name exists in both the base and derived classes, we can override the base member function in the derived class using the override keyword, but we should also mark the member function of the base class with the open keyword.

First example:

```kotlin
// baseclass
open class Animals {
    open fun run() {
        println("Animals runs")
    }
}
// derivedclass
class Tiger: Animals() {
    override fun run() {        // it overrides the
run method of base-class
        println("Tiger runs very fast")
    }
}
fun main(args: Array<String>) {
    val tg = Tiger()
    tg.run()
}
```

Similarly, we may override the property of the base class in the derived class.

Second example:

```kotlin
// baseclass
open class Animals {
    open var name: String = "Cat"
    open var speed = "30 km/hr"

}
// derivedclass
class Tiger: Animals() {
    override var name = "Lion"
    override var speed = "100 km/hr"
}
```

```
fun main(args: Array<String>) {
    val tg = Tiger()
    println(tg.name+" can run at speed "+tg.speed)
}
```

Calling Superclass Implementation

We may invoke the base class's member methods or attributes from the derived class using the super keyword. We call the base class's property color and function displayCompany() in the superclass using the super keyword.

```
// baseclass
open class Phones() {
    var color = "Rose Gold"
    fun displayCompany(names:String) {
        println("The Company is: $names")
    }
}
// derivedclass
class iphone: Phones() {
    fun displayColor(){
        // calling the base-class property color
        println("Color is: "+super.color)
        // calling the base-class member function
        super.displayCompany("Blackberry")
    }
}
fun main(args: Array<String>) {
    val ps = iphone()
    ps.displayColor()
}
```

COMPOSITION

The concepts of inheritance and composition are used to construct relationships between classes and objects. It is critical to understand which of them to prioritize to create a successful software design.

Composition is method in which we compose a class by adding private fields to it that refer to an instance of an existing class rather than extending it. As a result, a "has-a" relationship is created between the constructed class and the instances it contains. The class fulfills its obligation by forwarding to or calling non-private methods of its private fields.

- Recognize inheritance and composition.

- Write classes using an inheritance-based approach and learn about their limitations.

- Discover the patterns of delegation.

- The composition may be used to restructure inheritance-based classes.

- Discover Kotlin's by keyword.

We may modify the User_Mediator using a composition-based method, as demonstrated below:

```
class User_Mediator {
  private val cacheService: UserCacheService =
UserCacheService()
  private val apiService: UserApiService =
UserApiService()
  ...
}
```

Take note of how a private instance of the UserCacheService and the UserApiService are combined to form UserMediator.

Now that we have a fundamental knowledge of composition, let's look at how it may use to tackle design problems caused by implementation inheritance.

Substitution Principle of Liskov

The foundation of LSP is that subclasses must be interchangeable with their superclasses. And for this to happen, the superclass's contracts must be honored by its subclasses. Statically typed languages such as Java and Kotlin enforce contracts such as function signatures (function name, return types, and parameters) as compile-time errors.

However, operations that violate this concept include unconditionally throwing exceptions, such as UnsupportedOperationException, in over-ridden methods when not anticipated in the superclass.

We may see if the modification needs every invocation of the method in question to be wrapped with if statement to test whether the method in question should be called or not based on the newly added subclass.

Antipatterns of Implementation Inheritance

Implementation inheritance is a valuable technique for code reuse, but it may not be appropriate in many situations. Using implementation inheritance when it is not suitable may cause maintenance issues. These will be covered in the following sections.

Inheritance of a Single Implementation

Class cannot inherit from more than one parent class in Java Virtual Machine languages such as Kotlin and Java.

Increase the userservice package's size. It includes two service classes: UserCacheService, which keeps User records in an in-memory data structure, and UserApiService, which simulates a network call with a delay. For the time being, disregard UserMediator.

Assume we need to create a class that communicates with the UserCacheService and the UserApiService to obtain a User record. We must do the task quickly; therefore, we search for the user in UserCacheService and return if it exists. Otherwise, we must make a slow "network" call. When UserApiService produces a User, it is cached for later use. Is it possible to do this using implementation inheritance?

```
// Error: Only one class may appear in supertype list
/**
 * Mediates repository between the cache and server.
 * In case of the cache hit, it returns data from the
cache;
 * else it fetches data from API and updates cache
before returning the result.
**/
class User_Mediator: UserApiService(),
UserCacheService() {
}
```

First and foremost, the code above will not compile. The relationship would be meaningless even if it did since UserMediator utilizes UserCacheService and UserApiService as implementation details rather than an is-a relationship. Later, we'll see how to solve this.

Tight Coupling

Implementation Inheritance establishes a close bond between a parent and their children. Inheriting a class binds the child class to the parent class's implementation details. As a result, if the parent class changes – that is, if it becomes unstable – the child class may fail even though its code remains unchanged. As a result, each child class must grow with the parent class.

This necessitates making a broad assumption about future requirements. We must establish the hierarchy early on and maintain the relationship with each new demand. As a result, we may have to use a Big Design Up Front (BDUF) approach, resulting in over-engineering and complicated design.

Unnecessary Exposure of Superclass APIs

Implementation inheritance is only suitable when the subclass is truly a subtype of the superclass. In other words, class B should extend class A only if they have "is-a" connection. Otherwise, we unnecessarily expose the superclass's implementation information to the user. This allows our class's clients to break its internal invariants by directly altering the superclass.

Examine Exposure_Demo.kt, which is included in the exposuredemo package. The variable property is an instance of the java.util package's Properties class. It is derived from the concrete Hashtable. This implies that, in addition to its public fields and methods, we may access Hashtable's public fields and methods, such as put() and get(), through the instance of Properties.

Go to Properties.java (found under java.util) in our IDE and select the Structure tab to obtain an overview of the APIs offered by Properties.

Deselect "Show non-public" and select "Show inherited" using the icons at the top of the window. The light grayish methods are the inherited public methods that may access through a Properties instance.

// [Properties] class is an extend from Hashtable. As a result, the Hashtable methods can also be used.

```
val properties = Properties()
// Using the [Hashtable]'s methods
properties.put("put1", "val1")
properties.put("put2", 110)
// Using [Properties]'s methods
properties.setProperty("setProperty1", "val1")
properties.setProperty("setProperty2", "110")
```

Property's getProperty() method performs additional safety checks that Hashtable's get() method does not. Properties users might circumvent these checks and read straight from Hashtable.

```
Using Hashtable's get() setProperty2: 110
Using Properties' getProperty() setProperty2 :   110
Using Hashtable's get() setProperty1: val1
Using Properties' getProperty() setProperty1 :   val1
Using Hashtable's get() put2: 110
Using Properties' getProperty() put2 :   null
Using Hashtable's get() put1: val1
Using Properties' getProperty() put1 :   val1
```

When the value is not of the type String, the functions getProperty() and get() in the above example provide different results for the same key. As a result, the resultant API is perplexing and prone to incorrect invocations.

Exploding Numbers of Subclasses

Kotlin does not allow multiple inheritance. However, it does enable multilevel inheritance, which is often utilized. For example, the Android SDK includes a TextView class derived from View. To make TextView support HTML, build an HtmlTextView that derives from TextView.

```kotlin
abstract class VegPizza {
  abstract fun prepare()
}
abstract class CheesePizza : VegPizza()
abstract class VeggiesPizza : VegPizza()
class SmallCheesePizza : CheesePizza() {
  override fun prepare() {
    println("Prepared small cheese burst pizza")
  }
}
class MediumCheesePizza : CheesePizza() {
  override fun prepare() {
    println("Prepared medium cheese pizza")
  }
}

class LargeCheesePizza : CheesePizza() {
  override fun prepare() {
```

```
    println("Prepared large cheese pizza")
  }
}

class SmallVeggiePizza : VeggiesPizza() {
  override fun prepare() {
    println("Prepared small veggie pizza")
  }
}

class MediumVeggiePizza : VeggiesPizza() {
  override fun prepare() {
    println("Prepared medium veggie pizza")
  }
}

class LargeVeggiePizza : VeggiesPizza() {
  override fun prepare() {
    println("Prepared large veggie pizza")
  }
}
```

Composition Refactoring

Composition is the utilization of tiny elements to create a complex entity. This section will show us how to utilize this composition-based method to minimize or alleviate the design challenges caused by implementation inheritance.

UserMediator Class Is Being Refactored

Because we can't extend more than one parent class, the easiest fix for the broken User_Mediator would be to remove the open keyword from UserApiService and UserCacheService and replace it with private instance fields of User_Mediator, as seen in the example below:

```
class User_Mediator {
  private val cacheService: UserCacheService =
UserCacheService()
  private val apiService: UserApiService =
UserApiService()
  /**
    * Search for [User] with the [username] on cache
first. If not found,
```

```
   * make API calls to fetch [User] and persist it in
server.
   *
   * @throws UserNotFoundException if it is not in
"server".
   */
  fun fetchUser(username: String): User {
    return cacheService.findUserById(username)
?        : apiService.fetchUserByUsername(username)?
.also { cacheService.saveUser(it) }
?        : throw UserNotFoundException(username)
  }
}
```

From Composition to Aggregation

Remove these two fields and write a constructor for User_Mediator that takes these two instance variables as arguments:

```
class User_Mediator(
  private val cacheService: UserCacheService,
  private val apiService: UserApiService
) {
  // methods
}
```

And, in the main() function of User_Demo.kt, use the following code to initialize the mediator:

```
val mediator = UserMediator(
  cacheService = UserCacheServiceImpl(),
  apiService = UserApiServiceImpl()
)
```

User_Mediator now relies on the class's user to provide its dependencies. Furthermore, during testing, we may pass in test stubs specific to our test circumstance, making testing much easier.

Place the focus on the User_Mediator class definition and hit Control-Enter. Then, choose Create test. This produces a file in the test directory named User_MediatorTest.kt.

```
internal class User_MediatorTest {
  private lateinit var mockApi: UserApiService
```

```
private lateinit var realCache: UserCacheService
@BeforeEach
fun setup() {
  // 1
  realCache = UserCacheServiceImpl()
  // 2
  mockApi = object : UserApiService {
    private val db = mutableListOf<User>()
    init {
      db.add(User("test_user1", "Test User"))
    }

    override fun fetchUserByUsername(username:
String): User? {
      return db.find { username == it.username }
    }
  }
}
@Test
fun 'Given username when fetchUser then should
return the user from cache and save it in cache'() {
  // 3
  val mediator = User_Mediator(realCache, mockApi)
  val inputUsername = "test_user1"
  val user = mediator.fetchUser(inputUsername)
  assertNotNull(user)
  assertTrue { user.username == inputUsername }
  // Check if saved in the cache
  assertNotNull(realCache.
findUserById(inputUsername))
  }
}
```

Here's how the code above is broken down:

Create a new instance of UserCacheServiceImpl for realCache. We do not need to mock this class because it only uses in-memory data structures.

However, UserApiServiceImpl makes a "network" call, and we don't want the outcome of our test cases to depend on the server's response or availability. As a result, it is preferable to mimic or stub it. We've replaced it with a solution that leverages an in-memory data structure, allowing us to control the outcome and alter it to meet our test scenario.

Handling the Exposure Issue

In OOP, the general rule is to write shy class. The shy class does not divulge needless implementation to others. The Properties of java.util contriadict this. Instead, a composition-based method would have been an ideal way to accomplish it.

We will not be allowed to edit Properties because it is a built-in class given by JDK. So, using a reduced version as an example, we'll discover how it may have been improved.

```kotlin
class Hashtable_Store {
  // 1
  private val store: Hashtable<String, String> =
Hashtable()
  // 2
  fun getProperty(key: String): String? {
    return store[key]
  }
  fun setProperty(key: String, value: String) {
    store[key] = value
  }
  fun propertyNames() = store.keys
}
```

Here's how the code works:

Using a composition-based technique, we build a private field in HashtableStore and initialize it as a Hashtable instance. We must interact with this instance to offer data storage functionality. Remember the following rule of thumb: Write shy classes. Making the instance private prohibits others from accessing it, which aids in encapsulation.

We expose public methods that the class's user can utilize. This class exposes three such methods, each passing its operation to the private field.

Create main() in the same file and paste the following code within it:

```kotlin
val properties = Hashtable_Store()
properties.setProperty("setProperty1", "val1")
properties.setProperty("setProperty2", "110")
properties.propertyNames().toList().forEach {
  println("$it: ${properties.getProperty(it.
toString())}")
}
```

If we want all of Properties' capabilities while still having control over the "exposure area," we may put a wrapper over it and expose our methods. Make a new class called PropertiesStore and add the following code into it:

```
class Properties_Store {
  private val properties = Properties()
  fun getProperty(key: String): String? {
    return properties.getProperty(key)
  }
  fun setProperty(key: String, value: String) {
    properties.setProperty(key, value)
  }
  fun propertyNames() = properties.propertyNames()
}
```

Composition over Inheritance

In OOP, composition takes precedence over inheritance. Instead of implementing all of the required interface's features in a single monolithic class, these functionalities should be built separately in several instances, and then used to finally empower the target class with all of the offered functionalities. This idea improves the reusability and maintainability of the code.

> **Example:** Let me illustrate the concept with a simple example. Assume you work at an automotive firm and our job is to build automobiles depending on several specifications such as the color of the car (appearance), the maximum speed (performance), and the number of seats (interior).

The Kotlin Method

Before we continue, there are two fundamental Kotlin keywords that we must understand: object and by. The object keyword tells the Kotlin compiler to produce only one instance of the defined class. And the by keyword is mainly seen in the lazy loading examples and the lazy function. It is less common knowledge (at least to me) that we may also use the by keyword to delegate implementation of an interface to another object. Let's look at some codes in action.

First, we declare and implement functionality classes as objects.

```
object Yellow: Appearance {
    override fun getColor(): String {
        return "Yellow"
    }
}
```

```kotlin
object SixSeat: Interior {
    override fun getNumberOfSeats(): Int {
        return 6
    }
}

object Slow: Performance {
    override fun getMaxSpeed(): Int {
        return 180;
    }
}
```

Then we can create our Car class with only one line of code:

```kotlin
class YellowSlowSUV: Appearance by Yellow,
        Interior by SixSeat, Performance by Slow
```

Because the objects delegate the required interface implementations via the by keyword, we don't need to explicitly declare those methods already delegated by objects because the Kotlin compiler is sophisticated enough to build the required code for us under the hood. Let's look at them using the Kotlin byte code viewer.

```java
/// Decompiled code in Kotlin byte code viewer
public final class YellowSlowSUV implements
Appearance, Interior, Performance {
    // $FF: synthetic-field
    private final Yellow $$delegate_0;
    // $FF: synthetic-field
    private final SixSeat $$delegate_1;
    // $FF: synthetic-field
    private final Slow $$delegate_2;

    public YellowSlowSUV() {
        this.$$delegate_0 = Yellow.INSTANCE;
        this.$$delegate_1 = SixSeat.INSTANCE;
        this.$$delegate_2 = Slow.INSTANCE;
    }
    public String getColor() {
        return this.$$delegate_0.getColor();
    }
    public int getNumberOfSeats() {
        return this.$$delegate_1.getNumberOfSeats();
    }
```

```
public int getMaxSpeed() {
    return this.$$delegate_2.getMaxSpeed();
}
}
```

ENCAPSULATION

Encapsulation is the union of data and logic into a single unit that conceals data from external access. As a consequence, we have fewer couplings between software components, as well as more understandable and reliable code.

The following access modifiers are available:

- **Private:** name is only available within the class where it was declared.

- **Protected:** name is only accessible within the class and its subclasses.

- **Internal:** name is accessible to everyone within the same module.

- **Public:** name is open to the public; this is the default modification to omit it.

It is worth noting that in Kotlin, the outer class does not view the private members of its inner classes.

Protected members are not permitted within interfaces or objects in Kotlin.

Kotlin does not provide abstract private functions; only body functions are supported.

If we override a protected member without explicitly specifying the visibility, the overriding member will also have protected visibility.

Modifiers can apply to the class constructor.

```
open class Outer {
    private val c = 1
    protected open val d = 2
    internal val e = 3
    val f = 4  // public by default
    protected class Nested {
        public val e: Int = 5
    }
}
class Subclass : Outer() {
```

```
    // c is not visible
    // d, e and f are visible
    // Nested and g are visible
    override val d = 5    // 'd' is protected
}
class Unrelated(o: Outer) {
    // o.c, o.d are not visible
    // o.e and o.f are visible (same module)
    // Outer.Nested is not visible, and Nested::g is
not visible either
}
class C private constructor(c: Int) { ... }
```

POLYMORPHISM

Unlike Python, Kotlin needs the use of the override keyword when an element in a class/interface is being overridden, and tests are done at build time to verify if the element may override. Any class that may inherit from must be open, as any of its declared components can override. In src, add a new package called org.example.enpoly.doggie. Create a new Kotlin file named Dog in the package with the following contents:

```
package org.example.enpoly.doggie
import org.example.enpoly.AnimalBase
internal open class Doggie(var petName: String = "",
open protected val coat: String,
                          open protected val energy:
Int) : AnimalBase {
    override val MAX_AGE = 20
    override fun doMove() = "Walks/runs"
    override fun makeSound() = "Wooff"
    fun stats() = "Coat: $coat, Energy: $energy"
}
```

The absence of the open keyword in the stats function in the above example indicates that the function cannot alter. Create a new Kotlin file called SmallDoggie in the same package with the following contents:

```
package org.example.enpoly.doggie
internal open class SmallDoggie : Doggie(coat =
"Fluffy", energy = 12)
```

Create a new Kotlin file named LargeDoggie in the same package with the following contents:

```
package org.example.enpoly.doggie
internal open class LargeDoggie : Dog(coat = "Raggy",
energy = 2)
```

Now it's time for several classes that will cover two dog breeds. Create a new Kotlin file called Chiwawa in the same package with the following contents:

```
package org.example.enpoly.doggie
internal class Chiwawa(petName: String) :
SmallDoggie() {
    override fun makeSound() = "Yaap, yaap, yaap"
    init {
        this.petName = petName
    }
}
```

Create new Kotlin file called GreatDane in the same package with the following contents:

```
package org.example.enpoly.doggie
internal class GreatDane(petName: String) :
LargeDoggie() {
    override val MAX_AGE = 13
    override val coat = "Smooth"
    init {
        this.petName = petName
    }
}
```

Finally, a main Kotlin file must be written to link everything. Create a new Kotlin file named main in the org.example.enpoly package with the following contents:

```
package org.example.enpoly
import org.example.enpoly.doggie.*
fun main(args: Array<String>) {
    val chiwawa = Chiwawa("Fiifi")
    val greatDane = GreatDane("Earles")
```

```
    println("Chiwawa -  Name: ${chiwawa.petName}, Max
Age: ${chiwawa.MAX_AGE}")
    println("Chiwawa Stats - ${chiwawa.stats()}")
    println("Chiwawa Sound - ${chiwawa.makeSound()}")
    println("Chiwawa Move - ${chiwawa.doMove()}")
    chiwawa.petName = "Rippy"
    println("Chiwawa's New Name - ${chiwawa.
petName}\n")
    println("Great Dane: Name - ${greatDane.petName},
Max Age: ${greatDane.MAX_AGE}")
    println("Great Dane Stats - ${greatDane.stats()}")
    println("Great Dane Sound - ${greatDane.
makeSound()}")
    println("Great Dane Move - ${greatDane.doMove()}")
}
```

ENCAPSULATION AND PROCEDURAL PROGRAMMING IN KOTLIN

Encapsulation is a term used by software developers to describe the process of grouping related data and behavior into a single unit, usually referred to as a class. The class is the polar opposite of procedural-based programming, in which data and behavior are considered as separate concerns. It should highlight that both OOP and procedural programming have different benefits, and neither is superior to the other. Kotlin supports both types of programming, and it's not unusual to see a combination of procedural and OOP.

Example of Procedural Programming

Let's look at a procedural programming example. In this example, we'll use rectangle object. Its data is stored in a map (data structure that allows key-value pairs), and it is subsequently consumed by functions.

```
val rect = mutableMapOf("Width" to 12, "Height" to 12,
"Color" to "Yellow")
fun calcArea(shape : Map<String, Any>) : Int {
    return shape["Height"] as Int * shape["Width"] as Int
}
fun toString(shape : Map<String, Any>) : String {
    return "Width = ${shape["Width"]}, Height =
${shape["Height"]}, Color = ${shape["Color"]}, Area =
${calcArea(shape)}"
}
```

So we start with the rectangle object, which stores our rectangle's width, height, and color. Following the formation of the rectangle, there are two functions. They are calcArea and function toString(), respectively. It's worth noting that these are global functions that can accept any Map. This is risky since we cannot ensure that the map will include "Width," "Height," or "Color" keys. Another concern is that we have lost our type safety. Because we need to store both Integers and Strings in the rectangular map, our value must type Any, Kotlin's basic type.

OOP

Here's an example of the same problem tackled using an OOP approach.

```kotlin
class Rect(
    var width : Int,
    var height : Int,
    var color : String) {
    fun calcArea() = this.width * this.height
    override fun toString() =
            "Width = ${this.width}, Height = ${this.
height}, Color = ${this.color}, Area = ${calcArea()}"
}
```

Because the data and the activity associated with the data are gathered into a single object called a class, the OOP approach displays encapsulation. The data associated with a class is commonly referred to as "properties," and the actions described in the class are commonly referred to as "methods." Because all objects based on the Rectangle class contain width, height, and color, the calcArea() and function toString() methods are always guaranteed to function. We also keep our type safety since we may define each property as a separate variable within the class, along with its type.

When invoking the calcArea() and function toString() methods, the term 'this' relates to the object called. Unlike the preceding procedural program, we'll observe that no Rectangle parameter is sent to calcArea() or function toString(). Instead, the 'this' keyword is modified to refer to the presently active object.

Tips for Choosing between Procedural and OOP

It should mention that many software projects use both procedural and OOP. It's also worth noting that practically anything that can be done using OOP can almost certainly be done with procedural code, and vice versa.

However, certain issues are easier to address when using procedural rather than OOP, while others are better solved with OOP.

Procedural

When we operate in terms of pure mathematical functions, a function receives certain inputs and returns specific outputs without any side effects.

- **Multithreading:** Procedural programming can assist in resolving many issues that arise in a multithreading environment. Because the integrity of changeable data is always an issue in multithreading, functional programming works well as long as the functions are pure functions that do not modify data.

- **Input and output:** Using a class to persist or retrieve an item from a data storage is often unnecessary. The same may be said for printing to ordinary IO. Java has been widely chastised for writing text to the console via System.out.println(). Kotlin simplified this to println().

OOP and Encapsulation

- **GUI toolkits:** Objects such as buttons, windows, and web pages are extremely well represented as classes.

- **Grouping state or behavior:** We frequently find that entities in software have qualities or methods shared by other entities with comparable properties or methods. All road vehicles, for example, have wheels and move. Trucks are specialized vehicles with a box. Four-wheel drive trucks are specialist vehicles that have four wheels of drive. We can utilize OOP to organize all of the components shared by all cars into a Vehicle class. All things common to Vehicles may be classified as Trucks, while all items used solely in four-wheel drive trucks can be classified as FourByFourTruck.

- **Modularization:** OOP enables developers to modularize code into smaller, reusable software components. Because the code units in a system are small, the code is typically easier to maintain.

Putting Everything Together

A working program demonstrating both procedural programming and OOP is provided below.

```
package ch1
/**
```

```
* This is a form object that lacks OOP. Take note of
how the data is kept separate from the activity that
operates on the
* data. The information is saved in a Map object,
which employs key-value pairs. Then there are distinct
functions that
* alter the data.
*/

val rect = mutableMapOf("Width" to 12, "Height" to 12,
"Color" to "Yellow")
fun calcArea(shape : Map<String, Any>) : Int {
    // How can we ensure that this map object contains
the "Height" and "Width" properties?
    return shape["Height"] as Int * shape["Width"] as Int
}
fun toString(shape : Map<String, Any>) : String {
    return "Width = ${shape["Width"]}, Height =
${shape["Height"]}, Color = ${shape["Color"]}, Area =
${calcArea(shape)}"
}

/**
* This class represents a Rectangle. You'll see it
contains less code than the
* non-OOP implementation right away. This is because
the state (width, height, and color) is bundled with
the behavior.
* Kotlin goes this a step further by allowing us to
adjust our code's width, height, and color. We need to
add calcArea(), which we can ensure will always
function because
* we know width and height will always exist.
Similarly, we know that our function toString()
function will never fail us
* for the same reason!
*/

class Rect(
    var width : Int,
    var height : Int,
    var color : String){
    fun calcArea() = this.width * this.height
    override fun toString() =
```

```kotlin
        "Width = ${this.width}, Height = ${this.
height}, Color = ${this.color}, Area = ${calcArea()}"
}

fun main(args : Array<String>){
    println("Using procedural programming")
    println(toString(rect))
    println("Changing width")
    rectangle["Width"] = 15
    println(toString(rect))
    println("Changing height")
    rectangle["Height"] = 80
    println(toString(rect))
    println("Changing color")
    rectangle["Color"] = "Blue"
    println(toString(rect))
    println("\n**********\n")
    println("Now-using-OOP")
    val square = Rect(12, 12, "Yellow")
    println(square)
    println("Changing height")
    square.height = 80
    println(square)
    println("Changing width")
    square.width = 50
    println(square)
    println("Changing color")
    square.color = "Black"
    println(square)
}
```

This chapter introduced the notion of OOP, where we learned about Class and Object, Nested classes, Constructors, and Inheritances. In addition, we discussed Interfaces, Abstract classes, and Generics in Kotlin. Moreover, Composition, Polymorphism, and Encapsulation.

CHAPTER 3

Usability Aspects of Kotlin

IN THIS CHAPTER

➢ Nullable types

➢ Extension methods

➢ Overloading

➢ Enumeration and generics

In the previous chapter, we covered Objects and Classes, Inheritance, and Composition. Moreover, Polymorphism, Encapsulation, and Abstraction. This chapter will cover Nullable types, Extension methods, Overloading, Enumeration, and Generics.

NULL SAFETY IN KOTLIN

Null safety in Kotlin is a process that eliminates the possibility of a null reference in the code. If null argument is given, the Kotlin compiler instantly raises a NullPointerException without executing more lines.

Kotlin's type system aims to eliminate NullPointerException from the code. Only the following causes can result in a NullPointerException:

- An uninvited call to throw NullPointerException();

DOI: 10.1201/9781003308447-3

- An uninitialized version of this operator can find in a constructor and used someplace.

- The use of external Java code as Kotlin is an example of Java interoperability.

Nullable and Non-Nullable Types in Kotlin

The Kotlin types system distinguishes between references that can hold null (nullable references) and references that cannot contain null (non-null reference). String types are not normally nullable. To create a string with a null value, we must explicitly declare it by inserting a? behind the String as: String?

Nullable Types

Nullable types are declared by adding a? to the end of a String, as in:

```
var strg1: String? = "hello"
strg1 = null // ok
```

Example:

```
fun main(args: Array<String>){
var strg: String? = "Hello" // variable is
declared as nullable
strg = null
    print(strg)
}
```

Non-Nullable Types

Non-nullable types are regular strings that are specified as String types, such as:

```
val strg: String = null // compile error
strg = "hello" // compile error Val cannot be reassign
var strg2: String = "hello"
strg2 = null // compile error
```

What happens when we add a null value to a string that is not nullable?

```
fun main(args: Array<String>){
var strg: String = "Hello"
```

```
strg = null // compile-error
    print(strg)
}
```

Checking for Null in the Conditions

The if expression in Kotlin is used to check the condition and return the value.

```
fun main(args: Array<String>){
var strg: String? = "Hello"      // variable is
declared as nullable
var len = if(strg!=null) str.length else -1
println("strg is : $strg")
println("strg length is : $len")
strg = null
println("strg is : $strg")
len = if(strg!=null) strg.length else -1
println("b length is : $len")
}
```

SMART CAST

We have seen how to declare a nullable type in the previous course Kotlin nullable types and non-nullable types. We have the option of using smart casts to use these nullable classes. Smart cast is a feature that allows the Kotlin compiler to track circumstances within if expressions. If the compiler discovers that a variable is not null of type nullable, it will enable access to the variable.

Example: We get a compile error when attempting to access a nullable type of String without using safe cast.

```
var string: String? = "HelloEveryone"
    print(string.length) // Compile-error
```

We use a safe cast to solve the above expression:

```
fun main(args: Array<String>){
var string: String? = "HelloEveryone"
    if(string != null) { // smart cast
print(string.length) // It works now
    }
}
```

When we use is or !is to verify a variable, the compiler records this information and internally casts the variable to the target type. If is or !is returns true, something is done within the scope.

Use of is for the Smart Cast

```
fun main(args: Array<String>){
val objt: Any = "The variable objt is automatically
cast to a String in this scope"
    if(objt is String) {
                // No Explicit-Casting needed.
println("String length is ${objt.length}")
    }
}
```

Use of !is for the Smart Cast

```
fun main(args: Array<String>){
val objt: Any = "The variable objt is automatically
cast to a String in this scope"
    if(objt !is String) {
println("objt is not string")
    } else
    // No Explicit-Casting needed.
println("String length is ${objt.length}")
}
```

Smart cast function under the following conditions:

- A val variable always has a local property aspect.

- If a val property is private or internal, the check is done in the same module defined by the property.

- If the local var variable is not changed between the check and the usage, it will not be recorded in a lambda that updates it.

UNSAFE AND SAFE CAST OPERATOR

Unsafe Cast Operator: as

When a variable cannot cast and an exception is thrown, this is referred to as an unsafe cast. The infix operator as performs the unsafe cast.

If a nullable string (String?) is cast to a non-nullable string (String), an exception is thrown.

```
fun main(args: Array<String>){
val objt: Any? = null
val strg: String = objt as String
println(strg)
 }
```

The preceding program throws an exception:

Exception in thread "main" kotlin.TypeCastException: null cannot be cast to non-null type kotlin.String at ExampleKt.main.

When attempting to cast an integer value of any type into a string value, a ClassCastException is thrown.

```
val objt: Any = 321
val strg: String = objt as String
// Throws java.lang.ClassCastException: java.lang.
Integer cannot be cast to java.lang.String
```

For casting to work, the source and target variables must be nullable:

```
fun main(args: Array<String>){
val objt: String? = "String unsafe cast"
val strg: String? = objt as String? // Works
println(strg)
}
```

Safe Cast Operator: as?

For safe cast to a type, Kotlin includes a safe cast operator as? If casting is not feasible, it returns null rather than raising a ClassCastException exception.

Consider the following example: attempting to cast any kind of string value that is initially understood by the programmer but not by the compiler into nullable string and nullable int. If casting is feasible, it will cast the value or return null instead of throwing an exception if casting is not possible.

```
fun main(args: Array<String>){
val location: Any = "KotlinAdvanced"
val safeString: String? = location as? String
val safeInt: Int? = location as? Int
println(safeString)
println(safeInt)
}
```

(?:) Elvis Operator

Elvis operator (?:) is used to return a value that is not null even if the conditional expression is null. It is also used to ensure that values are not null.

We can declare a variable storing a null reference in specific instances. Assume a variable strg has a null reference; before utilizing strg in a program, we shall check its nullability. If variable strg is found to be non-null, its property will use; otherwise, another non-null value will be used.

```
var strg: String? = null
var strg2: String? = "May be declare nullable string"
```

In the above code, the String strg includes a null value; thus, before accessing the value of strg, we must run a safety check to see if the string contains a value or not. Traditionally, we conduct this safety check with an if... else sentence.

```
var len1: Int = if (strg != null) strg.length else -1
var len2:  Int = if (strg2 != null) strg.length else
-1
```

```
fun main(args: Array<String>){
var strg: String? = null
var strg2: String? = "May be declare nullable string"
var len1:  Int = if (strg != null) strg.length else -1
var len2:  Int = if (strg2 != null) strg2.length else -1
println("Length of strg is ${len1}")
println("Length of strg2 is ${len2}")
}
```

The Elvis operator(?:) in Kotlin returns a result that is not null even if the conditional expression is null. The following Elvis operator may be used to express the above if... else operator:

```
var len1:  Int = strg?.length ?: -1
var len2:  Int = strg2?.length ?:  -1
```

The Elvis operator returns the expression to the left to ?:, i.e. −1. (strg?. length) If it is not null, it returns the expression right to (?:) i.e. (−1). The expression on the right side of Elvis operator is evaluated only if the expression on the left side returns null.

Example:

```
fun main(args: Array<String>){
var strg: String? = null
var strg2: String? = "May be declare nullable
string"
var len1:  Int = strg ?.length? : -1
var len2:  Int = strg2 ?.length? :  -1
println("Length of strg is ${len1}")
println("Length of strg2 is ${len2}")
}
```

Because Kotlin throw and return expressions, they may also be used on the Elvis operator's right side. This may be used to check functional arguments such as:

```
funfunctionName(node: Node): String? {
val parent = node.getParent() ?: return-null
val name = node.getName() ?: throw
IllegalArgumentException("name-expected")
 // .....
}
```

Elvis Kotlin Operator using the throw and return expression:

```
fun main(args: Array<String>){
val fruitName: String = fruit()
println(fruitName)
}
fun fruit(): String{
val strg: String? ="xyz"
val strgLength: Int = if(strg!= null) strg.length else
-1
val strgLength2: Int = strg?.length ?: -1
var string = "strg = $strg\n"+
            "strgLength = $strgLength\n"+
            "strgLength2 = $strgLength2\n\n"
fun check(textOne: String?, textTwo: String?):
String?{
val textOne = textOne ?: return null
val textTwo = textTwo ?: IllegalArgumentException
("text exception")
```

```
            return "\ntextOne = $textOne\n"+
                   "textTwo = $textTwo\n"
    }
    string += "check(null,\"grapes\") =
${check(null,"grapes")}\n" +
           "check(\"apple\",\"kiwi\") =
${check("apple","kiwi")}\n"
        return string
}
```

EXTENSION FUNCTION

The Kotlin programming language enables the programmer to enhance the functionality of existing classes without inheriting them. This is performed by utilizing a feature known as extension. A function that is added to an existing class is referred to as an Extension Function.

Create a new function that is tied to the classname, as shown in the example below, to add an extension function to class:

```
// A example class demonstrating extension functions
class Circle (val radius: Double){
    // the member function of class
    fun area(): Double{
        return Math.PI * radius * radius;
    }
}
fun main(){
    // Created an extension method for the Circle
class.
    fun Circle.perimeter(): Double{
        return 2*Math.PI*radius;
    }
    // create a object for the class Circle
    val newCircle = Circle(13.4);
    // invoke the member function
    println("The Area of the circle: ${newCircle.
area()}")
    //invoke the extension function
    println("The Perimeter of the circle: ${newCircle.
perimeter()}")
}
```

Explanation: In this scenario, a new function with the function class Circle.perimeter() and a return type of Double is added to the class using dot notation. In the primary function, an object is created to instantiate the class Circle, and the function is called with the println() line. When the member function is invoked, it returns the circle's area, whereas the extension function returns the circle's perimeter.

Extended Library Class Using an Extension Function

Not only can user-defined classes be extended in Kotlin, but so can library classes. The extension function may be added to library classes and used the same way it can add to user-defined classes.

Example:

```
fun main(){
    // Extension function defined for the Int type
    fun Int.abs() : Int{
        return if(this < 0) -this else this
    }

    println((-8).abs())
    println(8.abs())
}
```

Explanation: We utilized an extension function to extend the library function in this situation. To do the modulus procedure, we utilized an Integer value. We entered the integer numbers −8 and 8 and got positive results for both. If argument value is less than zero, it returns − (value), else it returns the same value.

Extensions Are Resolved Statically

The extension functions are resolved statically, which means that whichever extension function is performed is fully dependent on the type of the expression on which it is called, rather than the type resolved during the expression's final execution at runtime.

Example:

```
// An Open class created to be inherited
open class E(val e:Int, val f:Int){
}
```

```
// Class F inherits E
class F():E(6, 6){}
fun main(){
    // Extension function operate defined for E
    fun E.operate():Int{
        return e+f
    }

    // Extension function operate defined for F
    fun F.operate():Int{
        return e*f;
    }

    // Function to display static dispatch
    fun display(e: E){
        print(e.operate())
    }
    // Calling the display function
    display(F())
}
```

Explanation: If we're aware with Java or any object-oriented programming language, you'll see that class D is an ancestor of class E. In the above program, the parameter sent to the display function is an instance of class D. The output should be 36 according to the dynamic method dispatch paradigm; however, because the extension functions are statically resolved, the operate function is called on type E. As a consequence, the outcome is a value of 12.

Nullable Receiver

The nullable class type can also use to construct extension functions. The correct value is returned when the check for null is inserted inside the extension method.

Example:

```
// A sample class to display name
class CDE(val name: String){
    override fun toString(): String {
        return "Name is $name"
    }
}
```

```kotlin
fun main(){
    // An extension function as a nullable receiver
    fun CDE?.output(){
        if(this == null){
            println("Null")
        }else{
            println(this.toString())
        }
    }
    val a = CDE("Charch")
    // Extension function called using an instance
    a.output()
    // Extension function called on null
    null.output()
}
```

Companion Object Extensions

If a class has a companion object, we may also provide extension methods and properties for the companion object.

Declaration of companion object:

```kotlin
class mynewClass {
    // the companion object declaration
    companion object {
        fun display(){
            println("The companion object's defined
function")
        }
    }
}
fun main(args: Array<String>) {
    // invoking the member function
    val obj = mynewClass.display()
}
```

Like regular member functions of the companion object, extension functions can be invoked with just the class name as the qualifier.

Example:

```kotlin
class mynewClass {
    companion object {
```

```
                //member function of the companion object
                fun display(strg :String) : String{
                    return strg
                }
            }
    }
        // the companion object's extension function
    fun mynewClass.Companion.abc(){
        println("The companion object's Extension
    function ")
    }
    fun main(args: Array<String>) {
        val objt = myClass.display("The Function
    declared in the companion object")
        println(objt)
        // invoking extension-function
        val objt2 = myClass.abc()
    }
```

OVERLOADING OF THE OPERATOR IN KOTLIN

Because Kotlin enables user-defined types, it may also overload conventional operators, making dealing with user-defined types easier. All unary, binary, and relational operators can be overloaded. Overloading the operators is accomplished by using either member functions or extension functions. The operator modifier precedes these functions. Every operator has typical functions that can be overloaded depending on the situation.

Unary Operators

The table below lists the many functions that may define for unary operators. These functions modify the caller instance.

Operator Expression	Corresponding Function
+r	r.unaryPlus()
−r	r.unaryMinus()
!r	r.not()

The type for which the operator is defined is represented by r in this example. The overloaded functionality is defined within the functions.

Unary operator overloading is demonstrated in the following Kotlin program:

```
class OverloadUnary (var str:String) {
    // the overloading function
    operator fun unaryMinus() {
        strg1 = strg1.reversed()
    }
}
// main-function
fun main(args : Array<String>) {
    val objt1 = OverloadUnary ("HELLOEVERYONE")
    println("Initial string is ${objt1.strg}")y
    //calling the overloaded function unaryMinus()
    -objt1
    println("String after applying unary operator
${objt1.strg1}")
}
```

Increment and Decrement Operators

The following methods can use to define type's increment and decrement operators. These methods return a new instance with the expression's result.

Operator Expression	Corresponding Function
++r	r.inc()
--r	r.dec()

These functions work well in either postfix or prefix notation, delivering the same expected output in both circumstances.

Kotlin program to demonstrate operator overloading:

```
class OverloadIncDec(var strg:String) {
    // overloading the increment-function
    operator fun inc():OverloadIncDec {
        val objt1 = IncDecOverload(this.str)
        objt.strg1 = objt1.strg1 + 'a'
        return objt1
    }
    // overloading the decrement-function
```

```
    operator fun dec(): IncDecOverload {
        val objt1 = IncDecOverload(this.strg)
        objt.strg1 = objt1.strg1.substring(0,objt1.
strg1.length-1)
        return objt1
    }
    override fun toString(): String {
        return strg1
    }
}
// main-function
fun main(args: Array<String>) {
    var objt1 = OverloadIncDec("Helloeveryone")
    println(objt1++)
    println(objt1--)
    println(++objt1)
    println(--objt1)
}
```

Binary Operators

The binary operators and their equivalent functions are shown in the table below. All of these functions affect the instance that is being called.

Operator Expression	Corresponding Function
r1 + r2	r1.plus(r2)
r1 − r2	r1.minus(r2)
r1 * r2	r1.times(r2)
r1/ r2	r1.div(r2)
r1 % r2	r1.rem(r2)
r1..r2	r1.rangeTo(r2)

Overload the plus function with the following code:

```
class Objects(var objtName: String) {
    // Overloading-function
    operator fun plus(r: Int) {
        objtNames = "Name is $objtNames and data is $r"
    }
    override fun toString(): String {
        return objtNames
    }
}
```

```
//main-function
fun main() {
    val objt1 = Objects("Chairs")
    // Calling-overloaded-function
    objt1+9
    println(objt1)
}
```

Although the relational operators have no predefined functions, the type must implement the Comparable interface to use relational operators on instances of a user-defined type.

Other Operators

Because Kotlin has many operators, declaring each for a type is not a good programming practice. The below table lists some of the other useful Kotlin operators that may be overloaded.

Operator Expression	Corresponding Function
r1 in r2	r2.contains(r1)
r1 !in r2	!r2.contains(r1)
r[i]	r.get(i)
r[i, j]	r.get(i, j)
r[i] = b	r.set(i, b)
r[i, j] = b	r.set(i, j, b)
r()	r.invoke()
r(i)	r.invoke(i)
r(i, j)	r.invoke(i, j)
r1 += r2	r1.plusAssign(r2)
r1 -= r2	r1.minusAssign(r2)
r1 *= r2	r1.timesAssign(r2)
r1 /= r2	r1.divAssign(r2)
r1 %= r2	r1.remAssign(r2)

Enum CLASSES IN KOTLIN

It is sometimes important for a type to hold only specific values in programming. To do this, the concept of enumeration was developed. An enumeration is a named list of constants.

In Kotlin, as in many other programming languages, an enum is a specific type that indicates that something has several desirable properties. In contrast to Java enums, Kotlin enums are classes.

Some important things to note about Kotlin enum classes:

- Enum constants are more than simply collections of constants; they can also have attributes, methods, and other properties.

- A comma represents each enum constant function as a separate class and instance.

- Enums improves code readability by giving constants predefined names.

- Constructors are not permitted to construct an instance of the enum class.

Enums are defined by appending the term 'enum' to the beginning of a class name, as seen below:

```
enum class TIMEOFWEEK{
    MONDAY,
    TUESDAY,
    WEDNESDAY,
    THURSDAY,
    FRIDAY,
    SATURDAY,
    SUNDAY
}
```

Enum Initializing

Kotlin enums, like Java enums, can have constructors. Enum constants may initialize by passing particular values to the main constructor since they are Enum class objects.

Here's an example of how to color-code cards:

```
enum class ColorCard(val colors: String) {
    Diamond("pink"),
    Heart("green"),
}
```

We can quickly determine the color of a card by using:

```
val colors = ColorCard.Diamond.colors
```

Enum Properties and Methods

Enum classes in Kotlin, like those in Java and other programming languages, contain a variety of built-in attributes and functions that the programmer may use. Some of the essential techniques and attributes are listed here.

Properties:

- **ordinal:** This property stores the ordinal value of the constant, which is usually a zero-based index.

- **name:** This property contains the name of the constant.

Methods:

- **values:** This method returns a list of all the constants in the enum class.

- **valueOf():** The enum constant defined in enum that matches the input string is returned. If the constant is not found in the enum, an IllegalArgumentException is thrown.

Example:

```kotlin
enum class WEEKDAY {
    MONDAY,
    TUESDAY,
    WEDNESDAY,
    THURSDAY,
    FRIDAY
}
fun main()
{
    // A straightforward demonstration of
properties and methods
    for (day in WEEKDAY.values()) {
        println("${day.ordinal} = ${day.name}")
    }
    println("${WEEKDAY.valueOf(" FRIDAY ")}")
}
```

Properties and Functions of the Enum Class

Kotlin's enum class introduces a new type. This sort of class has its own set of properties and methods. The properties can offer a default value; however, each constant must specify its value for the property if no default value is provided. Functions are frequently defined within companion objects to avoid dependence on particular class instances. However, they may define without the need of companion objects.

Example:

```
// A default value is provided for the property
enum class WEEKS(val isWeekend: Boolean = false){
    SUNDAY(true),
    MONDAY,
    TUESDAY,
    WEDNESDAY,
    THURSDAY,
    FRIDAY,
    // Default-value-overridden
    SATURDAY(true);
    companion object{
        fun today(obj: WEEKS): Boolean {
            return obj.name.compareTo("SATURDAY")
== 0 || obj.name.compareTo("SUNDAY") == 0
        }
    }
}
fun main(){
    // A simple demonstration of properties and
methods
    for(day in WEEKS.values()) {
        println("${day.ordinal} = ${day.name} and
is weekend ${day.isWeekend}")
    }
    val today = WEEKS.MONDAY;
    println("Is today a weekend ${WEEKS.
today(today)}")
}
```

Enums as Anonymous Classes

Enum constants, like anonymous classes, implement their methods and override the class's abstract functions. The most important aspect is that each enum constant is overridden.

```
// enum-class defining
enum class Seasons(var weather: String) {
    Summer("cold"){
        // if not override the function foo() compile
time error
        override fun fooo() {
            println("The cold days of year")
        }
    },
    Winter("hot"){
        override fun fooo() {
            println("The Hot days of year")
        }
    },
    Rainy("moderate"){
        override fun fooo() {
            println("The Rainy days of year")
        }
    };
    abstract fun fooo()
}
// the main function
fun main(args: Array<String>) {
    // calling fooo() function override be Summer
constant
    Seasons.Summer.fooo()
}
```

Usage of when Expression with the Enum Class

When enum classes in Kotlin are combined with the when expression, they provide considerable benefits. Because enum classes limit the values that a type can take when paired with the when expression and all of the constant definitions are given, the else clause is unnecessary. As a result, a compiler warning will be produced.

```
enum class WEEKDAYS{
    MONDAY,
    TUESDAY,
    WEDNESDAY,
    THURSDAY,
    FRIDAY,
    SATURDAY
    SUNDAY;
}

fun main(){
    when(WEEKDAYS.SUNDAY){
        WEEKDAYS.SUNDAY -> println("Today is Sunday")
        WEEKDAYS.MONDAY -> println("Today is Monday")
        WEEKDAYS.TUESDAY -> println("Today is
Tuesday")
        WEEKDAYS.WEDNESDAY -> println("Today is
Wednesday")
        WEEKDAYS.THURSDAY -> println("Today is
Thursday")
        WEEKDAYS.FRIDAY -> println("Today is Friday")
        WEEKDAYS.SATURDAY -> println("Today is
Saturday")
        // Adding an else clause will generate a
warning
    }
}
```

KOTLIN GENERICS

Generics are helpful features that allow us to create classes, methods, and properties that may be accessed using a variety of data types while still ensuring compile-time type safety.

Creating parameterized classes: A type-parameterized class or function is a generic type. We always use angle brackets () to define the type parameter in the program.

The following is the generic class definition:

```
class mynewClass<E>(text: E) {
    var name = text
}
```

To create an instance of this class, we must specify the following type arguments:

```
val my : mynewClass<String> = Mynewclass<String>("The
Hubtutors")
```

The type arguments can remove if the parameters can deduce from the constructor arguments:

```
val my = mynewClass("TheHubtutors ")
Because TheHubtutors has the type String, the compiler
figures out that we are discussing mynewclass<String>.
```

The generic has the following advantages:

- **Avoiding typecasting:** The object does not need to be typecast.

- **Type safety:** Generic allows just one type of object at a time.

- **Compile-time safety:** To avoid run-time problems, generics code is checked for parameterized types at build time.

Generic Usage in Our Program

We define a Company class with a single parameter and a primary in the following example. We try to send different data kinds, such as String and Integer, through the Company class object. The Company class's primary constructor accepts string types ("TheHubtutors") but returns a compile-time error when an Integer type is passed (19).

```
class Companie (text: String) {
    var d = text
    init{
        println(d)
    }
}
fun main(args: Array<String>){
    var name: Companie = Companie("TheHubtutors")
    var rank: Companie = Companie(19)//
compile-time-error
}
```

To address the issue raised above, we may create a user-defined generic type class that accepts many arguments in a single class. The Company type class is a general type class that accepts arguments of both int and String types.

Example:

```
class Companie<E> (text : E){
    var d = text
    init{
        println(d)
    }
}
fun main(args: Array<String>){
    var name: Companie<String> = Companie<String>(
"Thehubtutors")
    var rank: Companie<Int> = Companie<Int>(19)
}
```

Variance

Unlike Java, Kotlin makes arrays invariant by default. By extension, generic types are invariant in the Kotlin. The out and in keywords may be useful here. Invariance is the property that prevents a standard generic function/ class written for a single data type from taking or returning another data type. Any is the supertype of all extra datatypes.

There are several types of variation:

- Declaration-site variance (using in and out)

- **Use-site variance:** Type projection

The out Keyword

In Kotlin, we may use the out keyword on the generic type to assign this reference to any of its supertypes. The out value can only be generated and consumed by the defined class:

```
class OutClass<out E>(val value: E) {
    fun get(): E {
        return value
    }
}
```

Above, we defined an OutClass class that may return a value of type E. Then, for the reference that is a supertype of it, we create an instance of the OutClass:

```
val out = OutClass("string")
val ref: OutClass<Any> = out
```

The in Keyword

To assign it to the reference of its subtype, we might use the keyword in on the generic type. The in keyword may only use on parameters that are consumed rather than produced:

```
class InClass<in E> {
    fun toString(value: E): String {
        return value.toString()
    }
}
```

In this scenario, we've defined a function toString() function that accepts only D values. Then we may assign a Number reference to its subtype – int:

```
val inClassObject: InClass<Number> = InClass()
val ref<Int> = inClassObject
```

Note: The following statement would result in a compiler error if we had not used the in type in the preceding class.

Covariance

Subtypes is permitted but not supertypes, i.e., the generic function/class may take subtypes of the datatype for which it is already defined, e.g., a generic class made for Number can accept int, but a generic class built for int cannot accept Number. This may be done in Kotlin by using the out keyword, as seen below:

```
fun main(args: Array<String>) {
    val c: MyClass<Any> = MyClass<Int>()
// Error: Type-mismatch
    val d: MyClass<out Any> = MyClass<String>()
// Works since String is subtype of Any
    val e: MyClass<out String> = MyClass<Any>()
// Error since Any is supertype of String
}
class MyClass<X>
```

By appending the out keyword to the declaration site, we may instantly allow covariance. The code below is completely functional.

```
fun main(args: Array<String>) {
        val d: MyClass<Any> = MyClass<String>()
// Compiles-without-error
}
class MyClass<out X>
```

Contra Covariance

It is used to substitute a supertype value in subtypes, implying that the generic function or class may take supertypes of the datatype for which it is already defined. A generic class designed for Number, for example, cannot accept int, but a generic class defined for int can accept Number. It is performed in Kotlin by using the in keyword as follows:

```
fun main(args: Array<String>) {
        var c: Container<Dog> = Container<Animal>()
//compiles-without-error
        var d: Container<Animal> = Container<Dog>()
//gives-compilation-error
}
open class Creature
class Cat : Animal()
class Container<in C>
```

Type Projections

It is possible to copy all of the elements of an array of some type into an array of Any type, but for the compiler to compile our code, the input argument must annotate with the out keyword. Consequently, the compiler decides that the input argument can be of Any type.

Kotlin code for copying array members into another array:

```
fun copy(from: Array<out Any>, to: Array<Any>) {
    assert(from.size == to.size)
    // copying (from) array to (to) array
    for (d in from.indices)
        to[d] = from[d]
    // printing elements of array in which copied
    for (d in to.indices) {
    println(to[d])
    }
}
```

```
fun main(args :Array<String>) {
    val ints: Array<Int> = arrayOf(11, 22, 33,44)
    val any :Array<Any> = Array<Any>(44) { "" }
    copy(ints, any)
}
```

Star Projections

The star(*) projection is used when we don't know what kind of value we're looking for and just want to output all the elements in an array.

Example:

```
// star-projection in array
fun printArray(array: Array<*>) {
    array.forEach { print(it) }
}
fun main(args :Array<String>) {
    val name  = arrayOf("Worst","for","Good")
    printArray(name)
}
```

In this chapter, we learned Usability aspects where we discussed Nullable Types, Extension methods, Overloading and Enumeration, and Generics.

CHAPTER 4

Kotlin Functional Programming

IN THIS CHAPTER

➤ Lambdas

➤ Higher-Order functions

➤ Local functions

➤ Scope functions

➤ Lists and maps

In the previous chapter, we covered Usability Aspects. This chapter will cover functional programming with its relevant syntax and examples.

LAMBDA EXPRESSIONS AND ANONYMOUS FUNCTIONS IN KOTLIN

This topic will cover lambda expressions and anonymous functions in Kotlin. While they are syntactically similar, Kotlin and Java lambdas have vastly distinct characteristics.

Lambda expressions and Anonymous functions are function literals, which imply they are not declared but supplied as an expression.

DOI: 10.1201/9781003308447-4

LAMBDA EXPRESSION

As we all know, the syntax of Kotlin lambdas is quite similar to that of Java lambdas. An anonymous function does not have a name. We may call lambda expressions anonymous functions.

Example:

```
fun main(args: Array<String>) {
    val company = { println("PeeksforPeeks")}
    // invoking the function method1
    company()
    // invoking the function method2
    company.invoke()
}
```

Syntax:

```
val lambda_names : Data_type = { argument_List ->
code_body }
```

Curly braces always enclose a lambda expression, argument declarations are enclosed by curly braces and have optional type annotations, and an arrow -> sign encloses the code body. If the lambda's inferred return type is not Unit, the final expression inside the lambda body is considered the return value.

Example:

```
val sum = {x: Int,  y: Int -> x + y}
```

Except for the code body, the lambda expression in Kotlin has optional parts. The lambda expression is shown below after the optional component has been removed.

```
val sum:(Int,Int) -> Int = { x, y -> x + y}
```

It's worth noting that we don't always need a variable because it can be supplied directly as an argument to a method.

Program:

```
// with the type annotation in lambda expression
val sum1 = { x: Int, y: Int -> x + y }
// without type annotation in lambda expression
```

```
val sum2:(Int,Int)-> Int  = { x,  y -> x + y}
fun main(args: Array<String>) {
    val result1 = sum1(1,4)
    val result2 = sum2(2,5)
    println("Sum of two numbers is: $result1")
    println("Sum of two numbers is: $result2")
    // directly print return value of the lambda
    // without storing in variable.
    println(sum1(4,6))
}
```

Inference in Lambda Types

Type inference in Kotlin assists the compiler in determining the type of a lambda expression. The lambda expression used to compute the sum of two numbers is shown below.

```
val sum = {x: Int,  y: Int -> x + y}
```

In this case, the Kotlin compiler evaluates it as a function that takes two Int parameters and returns an Int value.

```
(Int,Int)  -> Int
```

If we want to return a String value, we may use the inbuilt function toString() method.

```
val sum1 = { x: Int, y: Int ->
    val num = x + y
    num.toString()      //convert the Integer to String
}
fun main(args: Array<String>) {
    val result1 = sum1(12,7)
    println("Sum of two numbers is: $result1")
}
```

The Kotlin compiler self-evaluates the preceding program into a function that accepts two integer values and returns a String.

Type Declaration in Lambdas

The type of our lambda expression must explicitly declare. If lambda does not return a value, we can use: Unit.

```
Pattern: (Input) -> Output
```

Lambdas examples with return type:

```
val lambda1: (Int) -> Int = (x -> x * x)
val lambda2: (String,String) -> String = { x, y ->
x + y }
val lambda3: (Int)-> Unit = {print(Int)}
```

Lambdas can be used as class extension:

```
val lambda4: String.(Int) -> String = {this + it}
```

It represents implicit name of single parameter.

Program when lambdas used as class extension:

```
val lambda4 : String.(Int) -> String = { this + it }
fun main(args: Array<String>) {
    val result = "Peeks".lambda4(40)
    print(result)
}
```

Explanation: The preceding example uses the lambda expression as a class extension. We used the format mentioned above to pass the parameters. This keyword is used for string and the Int parameter given in the lambda. The code body then concatenates both values and returns to the variable result.

it: Implicit Name of a Single-Parameter

In most cases, lambdas only have one parameter. It is used here to indicate the single parameter passed to the lambda expression.

Program utilizing lambda function shorthand:

```
val numb = arrayOf(1,-2,3,-4,5)
fun main(args: Array<String>) {
    println(numb.filter { it > 0 })
}
```

Program with lambda function in longhand:

```
val numb = arrayOf(1,-2,3,-4,5)
fun main(args: Array<String>) {
    println(numb.filter {item -> item > 0 })
}
```

Returning a Value from a Lambda Expression

The final value returned by lambda expression after execution. The lambda function can return any Integer, String, or Boolean values.

Kotlin program that uses a lambda function to return a String value:

```
val find =fun(numb: Int): String{
if(numb % 2==0 && numb < 0) {
    return "The number is even and negative"
   }
   else if (numb %2 ==0 && numb >0){
   return "The number is even and positive"
   }
   else if(numb %2 !=0 && numb < 0){
   return "The number is odd and negative"
   }
   else {
   return "The number is odd and positive"
   }
}
fun main(args: Array<String>) {
    val result = find(112)
    println(result)
}
```

ANONYMOUS FUNCTION

An anonymous function is quite similar to a regular function except for the omission of the function's name from the declaration. The anonymous function's body can be either an expression or a block.

First Example: Function body as an expression

```
fun(x: Int, y: Int) : Int = x * y
```

Second Example: Function body as a block

```
fun(x: Int, y: Int): Int {
    val mul = x * y
    return mul
}
```

Return Type and Parameters

The return type and parameters are also supplied in the same way as regular functions, although the parameters can be omitted if they can be deduced from the context.

If the function is an expression, the return type can be automatically deducted; otherwise, the anonymous function must explicitly provide a body block.

The Distinction between Lambda Expressions and Anonymous Functions

The only difference is how non-local returns behave. A return statement without a label always returns from the function declared function. This implies that a return within a lambda expression returns from the enclosing function, but a return within an anonymous function returns from the anonymous function itself.

Program to call the anonymous function:

```
// the anonymous function with body as an expression
val anonymous1 = fun(a: Int, b: Int): Int = a + b

// the anonymous function with body as a block
val anonymous2 = fun(x: Int, y: Int): Int {
            val mul = x * y
            return mul
            }
fun main(args: Array<String>) {
    //invoking functions
    val sum = anonymous1(13,4)
    val mul = anonymous2(5,6)
    println("Sum of two numbers is: $sum")
    println("Multiply of two numbers is: $mul")
}
```

HIGHER-ORDER FUNCTIONS IN KOTLIN

The Kotlin programming language provides excellent support for functional programming. Kotlin functions can be kept in variables and data structures, and they can be passed as parameters to and returned from Higher-Order functions.

Higher-Order Function

Higher-Order functions in Kotlin are functions that can receive a function as an argument or return a function. We shall pass anonymous functions or lambdas instead of passing Integer, String, or Array as function parameters. Lambdas are frequently passed as parameters in Kotlin functions for simplicity.

The lambda expression is passed as an argument to the Higher-Order function: A lambda expression can pass as a parameter to Higher-Order function.

There are two kinds of lambda expressions that may be passed:

- A lambda expression returns a unit.

- Lambda expression returns any of the values integer, string, etc.

Kotlin lambda expression program that returns Unit:

```
 // lambda expression
var lambda = {println("Huboftutors: A Computer Science
portal for Hub") }
     //the higher-order function
fun higherfunc( lmbd: () -> Unit ) {       // accepting
lambda as parameter
    lmbd()                                  //invokes the
lambda expression
}
fun main(args: Array<String>) {
    //invoke higher-order function
    higherfunc(lambda)                      // passing the
lambda as parameter
}
```

Explanation: Let's go over the above program step by step:

- In the top, we define a lambda expression that includes print() to print a string to standard output.

  ```
  var lambda = {println("Huboftutors: A Computer
  Science portal for Hub") }
  ```

- After that, we define a Higher-Order function with one parameter.

  ```
  lmbd: () -> Unit
  ```

- The receiving lambda parameter is known locally as lmbd.

- The symbol () indicates that the function does not accept any parameters.

- The unit symbol symbolizes that the function does not return any value.

- We called the Higher-Order function in the main function by supplying the lambda expression as a parameter.

```
higherfunc(lambda)
```

Kotlin lambda expression program that returns an integer value:

```
// lambda expression
var lambda = {x: Int,  y: Int -> x + y }
    // the higher order function
fun higherfunc( lmbd: (Int, Int) -> Int) {
// accepting the lambda as parameter

    var results = lmbd(2,4)    // invokes lambda
expression by passing parameters
    println("Sum of two numbers is: $results")
}

fun main(args: Array<String>) {
    higherfunc(lambda)              //passing lambda as
parameter
}
```

Explanation: Let's go over the program above step by step:

- At the top, we define a lambda expression that returns an integer value.

```
var lambda = int x, int y -> x + y
```

- Then we defined a Higher-Order function that takes the lambda expression as an argument.

```
lmbd: (Int, Int) -> Int
```

- The receiving lambda argument is known locally as lmbd.

- (Int,Int) indicates that the function accepts two integer parameters.

- Int indicates that the function returns an integer value.

We called the Higher-Order function in the main function by passing the lambda as a parameter.

```
higherfunc(lambda)
```

Passing function as a parameter to a Higher-Order function: A function can pass as a parameter to a Higher-Order function.

Two kinds of functions may pass:

- method that returns Unit

- function that returns any of the values integer, string, etc.

Kotlin function passing program that returns Unit:

```
// the regular function definition
fun printMe(s1:String) : Unit{
    println(s1)
}
    // the higher-order function definition
fun higherfunc( str1 : String, myfunc: (String) -> Unit){
    // invoke the regular function using local name
    myfunc(str1)
}
fun main(args: Array<String>) {
    // invoke the  higher-order function
    higherfunc("Huboftutors: A Computer Science portal
for Hub",::printMe)
}
```

Explanation: At the top, we build a normal method printMe(), which receives a String parameter and returns a Unit.

```
fun printMe(s1:String) : Unit
```

- (s1: String) is the only parameter

- Unit represents the return type

The Higher-Order function is thus defined as:

```
fun higherfunc( str1 : String, myfunc: (String) -> Unit)
```

It is given two parameters. One is the String type, and the other is the function:

- **Str1:** String denotes a string parameter.

- **myfunc:** (String) -> Unit indicates that it accepts function as a parameter and returns Unit.

The higher function is invoked from the main function by supplying the string and function as arguments.

```
higherfunc("Huboftutors: A Computer Science portal for
Hub",::printMe)
```

Program of passing function which returns integer value:

```
// the regular function definition
fun add(x: Int, y: Int): Int{
    var sums = x + y
    return sums
}
    //the higher-order function definition
fun higherfunc(addfunc: (Int,Int)-> Int){
    // invoke the regular function using local name
    var results = addfunc(13,6)
    print("The sum of two numbers is: $results")
}
fun main(args: Array<String>) {
    // invoke the higher-order function
    higherfunc(::add)
}
```

Returning a Function from a Higher-Order Function

A function can return from a Higher-Order function. When returning the function, we must define the normal function's argument types and return type in the Higher-Order function's return type.

Program of a function in Kotlin that returns another function:

```
// the function declaration
fun mul(x: Int, y: Int): Int{
    return x*y
}
```

```
        //the higher-order function declaration
fun higherfunc()  :  ((Int,Int)-> Int){
        return ::mul
}
fun main(args: Array<String>) {
        // invoke the function and store the returned
function into a variable
        val multiply = higherfunc()
        // invokes the mul() function by passing arguments
        val results = multiply(12,4)
        println("Multiplication of two numbers is:
$results")
}
```

KOTLIN LOCAL FUNCTIONS

The concept of functions is pretty simple: divide a huge program into smaller portions that can be reasoned about more efficiently and allow code reuse to minimize duplication. This second idea is known as the DRY principle, which stands for Don't Repeat Yourself. The more times we write the same code, the more likely a bug will creep in.

When we apply this theory to its logical conclusion, we will have produced a program that consists of many little functions, each of which accomplishes a single thing; this is analogous to the Unix principle of small programs, in which each program does a single job. The same principle applies to code included within a function. In Java, for example, a huge function or method may split down by calling many support functions defined in the same class or a helper class with static methods.

Example: Kotlin allows us to take this step further by defining functions inside other functions. These are referred to as local or nested functions. Functions can even be nested on top of each other. The following style may use to write an example of a printing area:

```
fun printAreaone(width: Int, height: Int): Unit {
        fun calculateArea(width: Int, height: Int): Int =
width * height
        val area1 = calculateArea(width, height)
        println("Area is: $area1")
}
```

As we can see, the calculateArea function is now included within printAreaone, and hence inaccessible to code outside of it. This is handy when we wish to hide functions that are only needed as details in implementing a bigger function. A similar result might obtain by marking a member function as private. So, are there any additional benefits to using local functions? They do, the parameters and variables declared in the outer scope can be accessed by local functions:

```kotlin
fun printAreatwo(width: Int, height: Int): Unit {
    fun calculateArea(): Int = width * height
    val area1 = calculateArea()
    println("Area is: $area1")
}
```

We've eliminated the arguments from the calculateArea function, and it now utilizes the parameters provided in the enclosing scope directly. This makes the nested function more legible and eliminates the need to repeat parameter descriptions, which is especially important for functions with many arguments. Let's look at an example of a function that might be decomposed using local functions:

```kotlin
fun fizzbuzz(start: Int, end: Int): Unit {
    for (x in start..end) {
        if (x % 2 == 0 && x % 4 == 0)
            println("Fizz Buzz")
        else if (x % 2 == 0)
            println("Fizz")
        else if (x % 4 == 0)
            println("Buzz")
        else
            println(x)
    }
}
```

This is known as the Fizz Buzz issue. The requirement instructs us to print the integers from the beginning to the finish value. However, if integer is a multiple of 2, we should print Fizz. We should print Buzz if it is a multiple of four. Print Fizz Buzz together if it is a multiple of 2 and 4.

The first solution is short and readable; however, it has some duplicated code. Because the modulo checks are coded twice, an error is likely doubled. Obviously, this example is relatively simple, so the possibilities of a typo are minimal; yet, it helps to show the issue for more complex issues. We may declare a local function for each modulo test, using only one line of code. This gets us to our next solution iteration:

```kotlin
fun fizzbuzz2(start: Int, end: Int): Unit {
  fun isFizz(x: Int): Boolean = x % 2 == 0
  fun isBuzz(x: Int): Boolean = x % 4 == 0
  for (x in start..end) {
    if (isFizz(x) && isBuzz(x))
        println("Fizz Buzz")
    else if (isFizz(x))
        println("Fizz")
    else if (isBuzz(x))
        println("Buzz")
    else
        println(x)
  }
}
```

In this case, our if...else branches now call the nested methods isFizz and isBuzz. However, passing x to the function each time is still a bit verbose. Is there any way to avoid this? Local functions can be defined not just directly within other functions, but also in for loops, while loops, and other blocks:

```kotlin
fun fizzbuzz3(start: Int, end: Int): Unit {
  for (x in start..end) {
    fun isFizz(): Boolean = x % 2 == 0
    fun isBuzz(): Boolean = x % 4 == 0
    if (isFizz() && isBuzz())
        println("Fizz Buzz")
    else if (isFizz())
        println("Fizz")
    else if (isBuzz())
        println("Buzz")
    else
        println(x)
  }
}
```

We've moved the function definitions within the for loop in this third iteration of our function. As a result, we may skip the parameter definitions and immediately access x. Finally, we could use Kotlin Basics to reduce some of the noise from the if...else keywords:

```kotlin
fun fizzbuzz4(start: Int, end: Int): Unit {
    for (x in start..end) {
        fun isFizz(): Boolean = x % 2 == 0
        fun isBuzz(): Boolean = x % 4 == 0
    when {
        isFizz() && isBuzz() -> println("Fizz Buzz")
        isFizz() -> println("Fizz")
        isBuzz() -> println("Buzz")
        else -> println(x)
        }
    }
}
```

This results in our final solution, which avoids code repetition and is more understandable than the initial iteration.

SCOPE FUNCTION IN KOTLIN

The Kotlin standard library has numerous methods that aid in executing a block of code within the context of an object. Using a lambda expression to call these functions on an object generates a temporary scope. These are known as Scope Functions. We can get to the object of these functions even if we don't know what it's named. That's perplexing! Let's look at the examples.

Without utilizing the scope function:

```kotlin
class Companie() {
    lateinit var name: String
    lateinit var objective: String
    lateinit var founder: String
}
fun main() {
    // without using the scope function
    // creating instance of the Companie Class
    val hft = Companie()
    // initializing members of the class
    hft.name = "Thehuboftutorials"
```

```
    hft.objective = "Computer science tutorials for
Students"
    hft.founder = "Akshita Jain"
    println(hft.name)
}
```

Using the scope function

```
class Companie() {
    lateinit var name: String
    lateinit var objective: String
    lateinit var founder: String
}
fun main() {
    // using the scope function
    val hft = Companie().apply {
        // don't need to use-object
        // name to refer members
        name = "Thehuboftutorials"
        objective = "Computer science tutorial for
Students"
        founder = "Akshit Jain"
    }
    println(hft.name)
}
```

Explanation: We've probably observed that when we don't use the scope function, we have to specify the object name every time we refer to a class member. We may use the scope function to refer to members without specifying the object name. This is one method of using the scope function.

SCOPE FUNCTIONS

Every scope function has well-defined use cases, even though they all have roughly the same conclusion. Let's take a closer look at each scope function and its associated use cases.

Utilization of Scope Functions

Scope functions make code more clear, legible, and succinct, which are key qualities of the Kotlin language.

Scope Function Types

Scope functions are classified into five types:

- let

- run

- with

- apply

- also

With a few exceptions, each function is relatively similar. It is sometimes difficult to choose which function to utilize and when. As a result, we must understand the distinctions between these functions and their cases.

Distinctions between these functions: There are primarily two distinctions between these functions:

- Return value (i.e. returns either 'context-object' or 'lambda-result') method of referring to a context object (i.e. using either 'this' or 'it' keyword).

  Please remember that the term "context object" refers to the object on which the scope functions are being used. As in the last example, our context object is 'hft.'

  Table of scope functions:

Function	Object Reference	Return Value
let	it	Lambda-result
run	this	Lambda-result
with	this	Lambda-result
apply	this	Context-object
also	it	Context-object

1. **let function**

- Context object: it

- Return value: lambda result

  Case in point: The let function is frequently used to give null safety checks. Use the safe call operator(?.) with 'let' for null safety. It only performs the block with a non-zero value.

Example:

```
fun main() {
    // nullable variable
    // with the value as null
    var x: Int? = null
    // using let function
    x?.let {
        // statements will
        // not execute as x is null
        print(it)
    }
    // re-initializing value of x to 2
    x = 2
    x?.let {
        // statements will execute
        // as x is not null
        print(x)
    }
}
```

Explanation: As we can see, if the value of 'a' is 'null,' the let function simply skips the code block. As a result, the programmers' worst fear – NullPointerException – is no longer a nightmare.

2. **apply function**

- Context object: this

- Return value: context object
  Case in point: "Apply these to the object," as the name suggests. It may be used to perform operations on receiver object members, primarily to initialize members.

Example:

```
class Companie() {
    lateinit var name: String
    lateinit var objective: String
    lateinit var founder: String
}
fun main() {
    Companie().apply {
```

```
        // same as founder = "Akshit Jain"
        this.founder = "Akshit Jain"
        name = "thehuboftutorials"
        objective = "Computer science tutorials
for Students"
    }
}
```

3. with function

- Context object: this

- Return value: lambda result
  Case in point: 'with' is recommended for invoking functions on context objects without passing the lambda result.

Example:

```
class Companie() {
    lateinit var name: String
    lateinit var objective: String
    lateinit var founder: String
}
    fun main() {
        val hft = Companie().apply {
            name = "thehuboftutorials"
            objective = "Computer science tutorials
for Students"
            founder = "Akshit Jain"
        }
        // with function
        with(hft) {
            // similar to println( "${this.name}" )
            println(" $name ")
        }
    }
```

4. run function

- Context object: this

- Return value: lambda result
  The 'run' function is a mix of the 'let' and 'with' functions.

Case in point: When the object lambda comprises both initialization and the computation of the return value, this method is used. We may use run to do null safety checks and other computations.

Example:

```
class Companie() {
    lateinit var name: String
    lateinit var objective: String
    lateinit var founder: String
}

fun main(args: Array<String>) {
    println("Companie Name : ")
    var companie: Companie? = null
    // body only executes if
    // company is non-null
    companie?.run {
        print(name)
    }
    print("Companie Name : ")
    // re-initialize companie
    companie = Companie().apply {
        name = "thehuboftutorials"
        founder = "Akshit Jain"
        objective = "Computer science tutorials
for Students"
    }
    // body executes as
    // 'companie' is non-null
    companie?.run {
        print(name)
    }
}
```

Explanation: The body of the run is simply ignored when the 'company' parameter is null. The body executes when it is non-null.

5. **also, function**

- Context object: it

- Return value: context object

Case in point: It is used when further operations must perform after the object members have been initialized.

Example:

```
fun main() {
    // initialized
    val list = mutableListOf<Int>(11, 22, 33)
    // later if we want to perform multiple-
operations on this list
    list.also {
        it.add(44)
        it.remove(22)
        // more operations if needed
    }
    println(list)
}
```

Object References

In scope functions, there are two methods for referring objects:

1. **this:** A lambda receiver keyword – 'this' can refer to the context object. This keyword performs object reference in the functions 'run,' 'with,' and 'apply.'

Example:

```
Company().apply {
    // same as : name = "thehuboftutorials"
    this.name = "thehuboftutorials"
    this.founder = "Akshit Jain"
    this.objective = "Computer science tutorials
for Students"
}
```

It is crucial to note that we can omit this keyword when referring to class members.

2. **it:** The 'let' and 'also' functions refer to the object's context as a lambda parameter.

Example:

```
Company().let {
    it.name = "thehuboftutorials"
    it.founder = "Akshit Jain"
    it.objective = "Computer science tutorials for
Students"
}
```

Return Values

A scope function can return one of two sorts of return values:

1. **Lambda result:** If we write any expression after the code block, it becomes the scope function's return value. The lambda result is the return value for the 'let', 'run', and 'with' functions.

   Example:

```
class Companie {
    var name: String = "thehuboftutorials"
    var founder: String = "Akshit Jain"
    var objective: String = "Computer science
tutorials for Students"
}
fun main() {
    val founderName: String = with(Companie()) {
        // 'founder' is returned by 'with' function
        founder
    }
    println("HfT's Founder : $founderName")
}
```

2. **Context object:** The context object is returned by the 'apply' and 'also' functions. We don't need to define the return value in this case. The context object is returned automatically.

   Example:

```
class Companie {
    var name: String = "thehuboftutorials"
    var founder: String = "Akshit Jain"
    var objective: String = "Computer science
tutorials for Students"
}
fun main() {
    val hft = Companie().apply {
```

```
        // any statements
    }
    // hft is an object of class Companie as
    // return of apply() is the context object
    print("HfT's Founder : ${hft.founder}");
}
```

Notes:

- Scope functions improve the readability, clarity, and conciseness of code.

- "This" and "it" are object references.

- The context object and lambda result are returned as the return value.

- To prevent NullPointerException, operate with nullable objects.

- Change the configuration of an item.

- run: execute lambda expressions on a nullable object.

- Additionally, other procedures can add.

- with: working with non-null items.

KOTLIN COLLECTIONS

The concept of collections is introduced in Kotlin, as it is in Java Collections. A collection frequently consists of several things of the same sort, known as elements or items in the collection. The Kotlin Standard Library includes a comprehensive set of collection managing functions.

Types of Collections

In Kotlin, collections are categorized into two kinds:

1. Immutable Collection
2. Mutable Collection

Immutable Collection

It denotes that it solely offers read-only capabilities and that its elements are not editable. Immutable collections and the strategies related to them are as follows:

- List – listOf() and listOf<T>()

- Set – setOf()

- Map – mapOf()

1. **List:** A list is an ordered collection in which we may access items or objects by using indices – integer numbers that identify the location of each entry. A list's elements can be repeated an infinite number of times. The immutable list cannot be added or removed. The immutable list is demonstrated in the following Kotlin program:

```
// example of an immutable list
fun main(args: Array<String>) {
    val immutableLists = listOf("Minakshi","Nitin",
"Pihu")
    // gives compile-time-error
    // immutableLists.add = "Ranidhi"
    for(item in immutableLists){
        println(item)
    }
}
```

2. **Set:** A set is an unordered collection of elements in which duplicates are not permitted. It is made up of one-of-a-kind components. In general, the order of set components has no significant impact. We cannot perform add or remove actions on it since it is an immutable Set. The immutable set is demonstrated in the following Kotlin program:

```
fun main(args: Array<String>) {
    // initialize with the duplicate-values
      // but the output with no-repeatition
    var immutableSets = setOf(17,88,88,11,0,"Ruhi",
"prithvi")
    // gives the compile-time-error
    // immutableSets.add(17)
    for(item in immutableSets){
        println(item)
    }
}
```

3. **Map:** Each key in a map is distinct and stores just one value; it is a collection of key-value pairs. Each key represents a single value. Values can duplicate, but keys must be unique. Maps are used to store the logical relationship between two objects, such as a student's ID and name. Because it is immutable, its size is fixed, and its methods give read-only access. The immutable map is demonstrated in the following Kotlin application:

```
// example for the immutable map
fun main(args : Array<String>) {
    var immutableMaps = mapOf(19 to "Mayank",18 to
"Pari",17 to "Ridhi")
    // gives compile-time-error
    // immutableMaps.put(19,"Radhika")
    for(key in immutableMaps.keys){
        println(immutableMaps[key])
    }
}
```

Mutable Collection

It is capable of both read and write. The following are examples of mutable collections and the strategies that go with them:

- List – mutableListOf(),arrayListOf() and ArrayList

- Set – mutableSetOf(), hashSetOf()

- Map – mutableMapOf(), hashMapOf() and HashMap

1. **List:** Because mutable lists may be read and written to, declared list elements can be removed or added. The mutable list is demonstrated in the following Kotlin program:

```
fun main(args : Array<String>) {
    var mutableLists = mutableListOf("Rahil","Lali
ta","Pihu")
    // we modify element
    mutableLists[0] = "Rajni"
    // add one more element in the list
    mutableLists.add("Anmol")
    for(item in mutableLists){
        println(item)
    }
}
```

2. **Set:** The mutable Set supports read and write operations. We may simply add or remove elements from the collections while keeping the order of the components. Write the following Kotlin code to demonstrate the mutable set:

```
fun main(args: Array<String>) {
    var mutableSets = mutableSetOf<Int>(61,20)
    // adding-elements in set
    mutableSets.add(14)
    mutableSets.add(55)
    for(item in mutableSets){
        println(item)
    }
}
```

3. **Map:** It can do operations such as put, remove, and clear since it is changeable. Create a Kotlin application to display the mutable map.

```
fun main(args : Array<String>) {
    var mutableMaps = mutableMapOf<Int,String>(1
to "Ruhi",2 to "Nikita",3 to "Prithvi")
    // we modify the element
    mutableMaps.put(1,"Pooja")
    // add one more element in the list
    mutableMaps.put(4,"Abhinav")
    for(item in mutableMaps.values){
        println(item)
    }
}
```

ArrayList IN KOTLIN

The ArrayList class in Kotlin is used to create a dynamic array. The phrase "dynamic array" refers to an array's ability to expand or decrease its size depending on its demands. It also can read and write. ArrayList is a non-synchronized list that may include duplicates. We use ArrayList to get the index of a specific item, convert an ArrayList to a string or another array, and other things.

Constructors:

1. **ArrayList<E>():** – It creates empty ArrayList.

2. **ArrayList(capacity: Int):** – It creates ArrayList of the specified size.

3. **ArrayList(elements: Collection<E>):** – It create ArrayList filled by collection elements.

Among the most important methods are:

- **add(index:Int, element: E): Boolean:** It adds a specified element to the ArrayList. The second input is the element to be added, which is necessary, and the first argument is the index to which the element is to be added, which is optional and defaults to 1 + the array's last index.

    Example:

    ```kotlin
    fun main(args: Array<String>) {
        // creation of empty arraylist using the
    constructor
        var arraylists = ArrayList<String>()
        //adding the String elements in the list
        arraylists.add("Piiks")
        arraylists.add("Piiks")
        // iterating-list
        println("Array list ---->")
        for(x in arraylists)
            println(x)
        arraylists.add( 1,  "of")
        println("Arraylists after the insertion:")
        for(x in arraylists)
            println(x)
    }
    ```

- **addAll(index: Int, elements: Collection): Boolean:** It is used to insert into the current list all elements of the given collection at the specified index. The first argument, which is also optional, is the index value.

    ```kotlin
    fun main(args: Array<String>) {
        // creating the empty arraylist using
    constructor
        var arraylist=ArrayList<String>()
        //adding the String elements in the list
        arraylists.add("Piiks")
        arraylists.add("of")
        arraylists.add("Piiks")
        // creation of new arraylist1
    ```

```
    var arraylists1=ArrayList<String>()
    //adding all the elements from arraylists to
arraylists1
    println("Elements in the arraylist1:")
    arraylist1.addAll(arraylists)
    for(c in arraylists1)
        println(c)
}
```

- **get(index: Int): E:** Its purpose is to return the element in the list at the specified index.

```
fun main(args: Array<String>) {
    // creating the empty arraylists using
constructor
    var arraylists=ArrayList<Int>()
    // adding the elements
    arraylists.add(22)
    arraylists.add(14)
    arraylists.add(99)
    arraylists.add(17)
    arraylists.add(56)
    // iterating through elements
    for(r in arraylists)
    print("$r")
    println()
    println("Accessing the index 2 of arraylists:
"+arraylists.get(3))
}
```

- **set(index: Int, element: E): E:** It is used to replace the elements in the current list at the given location with the elements passed as arguments.

```
fun main(args: Array<String>) {
    // creating the empty arraylist using the
constructor
    var arraylists=ArrayList<String>()
    // adding- elements
    arraylists.add("Piiks")
    arraylists.add("of")
    arraylists.add("Piiks:")
    arraylists.add("Portal")
```

```kotlin
    // iterating through the elements
    for(r in arraylists)
        print("$r")
    println()
    // set element at index 3 with the new string
    arraylist.set(3,"Computer Science tutorials
for students")
    // iterating through the elements
    for(r in arraylist)
        print("$r")
}
```

- **indexOf(element: E): Int:** It is used to return the index of the list's first occurrence of the given element, or −1 if the specified element does not appear in the list.

```kotlin
fun main(args: Array<String>) {
    // creating the empty arraylists using
constructor
    var arraylists=ArrayList<String>()
    // adding-elements
    arraylists.add("Piiks")
    arraylists.add("of")
    arraylists.add("Piiks")
     // iterating through elements
    for(r in arraylists)
        print("$r ")
    println()
    println("Index of the element is: "+arraylist.
indexOf("Piiks"))
}
```

- **remove(element: E): Boolean:** If it is present, it is used to remove the first occurrence of the specified element from the current collection. Similarly, removeAt(index) is used to remove the element at index c.

```kotlin
fun main(args: Array<String>) {
    // creating the empty arraylists using
constructor
    var arraylists=ArrayList<String>()
    // adding-elements
    arraylists.add("Piiks")
    arraylists.add("for")
```

```
        arraylists.add("Piiks")
        arraylists.remove("of")
        // iterating through the elements
        for(r in arraylists)
            print("$r ")
    }
```

- **clear():** Clear is used to remove all of the items from a list.

```
    fun main(args: Array<String>) {
        // creating the empty arraylists using
    constructor
        var arraylists=ArrayList<Int>()
        // adding-elements
        arraylists.add(40)
        arraylists.add(80)
        arraylists.add(10)
        arraylists.add(20)
        arraylists.add(30)
        // iterating through the elements
        for(r in arraylist)
            print("$r")
        arraylist.clear()
        println()
        println("Size of arraylist after clearing all
    the elements: "+arraylists.size)
    }
```

listOf() IN KOTLIN

List is a collection of elements that have been sorted in a specified order. Lists in Kotlin can be immutable (non-modifiable) or mutable (modifiable) (can be modified).

Read-only lists are created with listOf(), and their items cannot edit, but mutable lists are created with mutableListOf(), and their contents may be amended or modified.

In the Kotlin program list, integers are used:

```
fun main(args: Array<String>) {
    val r = listOf('1', '2', '3')
    println(r.size)
    println(r.indexOf('2'))
    println(r[2])
}
```

Strings are utilized in a Kotlin application using a list:

```kotlin
fun main(args: Array<String>) {
    //creating the list of strings
    val r = listOf("Veena", "Shivam", "Pihu", "Rajat")
    println("The size of the list is: "+r.size)
    println("The index of the element Rajat is: "+r.
indexOf("Rajat"))
    println("The element at index "+r[2])
    for(i in r.indices){
        println(r[i])
    }
}
```

Indexing List Elements in Kotlin

An index is assigned to each list element. The first element has an index of zero (0), and the last element has an index of len – 1, where 'len' is the length of the list.

```kotlin
fun main(args: Array<String>)
{
    val numbs = listOf(13, 43, 29, 22, 0, 9, 23,
54, 11)
    val numb1 = numbs.get(0)
    println(numb1)
    val numb2 = numbs[7]
    println(numb2)
    val index1 = numbs.indexOf(1)
    println("The first index of number is $index1")
    val index2 = numbs.lastIndexOf(1)
    println("The last index of number is $index2")
    val index3 = numbs.lastIndex
    println("The last index of the list is $index3")
}
```

The First and Last Elements

The list's first and last members can retrieve without using the get() method.

```kotlin
fun main(args: Array<String>)
{
    val numbs1 = listOf(14, 65, 33, 31, 0, 22, 9, 64, 19)
```

```
    println(numbs1.first())
    println(numbs1.last())
}
```

Iteration Methods for Lists

This process goes over each element of a list one by one.

There are several ways to achieve this in Kotlin.

```
fun main(args: Array<String>)
{
    val names1 = listOf("Guarav", "Rashmi", "Sneha",
"Payal",
        "Danih", "Isha", "Elisa")
    // method1
    for (name in names1) {
        print("$name, ")
    }
    println()
    // method2
    for (r in 0 until names1.size) {
        print("${names1[r]} ")
    }
    println()
    // method-3
    names.forEachIndexed({r, s -> println("names1[$r]
= $s")})
    // method 4
    val it: ListIterator<String> = names1.
listIterator()
    while (it.hasNext()) {
        val r = it.next()
        print("$r ")
    }
    println()
}
```

Explanation:

```
for (name in names1) {
        print("$name, ")
    }
```

The for loop traverses the list. In each cycle, the variable 'name' refers to the next element of the list.

```
for (r in 0 until names1.size) {
      print("${names[r]} ")
    }
```

This method makes use of the size of the list. The til keyword generates a collection of list indexes.

```
names1.forEachIndexed({r, s -> println("names1[$r] =
$s")})
```

Using the forEachIndexed() function, we loop over the list with index and value accessible in each iteration.

```
val it: ListIterator = names1.listIterator()
    while (it.hasNext()) {
        val r = it.next()
        print("$r ")
    }
```

To iterate across the list, we utilize a ListIterator.

Sorting the List's Elements

The following examples show how to sort a list in ascending or descending order.

```
fun main(args: Array<String>)
{
    val lists = listOf(33, 54,87, 32,92, 13, 0, 15, 69 )
    val asc1 = lists.sorted()
    println(asc1)
    val desc1 = lists.sortedDescending()
    println(desc1)
}
```

Explanation:

```
val asc1 = list.sorted()
```

The sorted() function is used to sort the list in ascending order.

```
val desc1 = lists.sortedDescending()
```

Using the sortedDescending() method, the list is sorted in descending order.

The Functions contains() and containsAll()
This method checks to see if element exists in the list.

```
fun main(args: Array<String>)
{
    val lists = listOf(81, 24, 37, 11, 27, 43, 0, 55,
7 6 )

    val rest1 = lists.contains(0)
    if (rest1)
        println("list contains 0")
    else
        println("list doesnt contain 0")
    val results = lists.containsAll(listOf(3, -1))
    if (results)
        println("list contains 3 and -1")
    else
        println("list does not contain 3 and -1")
}
```

Explanation:
```
val rest = lists.contains(0)
```

Checks if the lists include 0 and returns true or false, saving the result in rest1.

```
val result = list.containsAll(listOf(3, -1))
```

This function determines if the list contains the numbers 3 and –1.

setOf() in Kotlin

The Kotlin Set interface is a general, unordered collection of items containing duplicates. Sets are classified as changeable or immutable in Kotlin.

- setOf() is immutable, which means it can only perform read-only operations.
- SetOf() is mutable, suggesting that it can read and write operations.

Syntax:

```
fun <C> setOf( vararg elements: C): Set<C>
```

Description:

- This function creates a new read-only set of the specified items.
- The objects are iterated over in the order they were stored.

setOf() function Kotlin program:

```
fun main(args: Array<String>)
{
    //declaring set of strings
    val seta1 = setOf("Piiks", "of", "Piiks")
    //declaring set of characters
    val setb1 = setOf( "P", "o", "P" )
    //declaring set of integers
    val setc1 = setOf( 01, 02, 03, 04 )
    //traversing through the set of strings
    for(item in seta1)
        print( item )
    println()
    //traversing through the set of characters
    for(item in setb1)
        print( item )
    println()
    //traversing through the set of integers
    for(item in setc1)
        print( "$item " )
}
```

Set Indexing

The index functions indexOf() and lastIndexOf() can be used to determine the index of the specified element. We may alternatively use the elementAt() function to find elements at a certain index.

Index-using the Kotlin program:

```
fun main(args: Array<String>) {
    val captain = setOf("Kamal","Sidhi","Ritu","Payal"
,"Aman","Kamal")
    println("The element at index 2 is: "+captain.
elementAt(2))
    println("The index of element is: "+captain.
indexOf("Smridhi"))
    println("The last index of element is: "+captain.
lastIndexOf("Ruhi"))
}
```

Set the first() and last() element: To get the first and last element in a set, use the first() and last() functions.

Example:

```
fun main(args: Array<String>){
    val captain = setOf(01,02,03,04,"Smriti","Raman",
        "Pihu","Kalash","Rita","Disha")
    println("the first element of the set is:
"+captain.first())
    println("the last element of the set is:
"+captain.last())
}
```

Set Basics

We'll go through basic functions like count(), max(), min(), sum(), and average ().

Basic functions are used in Kotlin program:

```
fun main(args: Array<String>) {
    val nums = setOf(101, 202, 303, 404, 505, 606,
707, 808)
    println("Number of element in the set is: "+nums.
count())
```

```
    println("Maximum element in the set is: "+nums
.max())
    println("Minimum element in the set is: "+nums
.min())
    println("Sum of the elements in the set is:
"+nums.sum())
    println("Average of elements in the set is:
"+nums.average())
}
```

The Functions contains() and containsAll()

To determine whether or not element exists in the set, both procedures are employed.

Kotlin code that makes use of the contains() and containsAll() functions:

```
fun main(args: Array<String>){
    val captain = setOf(01,02,03,04,"Rashmi","Smriti",
        "Pihu","Koyal","Radhika","Disha")
    var names = "Disha"
    println("set contains element $name or not?" +
            "   "+captain.contains(names))
    var nums = 5
    println("set contains element $nums or not?" +
            "   "+captain.contains(nums))
    println("set contains given elements or not?" +
            "   "+captain.containsAll(setOf(1,3,
"Ruhi")))
}
```

Using the isEmpty() methods to check the equality of empty sets:

```
fun <C> setOf(): Set<C>
```

This syntax yields an empty set of the given type.

Kotlin code that employs the isEmpty() function:

```
fun main(args: Array<String>) {
    //the creation of an empty set of strings
    val seta1 = setOf<String>()
    //the creation of an empty set of integers
    val setb1 =setOf<Int>()
    //checking if the set is empty or not
```

```
    println("seta1.isEmpty() is ${seta1.isEmpty()}")
    // since Empty sets are equal
    //check if 2 sets are equal or not
    println("seta1 == setb1 is ${seta1 == setb1}")
    println(seta1) //printing first set
}
```

mutableSetOf() METHOD IN KOTLIN

The Kotlin Set interface is a generic, unordered collection of items containing duplicates. Kotlin distinguishes between two types of sets: changeable and immutable.

- setOf() is immutable, which means it can only perform read-only operations.

- SetOf() is mutable, which means it may do both read and write operations.

Syntax:

```
fun <C> mutableSetOf( vararg elements: C):
MutableSet<C>
```

Description:

- This function returns a collection of objects that can be read and written that were provided.

- The items' iteration order is kept in the returned set.

The mutableSetOf() method is implemented with the following Kotlin code:

```
fun main(args: Array<String>)
{
    //declaring the mutable set of integers
    val mutableSetA1 = mutableSetOf<Int>( 101,  202,
303,  404,  303);
    println(mutableSetA1)
    //declaring the mutable set of strings
    val mutableSetB1 = mutableSetOf<String>("Piiks",
"of",  "Piiks");
    println(mutableSetB1)
```

```
//declaring the empty mutable set of integers
val mutableSetC1 = mutableSetOf<Int>()
println(mutableSetC1)
}
```

Adding and deleting components from a set: To add elements to a mutable set, we may use the add() method, and to remove elements, we can use the remove() function.

Example:

```
fun main(args: Array<String>)
{
    //declaring the mutable set of integers
    val seta1 = mutableSetOf( 101,   202,   303,
404,   303);
    println(seta1);
    //adding the elements 606 & 707
    seta1.add(606);
    seta1.add(707);
    println(seta1);
    //removing the 303 from the set
    seta1.remove(303);
    println(seta1);
    //another way to add the elements is by using
listOf() function
    seta1 += listOf(808,909)
    println(seta1)
}
```

Set Indexing

The index methods indexOf() and lastIndexOf() can be used to determine the index of the provided element (). To discover elements at a certain index, we may also utilize the elementAt() function.

Index-using the Kotlin program:

```
fun main(args: Array<String>) {
    val captain = mutableSetOf("Radha","Smriti","Pihu"
,"Maya","Kamal","Disha")
    println("The element at index 2: "+captain.
elementAt(2))
```

```
    println("The index of element: "+captain.
indexOf("Smriti"))
    println("The last index of element: "+captain.
lastIndexOf("Kamal"))
}
```

Set the First and Last Element

The first() and last() methods can use to get the first and last element of a set, accordingly.

Example:

```
fun main(args: Array<String>){
    val captain = mutableSetOf(01,02,03,04,
"Karishma","Smriti",
        "Pihu","Maya","Rita","Disha")
    println("first element of the set: "+captain.
first())
    println("last element of the set: "+captain.
last())
}
```

Traversal in a mutableSet

To explore all the elements in a mutableSet, we may use a for loop and an iterator.

```
fun main(args: Array<String>)
{
    //declaring mutable set of the integers
    val seta1 = mutableSetOf( 101,  202,  303,
404,  303);
    //traversal of the seta1 using iterator 'item'
    for(item in seta1)
        println( item )
}
```

The Methods contains() and containsAll()

To determine whether or not an element exists in the set, both procedures are employed.

Kotlin code that makes use of the contains() and containsAll() functions:

```
fun main(args: Array<String>){
    val captain = mutableSetOf(01,02,03,04,"Ridhi",
"Disha",
```

```
        "Pihu","Kama;","Raman","Alka")
    var names = "Raman"
    println("The set contains element $names or not?"
+
              "   "+captain.contains(names))
    var nums = 5
    println("The set contains element $nums or not?" +
              "   "+captain.contains(nums))
    println("the set contains given elements or not?" +
              "   "+captain.containsAll(setOf(01,03,
"Root")))
}
```

Checking equality of empty sets and employing the isEmpty() functions:

```
fun <C> mutableSetOf(): mutableSet<C>
```

This syntax yields an empty set of the given type.
Kotlin code that employs the isEmpty() function:

```
fun main(args: Array<String>) {
    //creation empty set of strings
    val seta1 = mutableSetOf<String>()
    //creation empty set of integers
    val setb1 = mutableSetOf<Int>()
    //checking if tset is empty or not
    println("seta1.isEmpty() is ${seta1.isEmpty()}")
    // empty sets are equal
    //checking if two sets are equal or not
    println("seta1 == setb1 is ${seta1 == setb1}")
    println(seta1) //printing first set
}
```

hashSetOf() IN KOTLIN

Kotlin HashSet is a general, unordered collection of items with no duplicates. It is responsible for implementing the set interface. hashSetOf() is a function that returns a mutable hashSet that may be read and written to. To hold all of the components, the HashSet class use hashing.

Syntax:

```
fun <C> hashSetOf(vararg elements: C): HashSet<C>
```

It returns a new HashSet with the requested elements but offers no assurances about the order sequence specified when storing.

Example:

```
fun main(args: Array<String>)
{
    //declaring hash set of integers
    val seta1 = hashSetOf(11,22,33,33);
    //printing the first-set
    println(seta1)
    //declaration of hash set of strings
    val setb1 = hashSetOf("Piiks","of","piiks");
    println(setb1);
}
```

Adding and deleting elements from hashset:

- To add elements to a hashset, use the add() and addAll() methods.

- We may remove an element with the remove() function.

The following program use the add() and delete() methods:

```
fun main(args: Array<String>)
{
    //declaration of hash set of integers
    val seta1 = hashSetOf<Int>();
    println(seta1)
    //adding-elements
    seta1.add(101)
    seta1.add(202)
    //making extra set to add it in the seta
    val newsets = setOf(404,505,606)
    seta1.addAll(newsets)
    println(seta1)
    //removing 202 from the set
    seta1.remove(202)
    println(seta1)
}
```

hashSet Traversal

We can traverse hashSet in a loop using an iterator.

```
fun main(args: Array<String>)
{
    //declaration of hash set of integers
    val seta1 = hashSetOf(101,202,303,505);
    //traversing in set using a for loop
    for(items in seta1)
        println(items)
}
```

Indexing in a hashSet

The index of the specified element can be obtained using the index methods indexOf() and lastIndexOf(). We may alternatively utilize the element At() function to find elements at a certain index.

Index-using the Kotlin program:

```
fun main(args: Array<String>) {
    val captain = hashSetOf("Karishma","Sunita","Pihu"
,"Maya","Ritu","Rita")
    println("element at index 2: "+captain.elementAt(3))
    println("index of element: "+captain.indexOf
("Sunita"))
    println("last index of element: "+captain.
lastIndexOf("Ritu"))
}
```

The Functions contains() and containsAll()

Both techniques are used to determine whether or not a Hashset element exists.

Kotlin code that makes use of the contains() and containsAll() functions:

```
fun main(args: Array<String>){
    val captain = hashSetOf(01,02,03,04,"Raman",
"Smriti",
        "Naman","Maya","Ritu","Daman")
    var names = "Ritu"
    println("set contains the element $name or not?" +
            "  "+captain.contains(names))
    var nums = 5
```

```
    println("the set contains the element $nums or
not?" +
            "     "+captain.contains(nums))
    println("the set contains the given elements or
not?" +
            "     "+captain.containsAll(setOf(11,33,"Dam
an","Waner")))
}
```

Using the isEmpty() methods to check the equivalence of empty hash sets:

```
fun <C> hashSetOf(): hashSet<C>
```

This syntax yields an empty hash set of the specified type.

Kotlin code that employs the isEmpty() function:

```
fun main(args: Array<String>) {
    //creation of empty hash set of strings
    val seta1 = hashSetOf<String>()
    //creation of empty hashset of integers
    val setb1 =hashSetOf<Int>()
    //checking if set is empty or not
    println("seta1.isEmpty() is ${seta1.isEmpty()}")
    // Since the Empty hashsets are equal
    //checking if two hash sets are equal or not
    println("seta1 == setb1 is ${seta1 == setb1}")
}
```

mapOf () in Kotlin

A Kotlin map is a set of object pairs. A map's data is kept in the form of pairs, each of which has a key and a value. Map keys are unique, and the map maintains just one value for each key.

Kotlin distinguishes between immutable and mutable maps. Immutable maps produced by mapOf() are read-only, but mutable maps produced by mutableMapOf() may be read and write.

Syntax:

```
fun <C, D> mapOf(vararg pairs: Pair<C, D>): Map<C, D>
```

- The first value in the pair is the key, and the second is the value of the related key.

- If several pairs have the same key, the map will return the value of the last pair.

- The map entries are traversed in the specified order.

mapOf() Kotlin program:

```kotlin
fun main(args: Array<String>)
{
    //declaration of map of integer to string
    val map1 = mapOf(1 to "Piiks", 2 to "of", 3 to
"Piiks")
    //printing-map
    println( map1)
}
```

Map keys, values, and entries:

```kotlin
fun main(args: Array<String>)
{
    //declaration of map of integer to string
    val map1 = mapOf(1 to "One", 2 to "Two", 3 to
"Three", 4 to "Four")
    println("Map Entries : "+map1)
    println("Map Keys: "+map1.keys )
    println("Map Values: "+map1.values )
}
```

Map Size

A map's size may determine in two ways. Using size property of the map and the count() function.

```kotlin
fun main() {
    val ranks1 = mapOf(1 to "Canada",2 to
"WestAfrica",3 to "Russia",4 to "London")
    //method-1
    println("size of the map: "+ranks1.size)
    //method-2
    println("size of the map: "+ranks1.count())
}
```

Empty Map

We can build an empty serializable map using mapOf ().

MapOf() Example:

```
fun main(args: Array<String>)
{
    //creation of an empty map using the mapOf()
    val map = mapOf<String,  Int>()
    println("The Entries: " + map.entries)  //
entries of the map
    println("The Keys:" + map.keys)  //keys of the
map
    println("The Values:" + map.values)  //values
of the map
}
```

Get Map Values

The different methods indicated in the following code can be used to obtain values from a map.

```
fun main() {
    val ranks1 = mapOf(1 to "Kashmir",2 to "London",
3 to "Russia",4 to "Canada")
    //method-1
    println("The Team having rank #1: "+ranks1[1])
    //method-2
    println("The Team having rank #3: "+ranks1
.getValue(3))
    //method-3
    println("The Team having rank #4: "+ranks1
.getOrDefault(4, 0))
    // method-4
    val teams = ranks1.getOrElse(2, { 0 })
    println(teams)
}
```

Map Contains Keys or Values

We can determine if a map has a key or a value by using the containsKey() and containsValue() methods.

```
fun main() {
    val colorsTopToBottom = mapOf("pink" to 1, "orange"
to 2, "green" to 3,
        "purple" to 4,  "grey" to 5, "brown" to 6,
"blue" to 7)
```

```
var colors = "orange"
if (colorsTopToBottom.containsKey(colors)) {
    println("Yes, it contains color $colors")
} else {
    println("No, it does not contain color
$colors")
}
val values = 9
if (colorsTopToBottom.containsValue(values)) {
    println("Yes, it contains value $values")
} else {
    println("No, it does not contain value
$values")
}
}
```

Two Values and the Same Key

If two values have the same key value, the map will display the most recent value of those numbers.

Example:

```
fun main(args: Array<String>)
{
    //let's make the two values with the same key
    val map1 = mapOf(1 to "piiks1",2 to "of",  1
to "piiks2")
    // return-map-entries
    println("Entries of map is: " + map1.entries)
}
```

Explanation: In this scenario, key value 1 contains two values: piiks1 and piiks2, but because mapOf() can only have one value for a single key item, the map only keeps the most recent value, and piiks1 is erased.

HashMap IN KOTLIN

Kotlin HashMap is a collection of object pairings. Hash Tables are used to construct MutableMap in Kotlin. It stores information in the form of a key and value pair. Map keys are unique, and the map maintains just one value for each key. HashMap<key, value> or HashMap<K, V> is how it's written.

The hash table-based implementation of HashMap offers no assurances about the order of provided key, value, and collection items.

Kotlin HashMap class constructors are available:

Each of Kotlin HashMap's constructors has a public access modifier:

- **HashMap():** The built-in constructs for creating an empty HashMap object.

- **HashMap(initialCapacity: Int, loadFactor: Float = 0f):** This function is used to create a HashMap with the capacity specified. They will disregard if initialCapacity and loadFactor are not used.

- **HashMap(initialCapacity: Int):** This method generates a HashMap with capacity specify. If initialCapacity is not used, it will be ignored.

- **HashMap(original: Map <out K, V>):** This method creates a HashMap with the same mappings as the provided map.

HashMap Functions Use

Kotlin code that use the HashMap(), HashMap(original: Map), Traversing Hashmap, and HashMap.get() functions:

```
fun main(args: Array<String>) {
    //example of the HashMap class define
    // with empty "HashMap of <String, Int>"
    var hashMap1 : HashMap<String, Int>
            = HashMap<String, Int> ()
    //print empty hashMap
    printHashMap(hashMap1)
    //adding the elements to the hashMap1 using
    // put() function
    hashMap1.put("IronMan", 5200)
    hashMap1.put("Thor", 100)
    hashMap1.put("SpiderMan", 1100)
    hashMap1.put("NickFury", 1000)
    hashMap1.put("HawkEye", 1800)
    //print the non-Empty-hashMap1
    printHashMap(hashMap1)
    //using the overloaded print function of
    //Kotlin language to get the same results
    println("hashMap1 : " + hashMap1 + "\n")
    //hashMap1 traversal using a for loop
```

```
    for(key in hashMap1.keys){
        println("Element at key $key is :
${hashMap1[key]}")
    }
    //creation of another hashMap1 object with the
    //previous version of the hashMap1 object
    var secondHashMap : HashMap<String, Int>
            = HashMap<String, Int> (hashMap1)
    println("\n" + "Second HashMap : ")
    for(key in secondHashMap.keys){
        //using hashMap1.get() function to fetch
values
        println("The Element at key $key : ${hashMap1.
get(key)}")
    }
    //this will clear whole map and make it empty
    println("hashMap1.clear()")
    hashMap1.clear()
    println("After Clearing : " + hashMap1)
}
//function to print the hashMap1
fun printHashMap(hashMap1: HashMap<String, Int>){
    // isEmpty() function to check whether the
    // hashMap1 is empty or not
    if(hashMap1.isEmpty()){
        println("hashMap1 is empty")
    }else{
        println("hashMap1: " + hashMap1)
    }
}
```

Program of HashMap initial capacity, HashMap.size:

```
fun main(args: Array<String>) {
    //HashMap can also be initializing
    // with the initial capacity.
    //The capacity can be changed by
    // adding and replacing the element.
    var hashMap1 : HashMap<String, Int>
            = HashMap<String, Int> (4)
    //adding the elements to the hashMap1 using
put() function
```

```
    hashMap1.put("Iron-Man",  1300)
    hashMap1.put("Thor",  300)
    hashMap1.put("Spider-Man",  1900)
    hashMap1.put("Nick-Fury",  1200)

    for(key in hashMap1.keys) {
        println("Element at the key $key :
${hashMap1[key]}")
    }
    //return the size of hashMap1
    println("\n" + "hashMap1.size : " + hashMap1.size
)
    //adding new element in the hashMap
    hashMap1["Black-Widow"] = 3100;
    println("hashMap1.size : " + hashMap1.size + "\n")
    for(key in hashMap1.keys) {
        println("Element at key $key :
${hashMap1[key]}")
    }
}
```

Kotlin code that makes use of the HashMap.get(key), HashMap.replace(), and HashMap.put() methods:

```
fun main(args: Array<String>) {
    var hashMap1 : HashMap<String, Int>
            = HashMap<String, Int> ()
    //adding the elements to the hashMap1
    // using the put() function
    hashMap1.put("Iron-Man",  3100)
    hashMap1.put("Thor",  150)
    hashMap1.put("Spider-Man",  1700)
    hashMap1.put("Cap",  1200)
    for(key in hashMap1.keys) {
        println("Element at the key $key :
${hashMap1[key]}")
    }
    //the hashMap1's elements can be accessed like
this
    println("\nhashMap1[\"Iron-Man\"] : "
            + hashMap1["Iron-Man"])
    hashMap1["Thor"] = 2200
```

```
println("hashMap1.get(\"Thor\") : "
        + hashMap1.get("Thor") + "\n")
//replacing some value
hashMap1.replace("Cap",  909);
hashMap1.put("Thor",  2100);
println("hashMap1.replace(\"Cap\",  909)" +
        " hashMap1.replace(\"Thor\",  2100)) :")
for(key in hashMap1.keys) {
    println("Element at key $key :
${hashMap1[key]}")
    }
}
```

HashMap Time Complexity

Kotlin HashMap provides constant time or O(1) complexity for fundamental operations like get and put if the hash function is properly built and the objects are effectively distributed. When searching in a HashMap, containsKey() is simply a get() that discards the returned result; hence, it is O(1) (assuming the hash function works properly).

The Kotlin HashMap class also has the following features:

- **Boolean consistsKey(key: K):** If the map contains the specified key, this method returns true.

- **Boolean containsValue(value: V):** True is returned if the map maps one or more keys to the provided value.

- **void clear():** It removes all map items.

- **remove(key: K):** It removes the specified key and value from the map.

We discussed Lambdas Expressions and Anonymous Functions, the distinction between Lambdas expressions and Anonymous functions, the Local Function and the Scope Function in this chapter. Collections, Arraylist, setOf(), mutableSetOf(), hashSetOf(), mapOf(), and Hashmap were also discussed.

CHAPTER 5

Code Management and Exception Handling

IN THIS CHAPTER

> ➤ Exception handling

> ➤ Logging

> ➤ Unit testing

> ➤ "Nothing" type

We studied Functional Programming with its subparts and related examples in the previous chapter. This chapter will cover Exceptional Handling, Logging, Unit Testing, and the nothing type.

EXCEPTIONAL HANDLING | TRY, CATCH, THROW, AND FINALLY

An exception is an undesirable or unexpected occurrence that occurs during program execution, i.e., during run time, and disrupts normal flow of the program's instructions. Exception handling is an approach for dealing with errors and avoiding run-time crashes, which might cause our program to crash.

Exceptions are classified into two types:

- **Checked Exception:** IOException, FileNotFoundException, and other exceptions are often added to functions and verified at build time.

DOI: 10.1201/9781003308447-5

- **Unchecked Exception:** Exceptions, such as NullPointerException and ArrayIndexOutOfBoundException, are frequently produced by logical errors and are examined at run time.

Exceptions in Kotlin

Exceptions in Kotlin are unchecked and can only be discovered at run time. Throwable is the parent of all exception classes.

We frequently use the throw-expression to throw an exception object:

```
throw Exception("Throw-me")
```

Some of the more common exceptions are as follows:

- **NullPointerException:** We receive a NullPointerException when executing a property or method on a null object.

- **Arithmetic Exception:** This exception is raised when numbers are given to incorrect arithmetic operations. Divide by zero, for example.

- **SecurityException:** This exception is raised to indicate a security problem.

- **ArrayIndexOutOfBoundsException:** This exception is generated when we attempt to obtain the wrong index value of an array.

An arithmetic exception is thrown in a Kotlin program:

```
.fun main(args : Array<String>){
    var numb = 40 / 0        // throws-exception
    println(numb)
}
```

Although we know that division by zero is not permitted in arithmetic, we begin the numb variable with 40/0 in the preceding program. An exception is raised when we attempt to launch the program.

To solve this problem, we must use the try-catch block.

Exception Handling

In the example below, we divide an integer by 0 (zero), which results in an ArithmeticException. The catch block will be performed because this code is in the try block.

The ArithmeticException occurred in this case; therefore, the ArithmeticException catch block was executed, and "Arithmetic Exception" was printed in the output.

When an exception occurs, everything beyond that point is disregarded, and control is sent to the catch block, if one exists. The finally block is run always, regardless of whether or not an exception occurs.

```kotlin
fun main(args: Array<String>) {
    try {
        var numb = 50/0
        println("Beginners ")
        println(numb)
    } catch (c: ArithmeticException) {
        println("Arithmetic-Exception")
    } catch (c: Exception) {
        println(c)
    } finally {
        println("in any of case it will print.")
    }
}
```

What If We Don't Deal with Exceptions?

Assume that the program will crash if we do not handle the exception in the previous example.

The program terminated with an error in this scenario since we did not handle exceptions.

How to Throw an Exception in Kotlin

The term throw can also use to throw an exception. In the following example, the throw keyword is used to throw an exception. The statement preceding the exception was executed, but the statement after the exception was not performed since control was transferred to the catch block.

```kotlin
fun main(args: Array<String>) {
    try{
        println("Before-exception")
        throw Exception("Something wrong ")
        println("After-exception")
    }
    catch(c: Exception){
        println(c)
    }
```

```
finally{
    println("can't-ignore ")
}
}
```

NullPointerException Example
Here's an example of a NullPointerException raised when the length()
method of a null String object is called:

```
public class Exception_Example {
    private static void printLength(String strg) {
        System.out.println(strg.length());
    }
    public static void main(String args[]) {
        String myString = null;
        printLength(myString);
    }
}
```

In this example, the printLength() function utilizes the length() method
of a String without first performing a null check. Because the string
returned by the main() method has no value, the preceding code throws a
NullPointerException:

```
Exception in the thread "main" java.lang.
NullPointerException
    at Exception_Example.printLength(Exception_
Example.java:3)
    at Exception_Example.main(Exception_Example.java:8)
```

How to Avoid NullPointerException
The NullPointerException can avoid by using the following checks and
protections:

- Include a null check before referring to them to verify that an object's
  methods or properties are properly initialized.

- Using Apache Commons StringUtils for String operations, such as
  StringUtils.isNotEmpty(), to ensure that a string is not empty before
  using it.

- Use primitives rather than objects wherever possible since they cannot have null references, such as int instead of Integer and boolean
  instead of Boolean.

KOTLIN try-catch block

To manage exceptions in the program, we use the try-catch block in Kotlin. The try block contains the code that throws an exception, whereas the catch block handles the exception. This block must be present in either the main or other methods. There should be a catch block, a finally block, or both after the try block.

Syntax:

```
try {
    // the code that throw exception
} catch(c: ExceptionName) {
    // catch exception, handle it
}
```

A try-catch block program in Kotlin is used to handle arithmetic exceptions:

```
import kotlin.ArithmeticException
fun main(args : Array<String>){
    try{
        var numb = 40 / 0
    }
    catch(e: ArithmeticException){
        // caught, handles it
        println("not allowed divide by zero")
    }
}
```

Explanation: We used a try-catch block in the previous application. Because division by zero is not specified in arithmetic, the numb variable, which may throw an exception, is enclosed within the try block's braces. The catch block will execute the println() method when an exception is thrown.

Kotlin try-catch block as an Expression

As previously stated, expressions always return a value. We may use the Kotlin try-catch block as an expression in our software. The return result of the expression will be either the last expression of the try block or the final expression of the catch block. If an exception occurs in the function, the catch block returns the value.

In a Kotlin code, use try-catch as an expression:

```kotlin
fun test(x: Int, y: Int) : Any {
    return try {
        x/y
        //println("The Result is: "+ x / y)
    }
    catch(e:Exception){
        println(e)
        "Divide by zero not allowed"
    }
}
// the main function
fun main(args: Array<String>) {
    // invoke the test function
    var results1 = test(30,3  ) //execute try-block
    println(results1)
    var results = test(30,0 )    // execute catch-block
    println(results)
}
```

In the preceding code, we used try-catch as an expression. Declare a function test at the program's top and return a value via a try-catch block. The main method invoked the test function and provided the input values to it (30,3). After considering the parameters, the test method returns the try result (30/3 = 10). However, in the next call, we passed (b = 0), and this time the exception is caught and the expression of the catch block is returned.

Kotlin Finally Block

Whether or not the catch block handles an exception, the finally block is always run in Kotlin. As a result, it is used to carry out crucial code statements.

We may merge the finally and try blocks and eliminate the catch block.

Syntax:

```kotlin
try {
    //the code that can throw-exception
} finally {
    // code of finally-block
}
```

Kotlin program that includes a finally block and a try block:

```kotlin
fun main(args : Array<String>){
    try{
        var ar = arrayOf(11,22,33,44,55)
        var int = ar[6]
        println(int)
    }
  finally {
        println("This block will executes always")
    }
}
```

We used the try with finally block instead of the catch block in the previous program. In this scenario, the catch block ignores the exception and performs the finally block instead.

Finally block with the try-catch block Syntax:

```kotlin
try {
    // the code that throw-exception
} catch(c: ExceptionName) {
    // catch the exception, handle it.
} finally {
    // code of finally-block
}
```

Kotlin program that includes a finally block and a try-catch block:

```kotlin
fun main (args: Array<String>){
    try {
        var int = 30 / 0
        println(int)
    } catch (c: ArithmeticException) {
        println(c)
    } finally {
        println("This block will executes always ")
    }
}
```

Kotlin throw Keyword

In Kotlin, we use the throw keyword to throw an explicit exception. It also can throw a custom exception.

Program of throw keyword in Kotlin:

```
fun main(args: Array<String>) {
    test("cdefg")
    println("executes after the validation")
}
fun test(password: String) {
    // it calculate the length of entered password and
compare
    if (password.length < 6)
        throw ArithmeticException("Password short")
    else
        println("Password is strong ")
}
```

NESTED try block AND MULTIPLE catch block

Nested try block

This section will teach us about nested try-catch blocks and multiple catch blocks. A nested try block has one try-catch block within another try-catch block.

When an exception occurs in the inner try-catch block that is not handled by the inner catch blocks, the outer try-catch blocks are inspected for that exception.

Syntax:

```
// the outer try-block
try
{
    //the inner try-block
    try
    {
        //the code that can throw an exception
    }
    catch(c: SomeException)
    {
     //it catch the exception, handles it
    }
}
catch(c: SomeException)
```

```
{
// it catch the exception, handles it
}
```

nested try block Kotlin program:

```
fun main(args: Array<String>) {
    val numbs = arrayOf(11,22,33,44)
    try {
        for (i in numbs.indices) {
            try {
                var n = (0..4).random()
                println(numbs[i+1]/n)
            } catch (c: ArithmeticException) {
                println(c)
            }
        }
    } catch (c: ArrayIndexOutOfBoundsException) {
        println(e)
    }
}
```

Remember that this result is generated for a random integer. Don't be concerned if we get a different outcome because it will be decided by the random number generated at the time.

Multiple catch block

A try block may include several catch blocks. When we are unclear what type of exception may occur inside the try block, we may insert several catch blocks for the various exceptions and the parent exception class in the last catch block to handle all the remaining exceptions in the program that are not described by catch blocks.

Syntax:

```
try {
    // the code may throw-exception
} catch(c: ExceptionNameOne) {
    // catch the exception one, handle it
} catch(c: ExceptionNameTwo) {
    // it catch the exception two, handle it
}
```

Multiple catch blocks program in Kotlin:

```kotlin
import java.util.Scanner
object Tests {
    @JvmStatic
    fun main(args: Array<String>) {
        val scn = Scanner(System.'in')
        try {
            val n = Integer.parseInt(scn.nextLine())
            if (612% n == 0)
                println("$n is a factor of 612")
        } catch (c: ArithmeticException) {
            println(c)
        } catch (c: NumberFormatException) {
            println(c)
        }
    }
}
```

Expression in the catch block use: In Kotlin, an expression in a catch block can be used to replace several catch blocks. In the section that follows, we will demonstrate how to utilize when expression.

```kotlin
import java.lang.NumberFormatException
import java.util.Scanner
object Tests {
    @JvmStatic
    fun main(args: Array<String>) {
        val scn = Scanner(System.'in')
        try {
            val n = Integer.parseInt(scn.nextLine())
            if (612% n == 0)
                println("$n is a factor of 612")
        } catch (c: Exception ) {
          when(c){
            is ArithmeticException -> {
println("Arithmetic-Exception: Divide by zero") }
            is NumberFormatException -> { println
("Number Format Exception ") }
          }
        }
    }
}
```

LOGGING IN KOTLIN

Kotlin is a new programming language. JetBrains, the firm behind IntelliJ, Resharper, and other prominent development tools, released it as open source in 2012. Kotlin is a statically typed language with extensive functional programming features. It is frequently executed on the Java Virtual Machine (JVM) and supports Java libraries, although it may also be compiled to Javascript or native code.

We'll begin with the most basic example of Kotlin logging that can use. After that, we'll utilize better logging tools after exploring why logging is important and how it affects our ability to maintain our code. We'll also show how appropriate logging increases our capacity to troubleshoot issues, monitor our app, and provide better support to our clients.

The Easiest Kotlin Logging That Could Work

- Because the JetBrains team designed Kotlin, using IntelliJ for this lesson makes logical. We'll locate the community edition here if we don't already have it.

- Begin by making a new project. In the welcome page, select the new project menu option.

- Next, under the project settings, pick Kotlin and Kotlin JVM.

- Next, enter a name for our project and click Next.

- After we click Finish, IntelliJ will build our project.

- It's now time to make our first file and log a message. Right-click on the src folder in the project directory.

- This will open up a window where we can enter the file name. It should be called logging.

- Click OK, and we're ready to start writing code.

- We've already completed the difficult part by building the simplest Kotlin logging example that will run. Here's our first program's code:

```
import java.io.File
fun main() {
    File("application.log").writeText
("Hello-Logging")
}
```

- Enter that, and start our program by right-clicking the source file and selecting run.

- IntelliJ will compile and execute our code.

The findings are shown at the bottom of the IDE window by IntelliJ. Because we told Kotlin to create it there, our log file will locate in the project's working directory. To open our log file in the editor, double-click it, and we'll see the log message.

This code is adequate for simple logging, but it is not a long-term solution. Is the Kotlin keeping fit open in the background, or does it open it for each call? What would happen if hundreds of messages were sent? Is it threadsafe, or does accessing the file every time cause the application to crash? Would the file be corrupted if numerous threads ran concurrently?

After a quick explanation of what logging is, let's look at a better approach to do Kotlin logging.

What Is Application Logging?

Before we enhance logging in Kotlin, let's define it.

"Application logging is the process of writing information about our application's runtime activity to a more permanent media."

There's a lot packed into that sentence. Logging is used to record behavior. Messages are used to record events that occur within our app. Furthermore, because the term refers to runtime, it indicates that we generate logs with a time component. We should record the messages as they appear, together with information about when they occurred.

We also keep logs on a long-term medium. Why? As a result, we will review events as they occur. This is required for tasks that happen too rapidly to follow. A record of occurrences is helpful when trying to track out a mistake. Persistent storage may even require if we need to keep an audit trail. A disk, a relational database, or search platform like Scalyr is examples of persistent mediums.

Using Logback for Kotlin Logging
Add Logback to Our Project

- Our code may access any Java library when we execute Kotlin in the JVM. So, let's configure your application with Logback, one of Java's most popular logging frameworks.

- To begin, access the module settings for our project by right-clicking on the project name and selecting the module settings menu entry.

- Then, choose Add Library and locate the Plus button toward the top of the window.

- This button displays a menu. Choose from maven.

- A conversation will begin. Use this search feature to find and add the following three libraries:

```
org.slf4j:slf4j-api:1.7.26
ch.qos.logback:logback-classic:1.2.3
ch.qos.logback:logback-core:1.2.3
```

- After entering a name, click the disclosure indication to the right. IntelliJ will search maven for libraries and populate the list. Choose the proper one.

- IntelliJ will include it in the module. Rep for the last three libraries.

- We included the Simple Logging Facade for Java and two Logback libraries. The library we'll need from Kotlin is the Simple Logging Facade. Logback will handle the logging.

Calling LogBack from Kotlin

- Logback may now call from Kotlin. Add new Kotlin file to the project. Utilities are what it's named.
  The code is as follows:

```
fun getLogger(): Logger = LoggerFactory.
getLogger(Logger.ROOT_LOGGER_NAME)

fun getLogger(name: String): Logger =
LoggerFactory.getLogger(name)
```

- These two methods return instances of the Simple Logging Facade Logger. The first obtains the top-level or root logger. The second one looks for one based on an arbitrary name. We'll explain the distinction further down.
  Then, change the logging.kt to use a logger and rerun the code.

```
fun main() {
    getLogger().debug("Hello, Logging")
}
```

- Our output will look like this:

```
17:23:55.984 [main] DEBUG ROOT - Hello-Logging
```

We now have a timestamp, the name of the function, the logging level, the name of the logger, and the message. So, we've already enhanced our logging with only a few lines of code.

Why Log?

Kotlin is a valuable programming language. With more concise syntax and support for functional and object-oriented programming, it has full access to Java's vast ecosystem. That doesn't imply our Kotlin code is impenetrable. We'll still need the means to observe what's going on within the app. Even the finest Kotlin code contains flaws and will encounter unexpected circumstances. Kotlin logging is required.

The Kotlin is a popular programming language for Android. Android apps encounter a variety of unexpected scenarios. We may launch our app in a simulator to catch mistakes while it is still in development. A system for recording logs as part of problem reports, on the other hand, is a helpful tool. On our client devices, we may launch a remote debugging session. Logs are the closest thing to being there.

Logs may use for more than just isolating issues. We may use them to monitor our application while running and identify areas for improvement. And, of course, the use of logs does not end there. Logs are a business necessity if our code processes financial transactions.

What Logging Method Should We Use?

We've already transformed a single print statement into a complete log message. Let's speak about what we need in our log messages before concluding the work. How can we ensure that our logs are useful when it comes time to troubleshoot? In most logging systems, each log entry contains at least the following information:

- **Timestamp:** the time when the event in the log entry occurred. We'll see how to include this into messages in the section following.

- **The location of the event:** where did it take place? Whom are you addressing? During a debugging session, saying "It worked" or "It's broken" may be beneficial or funny. "Failed to connect to the database at 192.9.168.3:5000" is more useful in production.

- **Severity level:** Each entry requires a flag in context with other messages. ERROR, WARN, INFO, DEBUG, and TRACE are all defined by Logback.

Configuring Logger

We configure the Logback file, which we supply to the library through a Java property or by including it in the classpath. To make things easy, we'll utilize the classpath in this lesson.

Make a new file in our project's source directory. The default configuration file name is logback.xml. Include the following information:

```
<configuration>
    <appender name="FILE" class="ch.qos.logback.core.
FileAppender">
        <file>my_App.log</file>
        <encoder>
            <pattern>%date %level [%thread]
%logger{12} [%file:%line] %msg%n</pattern>
        </encoder>
    <appender name="STDOUT" class="ch.qos.logback.
core.ConsoleAppender">
        <encoder>
            <pattern>%msg%n</pattern>
        </encoder>
    </appender>
    <root level="debug">
        <appender-ref ref="FILE" />
        <appender-ref ref="STDOUT" />
    </root>
</configuration>
```

Logback will detect this file at runtime since the directory from where you execute your code is part of the project's classpath. It is divided into three pieces. They are all log appenders, save for two. The root logger is defined by the other.

A log appender is exactly what its name suggests. It's an item that adds to the end of a log. The first appender writes to a file, while the second writes to standard output; the terminal. Logback makes it simple to deliver logs to many destinations; simply add another appender. Each appender is equipped with an encoder. The encoder prepares the message before the appender sends the message to the logger. In a minute, we'll see how the two encoders vary.

Finally, the root logger is specified in the settings. When we introduced Logback to our code, we specified several loggers. Logback organizes logger instances into a hierarchical structure resembling an object-oriented hierarchy. The property of a logger is inherited from the hierarchy. We define the properties for all loggers in the application by configuring the root logger. Logback builds it with these attributes unless a logger overrides explicitly them.

This root logger will log all messages sent to it with a DEBUG or higher level. Both log appenders will get entries from Logback.

Formatting Kotlin Logging Messages

Restart the program using the configuration file.

The terminal output is as follows:

```
Hello-Logging
```

The program also produces log file called my_App.log in the project root. It is only one line:

```
2019-06-15 22:44:03,105 DEBUG [main] ROOT [logging.
kt:3] Hello-Logging
```

Both appenders received the logging output, but the messages were specified differently. The encoders are distinct.

Here's the STDOUT encoder:

```
<encoder>
    <pattern>%msg%n</pattern>
</encoder>
```

The encoder for the file is as follows:

```
<encoder>
        <pattern>
%date %level [%thread] %logger{12} [%file:%line]
%msg%n</pattern>
</encoder>
```

Logback includes a large number of conversion words for formatting log messages. Because we only see the log message's content in the terminal output, we can safely assume that %msg is the formatter for the log data. Here's a table with the rest of the information.

Word	Description
%date	date, including a timestamp
%level	log message level
%thread	thread logging the message
%logger	name of logger
%file	source code file name
%line	source code line number
%msg	Message contents
%n	Platform-specific linefeed character

Although these are merely the fundamental formatters, we've already met the requirements for useful log messages using the file encoder. It explains where the message originated in our source code. It has a date and time, as well as the log level.

Logging to a File

Our log files are also being stored to a persistent media.

```
<appender name="FILE" class="ch.qos.logback.core.
FileAppender">
    <file>my_App.log</file>
    <encoder>
        <pattern>%date %level [%thread] %logger{10}
[%file:%line] %msg%n</pattern>
    </encoder>
</appender>
```

With each program's execution, the file appender creates the file and opens and closes it. If we rerun it, we'll notice that a second line has been added.

Logback also features a RollingFileAppender. It will produce a new file and rename the old one for us so that our log files do not get too large to manage or create a new file at regular intervals.

Setting Kotlin Logging Levels

Make changes to the Logback configuration file.

```
<root level="info">
        <appender-ref ref="FILE" />
        <appender-ref ref="STDOUT" />
    </root>
```

Restart the program. The log message is suppressed because we set the root logger to INFO.

Messages can be routed to specified destinations using appenders and loggers. Assume we want to send just debug messages to the console and only information or higher to a file. Make a new logger and assign it the file appender:

```
<root level="debug" >
    <appender-ref ref="STDOUT" />
</root>
<logger name="productions" level="info">
    <appender-ref ref="FILE" />
</logger>
```

Modify the application such that it log two messages.

```
fun main() {
    getLogger("productions").info("Start log test")
    getLogger("test").debug("w00t")
}
```

We're replacing the root logger with two named loggers. One of these is the Logback configuration's production logger. Restart the program.

Both messages are sent to the console:

```
Start log test
w00t
```

However, just the first message is recorded in the log file:

```
2019-06-15 23:20:16,969 INFO [main] production
[logging.kt:3] Start log test
```

The output to terminal was sent down from the root logger to the new logger. However, because we changed its level to information, it did not inherit the debug messages. That's a lot of power in only a few lines of code.

UNIT TESTING

A unit test is a piece of code separate from our application. It can generate and invoke our application's public classes and methods. But why would we want to build code that we would never use in our application? Simply because we want to ensure that the application code works as expected. And we want to double-check it to ensure that you don't disrupt any current functionality. And, like me, we're probably lazy and don't want to do it manually. As a result, we may build test code to check our application behavior. Unit Tests are here to help.

Unit testing focuses on testing only a small number of classes (one or more) that perform a single function (domain) and do not rely on libraries or framework code. We don't want to test the libraries we use (at least not in a unit test); they should just function. We want to concentrate solely on our valuable code and demonstrate no hidden issues.

Simple Android Application

Before we begin writing any tests, we'd want to show us a simple Android app with a login screen. It accepts two inputs for login and password and validates them. When the inputs are accurate, we can sign in with the proper data or receive an error indicating wrong credentials. We chose MVP design since it would allow us to develop tests that are not dependent on the Android framework.

Project Setup

We can now write our first test when we have an application to test. The JUnit4 test runner and the Kotlin programming language will use. A test runner is a library that executes our test code and gathers the results in a user-friendly manner.

Our First Test

To begin, under the/src/test/kotlin folder, build a class with a public function annotated with @org.junit.Test. This tells JUnit4 where to find the test code. We may begin by determining whether our app allows us to login with the right info. To instrument LoginRepository, I must construct a LoginRepositoryTest class with a test function. At first want to see whether we can sign in with the right credentials, so we built a test function called login using the correct username and password.

```
class Login_Repository_Test {
    @Test
```

```
    fun 'login with the correct login and password'()
{
    }
}
```

We may name tests in Kotlin with natural names, such as login with the right username and password; however, this only applies to code that runs on the JVM. Fortunately, unit tests are run on the JVM, utilizing such descriptive names.

Test Structure

Each test should be built using the following blocks:

- **Arrange/Given:** We will prepare the necessary data for the test Act/When – we will invoke a single method on the tested object.

- **Assert/Then:** We will check the test result, whether it is pass or fail.

Because JUnit4 does not split test blocks, it is easy to add comments to test code, especially if we are starting off with testing.

```
@Test
fun 'login with the correct login and password'() {
    //given
    //when

    //then
}
```

Given Block

Our test will start with the supplied block, in which we will prepare our test data and build the tested object.

We're making a new instance of the tested object LoginRepository and assigning it to the read-only attribute. It's easier to distinguish between tested objects and test parameters, thus I'm naming it objectUnderTest. It can also be referred to as sut, topic, or target. Choose a name that best describes us, but keep it constant throughout our project.

When we have an instance of the tested object, we may proceed to testing the parameters. That is correctLogin with the value 'dabcisski' and correctPassword with the value 'correct'. It is critical to give each test parameter meaningful names; it must be evident what sort of values each one contains.

```
@Test
fun 'login with the correct login and password'() {
    //given
    val objectUnderTest = LoginRepository()
    val correctLogin = 'dabcisski'
    val correctPassword = 'correct'
    //when
    //then
}
```

When Block

In the when block, we must call the method we want to test using the parameters we prepared in the previous block. As a result, we invoke the function objectUnderTest.login (correctLogin, correctPassword). We should just have one line of code in the when block to make it obvious what is being tested.

```
@Test
fun 'login with the correct login and password'() {
    //given
    val objectUnderTest = LoginRepository()
    val correctLogin = 'dabcisski'
    val correctPassword = 'correct'
    //when
    objectUnderTest.login(correctLogin,
correctPassword)
    //then
}
```

Then Block

It's time to see if the tested object returns the expected result. However, we must first store the result of the tested method in a property val result and then analyze it in the then block. Now we can do an assertion to see whether the return value matches what we anticipate. If the assertion is not met, it will throw an error, and the test will fail.

In this situation, the returned object is a RxJava 2 Observable, but we can simply convert it to TestObserver, a class that includes assertion methods. I'm testing to see if the result value is true; otherwise, the test will fail.

```
@Test
fun 'login with the correct login and password'() {
    //given
    val objectUnderTest = LoginRepository()
    val correctLogin = 'dabcisski'
    val correctPassword = 'correct'
    //when
    val result = objectUnderTest.login(login,
password)
    //then
    result.test().assertResult(true)
}
```

Running Test

We can run a test in Android Studio/IntelliJ by hitting Ctrl + Shift + F10, or from a Terminal by typing ./gradlew test.

After running the test that we just wrote, we should see a green bar in the IDE or BUILD SUCCESSFUL in the Terminal.

NOTHING BY KOTLIN: ITS APPLICABILITY IN GENERICS

This section explores the use of Kotlin's Nothing type in generics. We'll look at how it relates to Java. Let's have a look at a linked list as an example.

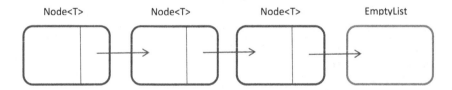

A LinkedList.

A LinkedList encloses a type C. The linked list can be either.

- A Node<C> with two properties: a T payload and a LinkedList<C> next.

- It's an empty list.

A sealed class requires the LinkedList to be of type 1 or type 2.

The sealed class and the Node<C> may be easily coded as follows:

```
sealed class LinkedList<out C>  {
    data class Node<C>(val payload: C, var next:
LinkedList<C> ) : LinkedList<C>()
}
```

Coding the empty list is a little more difficult. Every empty list is the same. As a result, an empty list is an object. EmptyList must be a subclass of LinkedList<T> as well. We could attempt to write.

Kotlin objects do not support type arguments. The above code will not compile. Instead, we may try to delete the type parameter from the EmptyList.

```
sealed class LinkedList<out C>  {
    data class Node<C>(val payload: C, var next:
LinkedList<C> ) : LinkedList<C>()
    object EmptyList : LinkedList<C>() // won't-compile
}
```

The code continues to fail to build. The C reference remains uncertain. We must provide a specific type for C.

C denotes the kind of payload wrapped by a node. See the diagram above. An empty list, on the other hand, encloses no payload. As a result, correct coding is required.

```
sealed class LinkedList<out C>  {
    data class Node<C>(val payload: C, var next:
LinkedList<> = EmptyList) : LinkedList<C>()
    object EmptyList : LinkedList<Nothing>()
}
val nonEmptyList = LinkedList.Node(payload = "D", next
= LinkedList.Node(payload = "E"))
```

What does the Kotlin Nothing type look like? Select Tools -> Kotlin -> Kotlin REPL from the Android Studio menu. Enter and run the command println in the REPL window (Nothing::class.java). As a result,

```
println(Nothing::class.java)
class java.lang.Void
```

Java's Void type backs up Kotlin's Nothing type. Nothing is a type in Kotlin that represents the absence of type.

Nothing's constructor is private. Contrast the preceding code with the Java equivalent:

```
public class GetVoidExamples {
    public Void getVoid() {
        return new Void(); // won't-compile
    }
}
```

The Void class in Java has a private constructor. Void cannot create. We are unable to return a Void. As a result, it appears reasonable that we cannot return Nothing in Kotlin.

Key Points
Nothing:

- Nothing is a non-open (final class) that cannot be expanded, and its constructor is also private, implying that we cannot create the object.

- This is typically used to represent a function's return type, which will always throw an exception.

- Nothing is the superclass of Any.

This chapter covered Exception Handling, Logging, Unit Testing, and "nothing" type in Kotlin with its relevant examples.

CHAPTER 6

Code Optimization Ideas

IN THIS CHAPTER

➤ Optimization tips

➤ Best coding practices

➤ Security and hardening ideas

In the previous chapter, we covered code management which we Learned Logging, Exceptional Handling, Unit Testing, and nothing type in Kotlin. This chapter will cover Optimization Tips, Writing Secure Code, Best Coding Practices and Security, and Hardening Ideas.

OPTIMIZATION TIPS

This chapter discusses approaches for building Android code in Kotlin that is both efficient and simple. JetBrains, the company behind the IntelliJ IDE, created Kotlin, a general-purpose language that compiles to Java bytecode.

Using Static Layout Imports in Kotlin

When we need to use one of the views in the activity, it is one of the most challenging aspects of dealing with Android. We must call the 'findView-ById()' function and then typecast it to the correct view type. Kotlin uses a different approach, allowing us to import all views in our layout file. Assume we have the layout file shown below.

```
<RelativeLayout xmlns:android="http://schemas.android
.com/apk/res/android"
```

```
    xmlns:tools="http://schemas.android.com/tools"
android:layout_width="match_parent"
    android:layout_height="match_parent"
android:paddingRight="@dimen/
activity_horizontal_margin"
    android:paddingLeft="@dimen/
activity_horizontal_margin"
    android:paddingBottom="@dimen/
activity_vertical_margin"
    android:paddingTop="@dimen/
activity_vertical_margin"
    tools:context="kotlineffiecienttechniques">
    <TextView android:id="@+id/maintextview"
        android:text="@string/helloo_world"
        android:layout_width="wrap_content"
        android:layout_height="wrap_content" />
</RelativeLayout>
```

And the activity code that uses static imports to change the text of the maintextview:

```
package kotlineffiecienttechniques
import android.support.v7.app.ActionBarActivity
import android.os.Bundle
import android.view.Menu
import android.view.MenuItem
import android.widget.Toast
import kotlinx.android.synthetic.main.
activity_main_activity2.*
public class MainActivity2 : ActionBarActivity() {
    override fun onCreate(savedInstanceState: Bundle?) {
        super.onCreate(savedInstanceState)
        setContentView(R.layout.
activity_main_activity)
        maintextview.text = "Helloo Static Import!"
    }
}
```

If we look at the code above, we'll notice that we've 'statically imported' all views using the import line.

```
import kotlinx.android.synthetic.main.activity_main_
activity.*
```

After that, we may change the text view as follows:

```
maintextview.text = "Helloo Static Import"
```

To get the preceding code to compile, add the following to our build.gradle dependencies:

```
dependencies {
    compile 'org.jetbrains.anko:anko-sdk21:0.9' //
sdk19, sdk21, sdk23 are available also
    compile 'org.jetbrains.anko:anko-support-v4:0.9'
// In case we need support-v4 bindings
    compile 'org.jetbrains.anko:anko-appcompat-v7:0.9'
// For appcompat-v7 bindings
}
```

Apply plugin:

```
apply plugin: 'kotlin-android-extension'
```

Also, include the following in our buildscript::dependencies:

```
dependencies {
        classpath "org.jetbrains.
kotlin:kotlin-android-extension:$kotlin_version"
    }
```

Creating POJO Classes in Kotlin

When converting JSON/XML to objects in several apps. When using REST services, we require classes that retain the contents of the JSON/XML. In Kotlin, defining such objects (also known as POJO in Java) is more convenient. Assume we want to create a POJO in Java to represent a book; the code follows:

```
public class Books {
    private String ISBN;
    private float prices;
    private int quantites;
    private String title;
    private String descriptions;
    public String getISBN() {
```

```java
        return ISBN;
    }
    public void setISBN(String ISBN) {
        this.ISBN = ISBN;
    }
    public float getPrices() {
        return prices;
    }
    public void setPrice(float prices) {
        this.prices = prices;
    }
    public int getQuantities() {
        return quantities;
    }
    public void setQuantities(int quantities) {
        this.quantities = quantities;
    }

    public String getTitle() {
        return title;
    }
    public void setTitle(String title) {
        this.title = title;
    }
    public String getDescriptions() {
        return descriptions;
    }
    public void setDescriptions(String descriptions) {
        this.descriptions = descriptions;
    }
}
```

If we want to define the same POJO with the same functionality in Kotlin, we may do it as follows:

```kotlin
public class Books {
    public var ISBN: String = ""
    public var prices: Float = 0.toFloat()
    public var quantities: Int = 0
    public var title: String = ""
    public var descriptions: String = ""
}
```

To be more specific, it may be defined as a data class as follows:

```
data class Books2(var ISBN: String, var prices: Float,
var quantities: Int,
                var title: String,  var descriptions:
String)
```

This POJO differs from the previous one because it has a main contractor. All arguments must be passed to the constructor when the object is created. Defining a data class includes the methods 'equals', 'hashCode', and contructor. This should be the preferable method for defining a POJO in Kotlin.

Constructors and Inheritance in Kotlin

Kotlin simplifies the creation of constructors for your classes. The primary constructor is included in the class header. It comes after the class's name. So, if we had a primary constructor for our Book class, the code would look like this:

```
public class Books (var ISBN: String, var prices:
Float, var quantities: Int,
                var title: String,  var
descriptions: String) {
}
```

The above code defines a primary constructor to which values are passed. The values are assigned to the members.

To construct an object of the Books class, do the following:

```
Val books1 = Books("564321", 43.0f, 4, "Kotlin for
us", " Kotlin Books ")
```

This eliminates the need for boilerplate code in the form of distinct constructor functions. The constructor just copies the parameters supplied to it into the member variables. If we were writing our Android app in Java, we would need to build such a constructor.

Inheritance in Kotlin is also safer; it cannot expand unless a class is specified as open.

So, if we want to expand Book, we should define it as follows:

```
open public class Books (var ISBN: String, var prices:
Float, var quantities: Int,
```

```
                  var title: String,   var
descriptions: String){
    open fun getShippingPrices():Float {
        return prices;
    }
}
```

Assume we have a HardCoverBooks subclass that extends the Books class and overrides the getShippingPrices method. That would be coded as follows:

```
class HardCoverBooks(ISBN: String, prices: Float,
quantities: Int,
                title: String,  descriptions:
String) :
        Book(ISBN, prices, quantities, title,
descriptions) {
    override fun getShippingPrice():Float {
        return prices + 3.0f;
    }
}
```

Using Lambda Functions in Kotlin

We frequently have functions in Android that accept one interface as a parameter. Very such instances, the Kotlin lambda functions come in handy. Look at how we can add an onClickListner to a view.

```
maintextview.setOnClickListener({ view -> Toast.
makeText(this, "Showing-Toast", Toast.LENGTH_SHORT).
show(); })
```

It's only one line. We don't even need to define the type of argument view because it can be deduced statically. In Java, the same code would be:

```
maintextview.setOnClickListener(new OnClickListener()
{
    @Override
    public void onClick(View v) {
        Toast.makeText(this, "Showing-Toast", Toast.
LENGTH_SHORT).show();
    }
});
```

Tail Recursion, Sealed Classes, Local, Infix, Inline Functions, and More Advanced Kotlin Tips

Local Functions

Local functions are useful for code reuse; nevertheless, they should not be used excessively to avoid confusion.

```
fun fooo(x: Int) {
    fun local(y: Int) {
        return x + y
    }
    return local(1)
}
```

Infix Functions

Infix functions are useful for readability since they allow us to type things like "test" foo "c" for example, which is pretty awesome.

```
infix fun String.fooo(s: String) {
    .....
}
// Call the extension function.
"test".fooo("c")
// Or call extension function using the infix
notation.
"test" fooo "c"
```

Infix functions can only have one parameter.

Inline Functions

An overhead occurs when a lambda expression in Kotlin is converted to Java anonymous classes in Java 6 or 7. Lambda calls affect the call stack, which influences performance.

Instead of initiating another method call and adding it to the call stack, inline functions can utilize to make direct calls. When we pass in the lambdas, it makes logical to utilize inline functions.

```
inline fun callBlock(block: () -> Unit) {
    println("Before-calling the block")
    block()
    println("After calling the block")
}
```

When we call the callBlock, it is converted into something like this:

```
callBlock { println("The block operation") }
// Rough java-bytecode
String var1 = "Before calling the block";
System.out.println(var1)
String var2 = "Block operation";
System.out.println(var2);
var1 = "After calling the block";
System.out.println(var1);
```

in comparison to the following if the function was not declared as inline

```
callBlock { println("Block operation") }
// Rough java-bytecode
callBlock((Functinos0)null.INSTANCE);
```

However, we must tread cautiously when using inline functions since it literally duplicates the method content when it is called, which is undesirable if the body of the functions is too lengthy.

Knowing that, the following will make no sense because it has no effect.

```
inline fun fooo(noinline block: () -> Unit) {// Single
lambda marked as the noinline
inline fun fooo() { // No-lambdas
```

Tail Recursion

We tell compiler that we want to replace the method call with a for loop or goto expression by using tailrec.

It can only use if the last call of a function is simply calling itself.

```
tailrec fun findFixPoint(r: Double = 1.0): Double
        = if (r == Math.cos(r)) r else
findFixPoint(Math.cos(r))
```

Sealed Classes

According to the Kotlin reference, we should use sealed classes to express restricted class hierarchies, which occur when an item has a limited set of types but cannot have any other type.

In other words, they are useful for returning types that are not identical but are related.

```
sealed class Responses
data class Success(val content: String) : Responses()
data class Error(val code: Int, val message: String) :
Responses()
fun getUrlPage(url: String) : Responses {
    val valid = // Some logic here!
    if (valid) {
        return Success("Content found")
    else {
        return Error("Not found")
    }
}
// Here is the beauty
val responses = getUrlPage("/")
when (responses) {
    is Success -> println(responses.content)
    is Error -> println(responses.message)
}
```

The definition of sealed classes must include in a single file.

Some More Helpful Tips
Local Return

They are most useful with lambdas, but let us explain with a simple code example.

```
fun fooo(list: List<String>): Boolean {
    list.forEach {
        if (...) {// Some-condition.
            return true
        }
    }
    return false
}
```

It gets fooo to return true. We may also limit the forEach scope just to return values.

```
fun fooo(list: List<String>): Boolean {
    list.forEach {
```

```
        if (...) {// Some-condition.
            return@forEach // Just like calling-break
        }
    }
    return false
}
```

If it doesn't make sense, consider the following code:

```
fun fooo() {
    Observable.just(1)
            .map{ intValue ->
                return@map intValue.toString()
            }
            ...

...
}
```

If we used return in the above code piece, it would return to foo, which makes no sense in this context. The return@map, on the other hand, returns the result of the map function, which is the desired behavior.

Operator Overloading

To override supported operators, use operator.

```
operator fun plus(time: Time) {
    ......
}
// This will allow following statement.
time1 + time2
```

It is important not to overuse operator overloading; it does not make sense to utilize it most of the time. Check out the list of conventions that govern operator overloading for various operators.

Lambda Extensions

They are just easier to read and type, much like markup.

```
class Status(var code: Int, var descriptions: String)
fun status(status: Status.() -> Unit) {}
// This will allow the following statement
```

```
status {
   code = 403
   descriptions = "Not-found"
}
```

lateinit

If a lateinit property is attempted to be used before it has been initialized, it will throw an exception of type UninitializedPropertyAccessException.

Companion Objects

Companion Objects are the equivalent of Java static methods.

```
class MykotlinClass {
  @Jvmstatic
  companion object Factory {
    fun create(): MyKotlinClass = MyKotlinClass()
  }
}
```

Members of the companion object may access by using the class name as the qualifier:

```
Val instance = MyKotlinClass.create()
```

Tips for Improving Kotlin Compilation Times

The Kotlin/Native compiler is regularly updated to increase speed. We may dramatically increase the compilation times of your projects with Kotlin/Native targets by using the newest Kotlin/Native compiler and a correctly configured build environment.

General Suggestions

Use the latest current Kotlin version. This way, we'll always get the most recent performance enhancements.

Avoid making large courses. During execution, they require a lengthy time to build and load.

Between builds, keep downloaded and cached components. Kotlin/Native downloads the necessary components and saves some of the results to the $USER HOME/.konan directory when we compile a project. The compiler uses this directory for subsequent compilations, helping them run faster.

When building in containers (such as Docker) or using continuous integration systems, the compiler may recreate the ~/.konan directory for each build. Configure your environment to keep ~/.konan between builds to avoid this step. For example, use the KONAN DATA DIR environment variable to change its location.

Configuration of Gradle

Due to the requirement to download dependencies, construct caches, and execute additional stages, the first Gradle compilation frequently takes longer than subsequent ones. To accurately assess the real compilation times, we need to compile your project at least twice.

Here are some suggestions for customizing Gradle to improve compilation performance:

- Increase the size of the Gradle heap. To gradle.properties, add org. gradle.jvmargs=-Xmx3g. If we use parallel builds, we may need to increase the heap size or use org.gradle.parallel.threads to select the appropriate number of threads.

- Create just the binaries we require. Run Gradle tasks that create the entire project, such as build or assemble, only when absolutely necessary. These jobs generate the same code several times, lengthening compilation times. The Kotlin tooling prevents conducting extraneous activities in common instances, such as running tests from IntelliJ IDEA or launching the program from Xcode.

If we have a non-typical scenario or build setup, we may need to select the job ourselves.

- **linkDebug*:** To execute our code during development, we normally only need one binary, therefore executing the associated linkDebug* task should suffice. Keep in mind that creating a release binary (linkRelease*) takes longer than compiling a debug binary.

- **packForXcode:** Because iOS simulators and devices have various processor architectures, it's usual to deliver a Kotlin/Native binary as a universal (fat) framework. Building the .framework for only the platform we're using will be faster during local development.

To create a platform-specific framework, use the packForXcode task provided by the Kotlin Multiplatform Mobile project wizard.

- Don't turn off the Gradle daemon unless we have a compelling cause to. By default, Kotlin/Native is executed by the Gradle daemon. When it is enabled, the same JVM process is utilized for all compilations, and there is no need to warm it up.

- Enable previously disabled Kotlin/Native functionality. The Gradle daemon and compiler caches can be disabled using the kotlin. native.disable option. CompilerDaemon=true and kotlin.native. cacheKind=none are set. Whether you had problems with these features in the past and put these lines to your gradle.properties or Gradle arguments, delete them and see if the build succeeds. It's conceivable that some characteristics were introduced in the past to work around concerns that have since been resolved.

- Make use of the Gradle build caches:

  - **Local build cache:** Add org.gradle.caching=true to your gradle. properties file or use the command line option – build-cache.

  - In continuous integration systems, remote build cache is used. Discover how to set up the remote build cache.

Configuration of Windows
Operating System Set up Windows Security. The Kotlin/Native compiler may slow by Windows Security. We may circumvent this by adding the .konan directory, which is by default placed in %USERPROFILE%, to Windows Security exclusions.

WRITING SECURE CODE

This codelab will develop our first Kotlin program using an interactive editor that we can run from our browser.

A program may be thought of as a set of instructions for the system to follow for it to do an action. We could, for example, develop a program that generates a birthday card. We could build the application to print congratulations text or compute someone's age based on their birth year.

Just like we use human language to interact with another person, we use a programming language to communicate with our computer's operating system (OS). Programming languages, fortunately, are less complicated than human languages and relatively reasonable.

Kotlin is the programming language used to create Android applications. Kotlin is a new language designed to help developers write code more effectively and fewer mistakes.

Learning to construct an app while also learning the fundamentals of programming will difficult; therefore, we will begin with programming before moving on to app creation. Learning the fundamentals of programming is not simply a necessary initial step in developing apps.

Set Up Source Code and Tests in Our Android Apps

Kotlin is a statically typed programming language for creating Android apps.

How Does Kotlin Code Look?

In Kotlin, we would declare a function like follows:

```
fun sum(x: Int, y: Int): Int {
  return x + y
}
```

As we can see, there are a few notable differences between Java and Python:

- The absence of semicolons (Yay right?)

- The return type is declared after function specification.

- After the parameter name, the type of the parameter is defined.

Why Is It Superior to Java?

Here's a brief rundown of Kotlin's advantages versus Java:

- Null Safety

- Lambdas

- Extension Methods

Adapting an Existing Android Project to Utilize Kotlin

1. Install the Kotlin Android Studio plugin:

   - Navigate to "Preferences" "Plugins," and then "Install JetBrains Plugin." In the search box, type "Kotlin." Install "Kotlin" by selecting it. We will most likely need to restart Android Studio for the adjustments to take effect.

2. Add the following line to the classpath section of our project's build. Gradle file.

```
buildscript {
    repositories {
        jcenter()
    }
    dependencies {
        classpath "com.android.tools.
build:gradle:2.0.0-alpha3"
        classpath 'com.github.
dcendents:android-maven-gradle-plugin:1.3'
        classpath "org.jetbrains.
kotlin:kotlin-gradle-plugin:1.0.0-beta-4584"
    }
}
```

3. Add the following to our app level build.gradle:

```
buildscript {
    repositories {
        maven { url 'https://maven.fabric.io/
public' }
    }
    dependencies {
        classpath 'io.fabric.tools:gradle:1.+'
    }
}
apply plugin: 'com.android.application'
apply plugin: 'kotlin-android'
android {
    .....
    sourceSets {
        main.java.srcDirs += 'src/main/kotlin'
    }
}
dependencies {
    .....
    compile 'org.jetbrains.
kotlin:kotlin-stdlib:1.0.0-beta-4584'

}
```

4. Make a kotlin folder in our app/src/main/folder. We may create a folder with our package name, such as org.bookdash. Android. (We may put Kotlin files in the same directory as Java files; we just like to keep them distinct per language.)

5. To create a new Kotlin class, right-click the package name and select "New -> Kotlin File or class." Give it a name, choose a type, and begin writing Kotlin code.

Existing Java Files Can Convert to Kotlin

To convert a Java class to Kotlin in Android Studio, perform the following:

- Open the file that we want to convert.

- Execute the command. (Continue to Action):

  - CMD + Shift + A on a Mac

  - CTRL + Shift + A on Linux and Windows

- Then, type "kotlin," and we should see an option to convert an existing Java file to Kotlin.

- This will convert the Java file you are now in into a Kotlin class. We'd double-check that the resulting code is correct.

- We converted the AboutActivity from my Book Dash App to Kotlin, and the outcome is as follows:

```
class About_Activity : BaseAppCompatActivity(),
AboutContract.View {
    private var aboutPresenter: AboutPresenter? = null
    override fun onCreate(savedInstanceState: Bundle?)
{
        super.onCreate(savedInstanceState)
        setContentView(R.layout.activity_about)
        aboutPresenter = AboutPresenter(this)
        val toolbar = findViewById(R.id.toolbar) as
Toolbar
        setSupportActionBar(toolbar)
        val actionBar = supportActionBar
        if (actionBar != null) {
            actionBar.setDisplayHomeAsUpEnabled(true)
```

```
            actionBar.setTitle(R.string.about_heading)
        }
        val textViewWhyBookDash = findViewById(R.
id.text_why_bookdash) as TextView
        textViewWhyBookDash.text = Html.
fromHtml(getString(R.string.why_bookdash))
        Linkify.addLinks(textViewWhyBookDash, Linkify.
ALL)
        ......
    }
    override fun showLearnMorePage(url: String) {
        val intent = Intent(Intent.ACTION_VIEW)
        intent.setData(Uri.parse(url))
        startActivity(intent)
    }
}
```

Writing Tests in the Kotlin

After writing some Kotlin code, we thought it would be cool to see if we could write some Android tests in Kotlin. Here's how to go about it:

- Make a kotlin folder in our androidTest folder.

- Make a package name that corresponds to the package we're testing.

- In our app build.Gradle file, add following:

```
android {
    ......
    sourceSets {
        main.java.srcDirs += 'src/main/kotlin'
        androidTest.java.srcDirs += 'src/
androidTest/kotlin'
    }
}
```

- After that, we may begin adding code to that folder. Here's an example of my AboutActivityTest in Kotlin, which performs some basic espresso testing.

```
@RunWith(AndroidJUnit4::class)
@SmallTest
```

```kotlin
class AboutActivityTest {
    @Rule
    fun getRule() = ActivityTestRule(AboutActivity
::class.java)
    @Before
    fun setUp() {
        Intents.init()
    }
    @After
    fun tearDown() {
        Intents.release()
    }
    @Test
    @Throws(Throwable::class)
    fun loadAboutBookDash_SeeInformation() {
        val about = Html.fromHtml(InstrumentationR
egistry.getTargetContext().getString(R.string.
why_bookdash))
        val headingAbout =
InstrumentationRegistry.getTargetContext()
.getString(R.string.heading_about)
        onView(withText(headingAbout))
.check(matches(isDisplayed()))
        onView(withText(about.toString()))
.perform(scrollTo()).check(matches(isDisplayed()))
    }
    @Test
    @Throws(Throwable::class)
    fun clickLearnMore_OpenBrowser() {
        onView(withText(R.string.learn_more)).
perform(scrollTo(), click())
        intended(allOf(hasAction(Intent.
ACTION_VIEW),
                hasData(Uri.parse("http://bookdash
.org"))))
    }


}
```

BEST CODING PRACTICES

It's normal for many Kotlin adopters from Java to begin writing Kotlin in the same way. After all, many of the techniques and libraries are the same, so it's simple to keep creating code in the same way. These Java standards typically detract from Kotlin's goal of saving time and enhancing code maintainability through readability.

Accept Immutability

Immutability is not explicitly stated in Java. While the final operator might be useful, it isn't usually employed consistently. Given that immutable programming is generally easier and less error-prone, it's a good idea to get into the habit of keeping everything immutable and only resorting to mutable objects when absolutely required.

```
public void main() {
    String someData = "Data";
    int someNumber = 63
    someData = null; // NPE!
    someNumber = 3;
}
```

Nothing in this example prevents the values inside someData and some-Number from being changed; they are mutable variables. If later code uses such values, there may be unforeseen effects. Long this is great for a single developer working on a project, teams or even individuals who have been away from a piece of code for a while might lose track of the usages of a value and accidentally create a problem.

Instead, Kotlin makes it extremely simple to declare things immutable from the start. In fact, if the value of a var variable isn't being changed elsewhere, IntelliJ Idea would often offer a quick-fix to convert it to val.

```
fun main() {
    val someData = "Data"
    var someMutableNumber = 63
    someData = "some other data" // Compiler-error,
val cannot be reassigned
    // This is ok since someMutableNumber was
specified as a mutable var.
    someMutableNumber = 3
}
```

In general, the presence of var in code should raise a red warning. There are situations when it is required; however, the vast majority of use cases may be refactored to be immutable.

Get Rid of ArrayList and HashMap

ArrayList and HashMap are perhaps two of the most often used collections among Java developers. However, we don't think either term is especially beneficial. We understand that these collections might change, but it's not natural or simple to read.

```
fun oldCollection() {
    val myLists = ArrayList<Int>()
    myLists.add(1)
    myLists.add(2)
    myLists.add(3)
    val myMap = HashMap<Int, Int>()
    myMap[0] = 0
}
```

Instead, Kotlin provides several handy tools over collection interfaces to abstract the underlying complexity in favor of readability.

```
fun newCollections() {
    val myLists = listOf(1, 2, 3)
    my mutableList = mutableListOf(4, 5)
    myList.add(4) // Error: List<Int> doesn't have the
method add()
    mutableList.add(4)
    val myMap = mapOf(0 to 0, 1 to 1)
    val mutableMap = mutableMapOf(2 to 2)
    mutableMap[3] = 3
}
```

We will admit that this conceals some details that may be relevant for performance on huge collections. We'll probably want to employ more particular implementations in specialized instances. However, it's probably not critical enough to sacrifice code readability most of the time.

Make Use of Functional Constructs

Functional structures aid in the integration of immutability and collections while also cleaning the code. When working with a collection, we frequently write code that looks something like this:

```
fun doubleList(values: Array<Int>) {
    for (x in 0..values.count()) {
        values[x] = values[x] * 3
    }
}
```

This method not only mutates the array that was handed in, but it also has a low signal-to-noise ratio. The for syntax is clear, but it introduces unnecessary noise that detracts from the "signal" in the method where the value multiplication occurs. This is a great location for an operation such as. map():

```
fun doubleList(values: Array<Int>): Array<Int> {
    return values.map { it * 3 }
}
```

This example is considerably shorter, with much less "noise" code surrounding the key multiplication part. The Another essential aspect to note here is that the original array is not altered in any way, but rather a duplicate of the array with the alterations is returned. Using different functional techniques such as .map() can frequently eliminate the need to abstract collection operations out to another method because using them in-line is usually sufficient.

Bonus:

```
fun getName(people: List<Person>): List<String> {
    return people.map { it.name }
}
```

Extraction of values from complicated objects is another area where. map() thrives. This is another case where we may loop over the complex objects and create a new list with the appropriate values, which .map() can perform in a single call.

Java does include these features, beginning with the Streams API in Java 8, and they are absolutely useful in Java applications. Unfortunately, the Streams API isn't available to individuals who must use earlier versions of Java, and the API itself isn't as user-friendly as Kotlin's.

javaClass

This one, in particular, falls into the category of "here's a neat suggestion" rather than "best practice." Some Java libraries, especially loggers, require a reference to the current class. This is done rather simply in Java:

```
LoggerFactory.getLogger(My_Class.getclass());
// Or
LoggerFactory.getLogger(this.getclass());
In Kotlin, :
LoggerFactory.getLogger(My_Class:class.java)
// Or
LoggerFactory.getLogger(this::class.java)
```

Both of them function perfectly. The first is prone to copy/paste difficulties, and both have a lot going on otherwise. Kotlin has a handy little shorthand for this, javaClass:

```
LoggerFactory.getLogger(javaClass)
```

String Interpolation

Concatenating strings is not just one of the core programming concepts that individuals learn early on, but it is also employed in some way in practically every programming project. Many languages offer a few variants to normal concatenation to aid in formatting or efficiency, but there is usually a cost in readability.

```
System.out.println("The Processing error at " +
DateTime.now() +
    " with message : " + ex.message + ".");
```

Concatenation is simple: take these string sections and put them together, but this comes with a slew of extra symbols that can be difficult to remember. Finally, the most legible aspect of string concatenation is the overall end string; thus the code should get as near as possible. To do this, Kotlin offers string interpolation (also known as string templating), which makes string composition considerably easier to read.

```
println("The Processing error at ${DateTime.now()}
with message: ${ex.message}.")
```

Infer Types

This is a nice feature in Kotlin, but it might be a bit tricky if you're not used to a language where types aren't explicitly specified. The Kotlin compiler is intelligent enough to infer the type of most things while retaining the power of those types in reality (unlike JavaScript where the type system is somewhat rudimentary). We won't get into whether static or dynamic typing is preferable, but it should go without saying that type checking can assist eliminate issues, although at the expense of readability. As an example:

```
User currentUsers = new User(usernames, email,
profileUrl);
```

Declaring currentUsers as a type User here is superfluous. The variable is instantly initialized to a User object, which a maintainer may see while reading through. Kotlin is both flexible enough to enable the type to be omitted in this scenario and smart enough to infer the type in most other cases.

```
Val currentUsers = User(usernames, email, profileUrl)
```

Of course, this is a contrived and rather simplistic example. At the end of the day, "User" isn't that many more letters, and limited keystrokes apart, it doesn't take long. Remember that readability is important, and time spent mentally filtering out redundant types is not spent deciphering the meaning of a piece of code. Furthermore, Java class names can get extremely lengthy; consider the following example of obtaining the settings of an AWS Lambda function:

```
public String getLambdaArn(String functionNames) {
    GetFunctionConfigurationRequest req = new
GetFunctionConfigurationRequest()
        .withFunctionName(functionNames);
    GetFunctionConfigurationResult results = client
.getFunctionConfiguration(req);
    return results.getFunctionArn();
}
```

This code isn't doing anything particularly complicated, and the types themselves make sense, but repeating GetFunctionConfigurationRequest isn't a wise use of time or mental capacity. Furthermore, while knowing that the result would be of type GetFunctionConfigurationResult is useful, someone reading this code could probably infer relatively simply that it will hold the result of retrieving the function configuration without the type declaration. Remember that we are writing code for humans, not machines.

```
fun getLambdaArn(functionNames: String): String {
    val req = GetFunctionConfigurationRequest()
        .withFunctionNames("myFunction")
    val results = client.getFunctionConfiguration(req)
    return results.functionArn
}
```

Semantic Test Naming

While ordinary method naming conventions call for short and descriptive names, test methods typically have extensive names that reflect the specific situation covered by the test. For example, we've probably all created and combed through tests that look something like this:

```
@Test
fun
handlerShouldSaveRecordToDbOnUpdatedEventProcessed()
{ ...... }
```

This is detailed and difficult to read. The rules of Kotlin allow for the naming of test methods in natural language style with spaces (or underscores).

```
fun 'handler should save the record to db on updated
event processed'() { ..... }
```

Safe Operator?

One of the most notable aspects of Kotlin is its handling of compile-time null safety. Kotlin includes a number of utilities to make dealing with nullable types simple and clean by implementing its null system. The following is an example of traditional Java convention in Kotlin:

```
fun getNameFromDb(): String? {
    val dbRow: DbRow? = selectFromDbById(3)
    if (dbRow != null) {
```

```
        if (dbRow.person != null) {
            if (dbRow.person.names != null) {
                return dbRow.person.names
            }
        }
    }
    return null
}
```

Instead, Kotlin includes aids that are comparable to those found in other languages that enable nullable types:

```
fun getNameFromDb(id: Int): String? {
    val dbRow: DbRow? = selectFromDbById(id)
    return dbRow?.person?.names
}
```

If the parent container is not null, the? access operator will continue to access the field. If any of values in the chain are null, the entire line returns null.

Elvis Throws

Following the lead of safe calls, the Elvis Operator may convert a nullable value to a non-null value. In the above example, getNameFromdb() returns a nullable string and expects the caller to handle the scenario where a null result is returned. We may assert that getNameFromDb() will always return a non-null string or throw a more thorough error if the value cannot retrieve using the Elvis operator.

```
fun getNameFromDb(id: Int): String {
    val dbRow: DbRow? = selectFromDbById(id)
    return dbRow?.person?.names
        ?: throw NotFoundException("Unable to find
user with the id $id")
}
```

List Literals in Annotations

Some controller annotations in Spring can accept multiple values for a field. @RequestMapping, for example, may accept several values for the method of the call, and the Kotlin code for it would look like this:

```
@RequestMapping(value = "/endpoint", method =
arrayOf(RequestMethod.POST))
fun updateEndpoint() {}
```

The use of arrayOf() is required here; however, it is lengthy. Kotlin, on the other hand, supports list literals in annotations:

```
@RequestMapping(value = "/endpoint", method =
[RequestMethod.POST])
fun updateEndpoint() {}
```

Collection Helpers

Collections in Kotlin contain strong helper methods that may make working with collections cleaner and more "Kotlin-y." Looping is a common operation on collections, sometimes with a changeable accumulator collection that saves the result.

```
fun searchForElemt(searchElemt: Any, list: List<Any>):
Any? {
    for (elemt in list) {
        if (searcnElemt == elemt) {
            return elemt
        }
    }
    return null
}
fun profilesWithPictures(profiles: List<Profile>):
List<Profile> {
    var foundProfiles: List<Profile> = mutableListOf()
    for (profile in profiles) {
        if (profile.picture != null) {
            foundProfiles.add(profile)
        }
    }
    return foundProfiles
}
```

These and other procedures are frequent, and they usually result in the creation of some form of utility class or library so that they may reuse. ProfilesWithPictures(), the latter of the instances, also necessitates the usage of a changeable list, which deviates from immutability as a best practice. Kotlin's standard library includes many utility methods on built-in collections to save time and encourage immutable practices. These accept a function reference or a lambda that is executed on each element of the collection. We usually use lambda syntax:

```
fun searchForElemt(searchElemt: Any, list: List<Any>):
Any? {
    return list.firstOrNull { it == searchElemt }
}
fun profilesWithPictures(profiles: List<Profile>):
List<Profile> {
    return profiles.find { it.pictures != null }
}
fun checkAllProfilesHavePictures(profiles:
List<Profile>): List<Profile> {
    return profiles.all { it.pictures != null }
}
```

On Kotlin collections, there are many additional operations available, such as .contains(), .isEmpty(), .filter(), and others. The Kotlin documentation for List covers them, and most of them are transferable to other sorts of collections.

No more .equals()

As someone from a Python and C# background, the way Java handles equality testing caused me a lot of agony and debugging. In those languages, the == operator determines value equality or invokes an equals method on a complicated object. This means that == can be used to check the equality of everything, from integers to strings to objects.

Because there are no operator overloads in Java, == determines reference equality (which I've never been inclined to check for). This means that only primitives may be tested using ==, whereas complicated objects (such as Strings) require the usage of .equals (). Consider sorting through code that looks something like this:

```
if (input.equals("some other string")) {}
if (numberInput == 8) {}
```

Because Kotlin supports operator overloading, == effectively becomes an alias for .equals(). This enables the operator to use both built-in Java and custom types that have previously implemented the .equals() method.

Data classes will implement a default.equals() function for us for new Kotlin objects, which will check the equality of each field.

In the end, this makes Kotlin code easier to comprehend, pick up, and transfer for those who are used to non-Java equality.

```
if (input == "some other string") {}
if (my_Class == other_Class) {}
```

Method Readability – Named Parameters

When building objects with several fields, object-oriented approaches, notably in Java, require using what is known as the builder pattern. While this improves a constructor's call-site readability, it results in a sprawl of code that must write in another class whose primary goal is to build other classes more cleanly. By allowing named arguments on constructors and standard methods, Kotlin eliminates this requirement.

```
val profile = Profile(
    firstName = "Bobby",
    lastName = "Sharma",
    profileUrl = "https://google.com/",
    email = "bob.sharma@test.com"
)
```

Rather than depending on positional indexing, this may make what value is going where on a constructor extremely apparent. While methods with a high number of arguments are often considered an anti-pattern, named parameters allow you to add more parameters as needed without sacrificing readability.

```
Val apiResults = getFromApi(
    client = apiClient,
    baseUrl = API_URL,
    endpoint = API_ENDPOINT,
    headers = customHeaders,
    authToken = token,
    queryString = null
)
```

This is a contrived example that probably lends itself to better design. Still, it demonstrates how a method with that many arguments may become challenging to comprehend and debug if the parameter names aren't helpful.

HOW KOTLIN OUTPERFORMS JAVA IN SOLVING LONG-STANDING SECURITY ISSUES

Java is a well-known name. According to PYPL's study of Google Trends, it ranks second after Python in terms of popularity, accounting for 17.17 percent of total language tutorials searches. Because of its lengthy history, general stability, and ongoing support, Java has been a staple of application stacks since 1995.

It is the language of choice for Android programming and server-side and back-end development projects. Java is well-established in desktop, mobile, and gaming environments. So, where does Kotlin enter come in?

JetBrains introduced Kotlin in 2011 as a cross-platform, statically typed, general-purpose programming language meant to interoperate with Java completely. Unlike other types of 'cross-platform' compatibility, Kotlin's is at the machine code level. This implies that Kotlin is not packaged in a container and does not require bridging to run on supported systems. JavaScript frameworks that claim to be cross-platform, for example, nonetheless require some type of container to function. Cross-platform JavaScript apps are not native programs; instead, they operate in a created container with APIs that connect them to the different hardware characteristics.

Kotlin, on the other hand, is native by design and can run on every platform that Java can. Kotlin, along with Java, has been considered a first-class and supported language for Android development since October 2017.

But Kotlin is not Java; in fact, it is considered safer than Java. This leads to the issue of how and why and what this means for the security of our projects when utilizing Java or Kotlin.

Typing, Syntax, and Speed Compared

Android has changed its attention from Java to Kotlin in recent years. So, what makes Kotlin unique?

Kotlin app development, it turns out, takes less time to build and is physically lighter than Java. Kotlin code is substantially smaller, resulting in fewer defects and faster debugging. The main advantage of Kotlin is that its bytecode can be executed with the JVM, allowing it to leverage and access Java-based libraries and frameworks without significant compromise. It also includes coroutines, making it compatible and interoperable with JavaScript and thus web development.

In Kotlin, security against NullPointerException is implemented via a null safety mechanism, but the developer must write catches in Java. NullPointerException is a security concern since it can crash a program and is frequently regarded as a significant bug when null is permitted in areas where it should not be, vulnerabilities in Java increase.

Null Reference Exceptions Pose Security Risks

Null reference exceptions, also known as null dereference, are one of the top security vulnerabilities to watch for in an application, according to OWASP. The issue with null is that it is a value that has no meaning. It lacks an intrinsic data type in Java and needs specific processing.

For example, suppose we're creating a function to locate a user in a database. The terrible but typical approach is to return null when nothing is discovered. While it appears to make logical because null is meant to symbolize the absence of anything, it distorts the anticipated object returned type, which might lead to possible crashes further down the code.

When it comes to object-oriented thinking, the consensus opinion is that objects should design with immutability in mind. When an object's state changes, it exposes data structures and integrity to vulnerabilities. The object is both incomplete and changeable when null is used. When null is raised, Java crashes the program by default, resulting in a null pointer exception. However, developers frequently include catch exception handling to mitigate this issue, which helps the program avoid the possibility of null being accepted in areas where it should not be.

The code below, for example, is an example of a developer dismissing the possibility of a null slipping through by creating a NullPointerException catch. This catch discreetly fails the application, allowing it to continue running.

```
boolean isName(String s1) {
  try {
    String names[] = s1.split(" ");
    if (names.length != 3) {
      return false;
    }
    return (isCapitalized(names[0]) &&
isCapitalized(names[1]));
  } catch (NullPointerException e) {
    return false;
  }
```

The correct pattern for preventing a null is to explicitly make tests against the existence of null. Here's how the code should look:

```
boolean isName(String s1) {
  if (s1 == null) {
    return false;
  }
  String names[] = s1.split(" ");
  if (names.length != 3) {
    return false;
  }
  return (isCapitalized(names[0]) &&
isCapitalized(names[1]));
  }
```

We don't have this problem with null handling in Kotlin since it incorporates the idea of null safety into its general design and implementation. While null pointer exceptions can still arise in Kotlin, there are only a few methods for this to happen.

One method is to invoke the NullPointerException() function in the code directly. Another approach is to use them!! (not null) operators. Finally, null pointers appear in Kotlin only when there is data discrepancy during startup.

The Kotlin type system is designed to throw exceptions if a cast is deemed unsafe, hence rendering the type un-nullable.

In Java, this is impossible. Unsafe casts are considered because they provide an erroneous definition of the typed item, resulting in undefined errors on static targets.

Kotlin Has Everything That Java Needs

In addition to null safety, Kotlin has a vast range of features that Java lacks. This includes the following:

- lambda expressions and inline functions
- smart casting
- string templates
- extension functions
- primary constructors

- first-class delegation

- type inference for variable and property types

- range expressions

- operator overloading

- singletons

- data classes

- companion objects

- separate interfaces for read-only and mutable collections

- coroutines

In comparison, the list of Java capabilities that aren't accessible in Kotlin is substantially less. However, Kotlin's replacement and alternative features compensate for the 'missing' functionalities.

These features are as follows: static members in Java are replaced by companion objects, top-level functions, extension functions in Kotlin wildcard-types are replaced by declaration site variance and type projections, and ternary operators are replaced by if expressions.

Finally, There Is More to It Than Simply Null

The problem with null is only one of numerous security flaws that come with Java by default. While Kotlin does not prohibit the use of null, its handling of it is far superior and makes it less attractive for developers just to use a NullPointerException catch.

Raw types, for example, are still supported in Java for compatibility reasons but are strongly discouraged since the advent of generics. While raw types are acceptable during runtime, they constitute a security risk since manual checks are necessary when they include anything other than the intended type. In some ways, it's just another muddled form of null, but with types involved.

Raw type is only one example of something Java knows it should no longer support or have, but it does for various reasons. Because it is a newer language, Kotlin can mitigate this by looking at everything Java is excellent at, taking the best aspects, and removing the harmful and unnecessary. As a result, Kotlin's overall security is far superior to Java.

WHAT EXACTLY IS APPLICATION HARDENING?

Application hardening is similar to system hardening. It is possible to remove any unnecessary functions or components by restricting access and ensuring the application is maintained up to date with updates. Maintaining application security is critical to make apps available to users. Most apps contain buffer overflow issues invalid user input areas; therefore, fixing the application is only to protect it from assault.

What Is the Purpose of Application Hardening?

Here are some of the reasons why application hardening is important:

- Application hardening is a critical component of the protective business infrastructure for building a secure mobile environment with a safe software development lifecycle process.

- Determine what measures to take if the app is attacked or a tool is determined to be hacked.

- To safeguard user credentials, allow your application to execute in zero trust contexts.

- Prevent hackers from studying internal values, monitoring, or interfering with the program.

- Protect the program against a hacker attempting to reverse engineer it back to an ASCII text file.

Is Our Application in Need of Hardening?

Determine whether or not it is essential to protect the application from hackers based on the application's needs. For this purpose, several criteria are also used to make a decision, such as:

- If the application has a cost-effective property to protect.

- If the program has access to the user's sensitive info.

- Application hardening is primarily useful in the early phases of security considerations.

- If our application involves financial transactions or business data that we do not want others to see.

Today's applications operate on a variety of devices in a variety of situations. It's difficult to keep an eye on all of those gadgets and environments, which are putting our copyrights and expertise outside the control of our company. Application hardening also helps defend the company's image; data breaches can have significant consequences for the company's brand.

Application Hardening Methods

We'd want to employ several strategies to safeguard our application from various threats. Among them are the following:

1. **Data Obfuscation:** The substitution of difficult-to-decipher identifiers within the code for simple identifiers. Renaming class and variable names to something else. Encrypt some code to prevent attackers from easily deciphering it. To prevent attackers from seeing a functional representation of an application, binary-level code obfuscation might be utilized.

2. **Anti-Debug:** A debugger is software that analyzes other programs while they are executing. A debugger might be attached to a mobile banking application method and analyzed how it works. Typically, debuggers will use a debug API within the OS. They'll also set various flag registers. To avoid this, an app should prepare to recognize and respond to the presence of a debugger.

3. **Binary Packing:** Binary packing is a strategy to guard against static analysis. The software downloaded from the app store is encrypted and is only unpacked at runtime, making static analysis exceedingly difficult.

4. **Arithmetic Obfuscation:** Converting basic arithmetic and logical phrases into complicated equivalent expressions that are difficult to interpret using simple procedures.

5. **Android Rooting Detection:** Rooting an Android smartphone allows an attacker to get root access to the device. Rooting an Android smartphone successfully may pose a security risk to applications that affect sensitive data or impose specific limitations. Android rooting detection methods use anti-rooting techniques to determine the validity of the OS and deploy security measures appropriately.

Benefits of Application Hardening

The following are some of the advantages of application hardening:

1. **To prevent financial loss:** If the program accesses sensitive information of users or organizations, data breaches can cost the corporation millions of dollars. If attackers use corporate financial information, they will frequently execute a number of acts, including openly selling information on the Internet.

2. **Protect brand image:** If attackers regularly infiltrate a corporation, the company's brand image will suffer in the future.

3. **Increase software sales:** Numerous users may use secure software with little or no impact on security concerns.

4. **Close security gaps:** Hardening adds to the several levels of protection that protect users and their servers. Hardening also eliminates deactivated files and frequently overlooked applications, providing attackers with veiled access to the application.

Application Patches

Application patches are likely to come in three flavors: hotfixes, patches, and upgrades.

1. **Hotfixes:** These are often tiny bits of code intended to repair a specific problem. As an example, a hotfix may be provided to address a buffer overflow within an application's login procedure.

2. **Patches:** These are generally sets of fixes that are significantly bigger in size and are generally provided regularly or when sufficient problems have been solved to allow a patch release.

3. **Upgrades:** These are another common technique of patching apps, and they are more likely to be accepted than patches. The phrase "upgrade" has a positive role. We're progressing to a lot better, more useful, and safer application.

In this chapter, we explored code optimization, where we learned about Optimization Tips, Writing Secure Code, Best Coding Practices, and Security and Hardening.

CHAPTER 7

Kotlin for Android Development

IN THIS CHAPTER

> ➢ Building Android apps in Kotlin

> ➢ Advantages and features

> ➢ Integration with Android Studio

In the previous chapter, we covered Code Optimization in Kotlin. This chapter will discuss Building Android apps in Kotlin, Advantages and Features, and Integration with Android Studio.

BUILDING ANDROID Apps IN KOTLIN

In this codelab, we'll learn how to use the Kotlin programming language to create and launch our first Android app. Kotlin is a Java-compatible statically typed programming language that runs on the JVM. Along with Java, Kotlin is an officially recognized language for creating Android apps.

- **What we must already be aware of:** This codelab is intended for programmers and assumes that are familiar with the Java or Kotlin programming languages. Even though we don't have much expertise with Kotlin, if we're experienced programmers who can read code, we should follow this codelab.

DOI: 10.1201/9781003308447-7

- **What we'll discover:**

  - How to create an App using Android Studio

  - How to execute our application on a device or in an emulator

  - How to include Interactive Buttons

  - When a button is pressed, how to display a second screen

- **To create Android apps, use Android Studio with Kotlin:** Android apps are written in the Kotlin or Java using Android Studio, an integrated development environment. Android Studio is an IDE for Android programming based on JetBrains' IntelliJ IDEA software.

Download and Install Android Studio

Android Studio 3.6 may be downloaded from the Android Studio website: https://developer.android.com/studio/.

Android Studio includes a complete IDE, a sophisticated code editor, and app templates. It also provides development, debugging, testing, and performance tools to make app development faster and easier. Android Studio allows us to test our apps on various preset emulators or mobile devices. We may also create production applications and publish them on Google Play.

Android Studio is accessible for Windows and Linux PCs and Macs running macOS. Android Studio includes the OpenJDK (Java Development Kit).

The installation process is same for all the systems. Any discrepancies are listed below:

- To download and install Android Studio, go to the Android Studio download page and follow the instructions.

- Accept the default configurations for all steps and check that all components are installed.

- Following the completion of the installation, the setup wizard downloads and installs other components, including the Android SDK. Be patient, since this procedure may take some time depending on our internet speed.

- When the installation is finished, Android Studio will launch, and we will build our first project.

Create Our First Project

We will establish a new Android project for our first app in this stage. This basic app displays the string "Hello Everyone" on an Android virtual or real device's screen.

- **Step 1: Begin by creating a new project**

  - Launch Android Studio.

  - Click Start a new Android Studio project in the Welcome to Android Studio window.

  - Choose Basic Activity (not the default). Next, click the button.

  - Name your application, e.g., My First App.

  - Check that the Language is set to Kotlin.

  - Leave the other fields at their default values.

  - Finally, click Finish.

  Following these steps, Android Studio:

  - This command creates a folder for your Android Studio project. This is normally in a folder named AndroidStudioProjects, which is located beneath our home directory.

  - Constructs our project (this may take a few moments). Gradle is the build mechanism used by Android Studio. The build progress may be seen at the bottom of the Android Studio window.

  - Opens the code editor showing our project.

- **Step 2: Get our screen set up**

  When we initially launch our project in Android Studio, there may be several windows and panes open. Here are some recommendations for customizing the layout to help us get started with Android Studio.

  To conceal a Gradle window open on the right side, click the minimize button (—) in the top right corner.

  Consider adjusting the pane on the left that displays the project folders to take up less space, depending on the size of our screen.

  Our screen should be less busy at this stage.

- **Step 3: Investigate the project's structure and layout**

  The upper left side of the Android Studio window.

  Android Studio has created several files for us based on our selection of the Basic Activity template for our project. We may examine the file structure for our app in various ways, one of which is under Project view. Project view organizes our files and folders to make working with an Android project easier. (This may not always correspond to the file hierarchy! Select the Project files view by clicking to examine the file structure.

  - Double-click the app folder to expand the app file structure.

  - We may hide or reveal the Project view by clicking Project.

  - The currently selected Project view is Project > Android.

    In the Project > Android view, three or four top-level files appear beneath our app folder: manifests, java, java (generated), and res. It's possible that we won't see java (produced) immediately away.

    I. Expand the manifests directory. AndroidManifest.xml is located in this folder. This file specifies all Android app's components and is read by the Android runtime system when your app is performed.

    II. Expand java folder. All of our Kotlin language files are stored in this folder; Android projects store all Kotlin language files in this folder, along with any Java sources. The java subdirectory is divided into three subfolders:

        - com.example.myfirstapp (or whatever domain name we've chosen): This folder includes our app's Kotlin source code files.

        - (androidTest) com.example.myfirstapp: This is the location for instrumented tests, which run on an Android smartphone. It begins with a skeleton test file.

        - com.example.myfirstapp (test): This is the location for your unit tests. Unit tests do not require the use of an Android smartphone to execute. It all begins with a skeleton unit test file.

III. Unzip the res folder. This folder holds all of our app's resources, including photos, layout files, strings, icons, and style. It contains the following subfolders:

– **Drawable:** This folder will hold all of our app's pictures.

– **layout:** The UI layout files for our activities are stored in this folder. Our app currently has one activity with a layout file called activity_main.xml. The content_main.xml, fragment first.xml, and fragment_second.xml are also included.

– **menu:** In this folder, we'll find XML files that describe any menus in our program.

– **mipmap:** This folder holds our app's launcher icons.

– **navigation:** This folder includes the navigation graph, which instructs Android Studio on how to move between various portions of your application.

– **values:** Contains resources utilized in our app, such as strings and colors.

- **Step 4: Construct a virtual device (emulator)**

  - This work will develop a virtual device (or emulator) that replicates the setup of a specific type of Android device using the Android Virtual Device (AVD) manager.

  - The first step is to establish a configuration for the virtual device.

  - Select Tools > AVD Manager in Android Studio, or click the AVD Manager icon in the toolbar.

  - Click the +Create Virtual Device button. (If we've already created a virtual device, the window displays all of our current devices, with the +Create Virtual Device button at the bottom.) The Select Hardware window displays a list of hardware device definitions already been setup.

  - Select a device definition, such as Pixel 2, and press the Next button.

- Select the most recent version from the Recommended option in the System Image dialog.

- If a Download link appears next to a recent release, it is not yet installed and must be downloaded. If required, click the link to begin the download and click Next after it is completed. Depending on our connection speed, this may take some time.

- Accept the defaults in the following dialogue box, then click Finish.

- The virtual device we installed is now visible in the AVD Manager.

- Close the Virtual Devices AVD Manager window if it is still open.

- **Step 5: Run our app on our new emulator**

  - Select Run > Run 'app' in Android Studio, or click the Run button in the toolbar. When our app is operating, the icon changes.

  - If a dialogue box appears stating, "Instant Run requires that the platform matching to our target device be installed," click Install and proceed.

  - Select the virtual device configured under Available devices in Run > Select Device. In addition, a dropdown menu is displayed in the toolbar.

  - The emulator begins and boots in the same way as a hardware device would. This may take some time, depending on the speed of your machine. To view the progress, look for messages in the little horizontal status bar at the very bottom of Android Studio.

EXPLORE LAYOUT EDITOR

Each screen in our Android app is often coupled with one or more pieces. One fragment, named FirstFragment, creates the single screen that displays "Hellofirstfragment." When we created our new project, this was generated for us. Each visible fragment in an Android app has a layout that specifies the fragment's user interface. We can design and specify layouts with Android Studio's layout editor.

XML is used to define layouts. The layout editor allows us to design and alter our layout using either XML code or the interactive visual editor.

A view is an element of a layout. In this work, we'll look at some of the layout editor's panels and learn how to adjust the characteristics of views.

- **Step 1: Open layout editor**

  i. Locate and access the layout folder (app > res > layout) in the Project panel's left side.

  ii. fragment first.xml should be double-clicked.

     The layout editor is comprised of the panels to the right of the Project view. They may organize differently in our version of Android Studio, but the purpose remains the same.

     A Palette of views that we may add to our app can be seen on the left.

     Under that is a Component Tree that shows the views currently in this file and how they are organized about one another.

     The Design editor is in the middle, and it displays a visual depiction of what the contents of the file will look like when combined into an Android app. We have the option of seeing the visual representation, the XML code, or both.

  iii. The three icons are located in the top right corner of the Design editor, above Attributes:

     These are the views for Code (code only), Split (code + design), and Design (design just).

  iv. Try with the various modes. Depending on our screen size and our working style, we may opt to switch between Code and Design or stay in Split view. Hide and expose the Palette if our Component Tree vanishes.

  v. The + and − buttons for zooming in and out are located in the lower right corner of the Design editor. Adjust the size of what we see using these buttons, or use the zoom-to-fit button to make both panels fit on our screen.

     The design layout displays how our app will appear on the device on the left. The schematic representation of the layout is presented on the right in the Blueprint layout.

  vi. Try with displaying the design view, the blueprint view, and both views side by side using the layout menu in the upper left of the design toolbar.

Depending on our screen size and our preferences, we may choose to show simply the Design view or the Blueprint view rather than both.

vii. To modify the direction of the layout, click the orientation symbol. This allows us to see how our design will look in portrait and landscape orientations.

View the layout on different devices by using the device menu. (This is fantastic for testing!)

The Attributes panel is on the right.

- **Step 2: Navigate and resize the Component Tree**

   i. Examine the Component Tree in fragment_first.xml. If it isn't visible, change the mode to Design rather than Split or Code.

   This panel displays the view hierarchy in our layout, or how the views are organized about one another.

   ii. Resize the Component Tree if required to read at least some of the strings.

   iii. In the upper right corner of the Component Tree, click the Hide symbol.

   The Component Tree is now closed.

   iv. Click the vertical label Component Tree on the left to restore the Component Tree.

- **Step 3: Evaluate view hierarchies**

   i. Notice that the root of the view hierarchy in the Component Tree is a ConstraintLayout view.

   Every layout must include a root view that includes all other views. A view group, which is a view that contains other views, is always the root view. A view group is an example of a ConstraintLayout.

   ii. Take note that the ConstraintLayout includes a TextView named textview first and a Button named button first.

   iii. If the code isn't visible, use the icons in the upper right corner to switch to Code or Split view.

iv. The root element in the XML code is

```
<androidx.constraintlayout.widget.
ConstraintLayout>. A <TextView> element and a
Button> element are contained in the root
element.
<androidx.constraintlayout.widget.
ConstraintLayout
    ...
    >

    <TextView
      ...
     />
    <Button
      ...
     />
</androidx.constraintlayout.widget.
ConstraintLayout>
```

- **Step 4: Modify the property values**

    i. Examine the TextView element's attributes in the code editor.

    ```
    <TextView
        android:layout_width="wrap_content"
        android:layout_height="wrap_content"
        android:text="Hellofirst fragment"
        ...
      />
    ```

    ii. When we click on the string in the text property, we'll see that it corresponds to a string resource called hellofirst_fragment.

    ```
    android:text="@string/hellofirst_fragment"
    ```

    iii. Go To > Declaration or Usages values/strings.xml opens with the string highlighted when we right-click on the property.

    ```
    <string name="hellofirst_fragment">Hellofirst
    fragment</string>
    ```

    iv. Change the string property's value to Hello Everyone.

    v. Return to fragment first.xml.

    vi. In the Component Tree, choose textview_first.

vii. Examine the Attributes panel on the right, and, if necessary, open the Declared Attributes section.

viii. Notice that the string resource @string/hellofirst_fragment is still referred to in the text field of the TextView in Attributes. There are various advantages to storing the strings in a resource file. We may modify the value of string without changing any other code. Because our translators don't need to know anything about the app code, this simplifies translating our app to different languages.

ix. To view the modification we made in strings.xml, restart the program. "Hello Everyone" appears in our app now.

- **Step 5: Modify the text display settings**

   i. With textview_first still selected in the Component Tree, expand the textAppearance field in the layout editor's list of attributes, under Common Attributes.

  ii. Modify the text's appearance attributes. Change the font family, raise the text size, and pick the bold style, for example. (We may need to scroll across the panel to see all fields.)

      Change the color of the text. Enter g in the textColor field by clicking on it.

 iii. A menu appears with possible completion values beginning with the letter g. Predefined colors are included in this list.

  iv. Press Enter after selecting @android:color/darker_gray.

   v. Examine the TextView's XML. The additional homes have been added, as we can see.

```
<TextView
    android:id="@+id/textview_first"
    android:layout_width="wrap_content"
    android:layout_height="wrap_content"
    android:fontFamily="sans-serif-condensed"
    android:text="@string/hellofirst_fragment"
    android:textColor="@android:color/darker_gray"
    android:textSize="25sp"
    android:textStyle="bold"
```

  vi. Run the app again and see the changes applied to our Hello Everyone.

- **Step 6: Show all attributes**

  i. Scroll down until we locate All Attributes in the Attributes panel.

  ii. Scroll through the list to get a sense of the properties a TextView may have.

ADD COLOR RESOURCES

So far, we've learned how to update the values of properties. We will then learn how to construct more resources, such as the string resources we dealt with previously. Using resources allows us to reuse data in numerous locations and specify values and have the UI update automatically any-time the value changes.

- **Step 1: Include color resources**

  To begin, we'll discover how to add new color resources.
  Change the TextView's text color and backdrop color.

  i. In the left-hand Project panel, double-click res > values > colors. xml to view the color resource file.

```
<resources>
    <color name="colorPrimary"> #7e43e6</color>
    <color name="colorPrimaryDark"> #9c8cba<//
color>
    <color name="colorAccent"> #75154f</color>
</resources>
```

  The editor opens the colors.xml file. Three colors have been defined thus far. These are the colors we'll see in our app's design (e.g., purple for the app bar).

  ii. Return to fragment_first.xml to view the layout's XML code.

  iii. Add a new android:background property to the TextView and begin typing to change its value to @color. This attribute may add anywhere in the TextView code.
  A menu appears, displaying the predefined color resources.

  iv. Select @color/colorPrimaryDark.

  v. Change the value of the android:textColor property to @ android:color/white.

We don't have to specify white because the Android framework provides a variety of colors, including white.

vi. In the layout editor, we can observe that the TextView now has a dark blue or purple background with white text.

- **Step 2: Create a new color to use as the screen backdrop**

    i. Create a new color resource named screenBackground in colors. xml.

    ```
    <color name="screenBackground"> #FFEE59</color>s
    ```

    A color is defined as three hexadecimal digits (#00-#FF, or 0-255) representing the red, blue, and green (RGB) components. The colors associated with the code are displayed in the editor's left margin.

    It's worth noting that a color may also be defined with an alpha value (#00-#FF), which signifies transparency (#00 = 0% = entirely transparent, #FF = 100% = fully opaque). When the alpha value is included, it is the first of four hexadecimal numbers (ARGB).

    The alpha value measures transparency. #88FFEE58, e.g., makes the color semi-transparent, whereas #00FFEE58 makes it completely translucent and disappears from the left-hand bar.

    ii. Return to fragment_first.xml.

    iii. Select the ConstraintLayout component from the Component Tree.

    iv. Select the background property in the Attributes window and hit Enter. In the field that displays, type "c."

    v. Select @color/screenBackground from the color choice that opens. To finish the selection, press Enter.

    vi. Click on the yellow patch.

    It displays a list of the colors specified in colors.xml. Click the Custom tab to use an interactive color chooser to select a custom color.

    vii. Change the value of the screenBackground color as desired, but make sure that the final color is visibly different from the colors colorPrimary and colorPrimaryDark.

- **Step 3: Investigate the width and height parameters**

  i. Now that we have a new screen backdrop color, we will adjust the width and height parameters of views to see what happens.

     Select ConstraintLayout component in the Component Tree of fragment first.xml.

  ii. Locate and expand the Layout section in the Attributes panel.

     Both the layout width and layout height attributes have the value match parent. Because the ConstraintLayout is the Fragment's root view, the "parent" layout size is the size of our screen.

  iii. Note that the screenBackground color is used across the background.

  iv. Choose textview first. The width and height of layout are now wrap content, which tells the view to be only large enough to contain its content (plus padding).

  v. Set both the layout width and layout height to match constraint, which instructs the view to be as large as the constraint.

     The width and height show 0dp, and the text is moved to the upper left, while the TextView expands to meet the ConstraintLayout except for the button. Because the button and the text view are on the same level of the view hierarchy within the constrained layout, they share space.

  vi. Try with what occurs when the width is match constraint and the height is wrap_content, and vice versa. The width and height of the button_first can also adjust.

  vii. Return the TextView and the Button's width and height to wrap_content.

ADD VIEWS AND CONSTRAINTS

We will add two more buttons to our user interface and update the existing button in this task.

- **Step 1: View the constraint properties**

  i. View the constraint attributes for the TextView in fragment first.xml.

     ```
     app:layout_constraintBottom_toTopOf="@id/
     button_first"
     ```

```
app:layout_constraintEnd_toEndOf="parent"
app:layout_constraintStart_toStartOf="parent"
app:layout_constraintTop_toTopOf="parent"
```

ii. In the Component Tree, choose textview_first and look at the Constraint Widget in the Attributes panel.

The square represents the selected view. Each gray dot indicates a constraint, from top to bottom, left to right; in this case, from the TextView to its parent, ConstraintLayout, or the Next button for the bottom constraint.

iii. When a specific view is selected, the limitations are also displayed in the blueprint and design views. Some limitations are jagged lines, but the one closest to the Next button is a squiggle since it's unusual. We'll find out more about that in a moment.

- **Step 2: Add the buttons and constrain their positions**

  We will add buttons to the layout to understand how to utilize constraints to connect the locations of views. Our first objective is to create a button and some limitations and update the constraints on the Next button.

  i. Take note of the Palette in the layout editor's upper left corner. If necessary, adjust the edges so that we can see most of the objects in the palette.

  ii. Select some of the categories and, if necessary, peruse through the listed items to get a sense of what's available.

  iii. Drag and drop Button, which is toward the top, into the design view, positioning it beneath the TextView near the other button.

- **Step 3: Add a constraint for the new button**

  The top of the button will now constrain to the bottom of the TextView.

  i. Move the mouse over the top of the Button's circle.

  ii. Click and drag the top circle of the Button onto the bottom circle of the TextView.

  Because top of the button is now confined to the bottom of the TextView, it moves up to sit just below it.

iii. Examine the Constraint Widget in the Attributes panel's Layout pane. It displays certain Button limitations, such as Top -> BottomOf textView.

iv. Check the XML code for the button. It now has the property that restricts the button's top to the bottom of the TextView.

```
app:layout_constraintTop_toBottomOf="@+id/
textview_first"
```

v. We may get the message "Not Horizontally Constrained." Add constraint from the left side of the button to the left side of the screen to remedy this.

vi. Add a constraint to keep the bottom of the button at the bottom of the screen.

Before adding another button, rename this one, so it's easier to tell which one is which.

i. Click on the newly added button in the design layout.

ii. Notice the id field in the Attributes tab on the right.

iii. Rename the button to the toast button.

- **Step 4: Make changes to the Next button**
  We will change the Next button that Android Studio built for us when we created the app. The restriction between it and the TextView is a wavy line rather than a jagged one, with no arrow. This denotes a chain, in which the constraints connect two or more items rather than simply one. For the time being, we will remove the chained restrictions and replace them with regular constraints.
  To delete a constraint:

  - In the design or blueprint view, hold the Ctrl key (Command on a Mac) and drag the cursor over the constraint's circle until it highlights, then click the circle.

  - Alternatively, choose one of the constrained views, then right-click on the constraint and select Delete from the menu.

  - Alternatively, in the Attributes panel, slide the mouse over the constraint's circle until it shows an x, then click it.

- If we delete a constraint and then want it back, we must either undo the operation or establish a new constraint.

- **Step 5: Remove the chain limitations**

    Click the Next button, then erase the constraint from the button's top to the TextView.

    Remove the constraint from the bottom of the text to the Next button by clicking on the TextView.

- **Step 6: Add new constraints**

    i. If it isn't already, move the right side of the Next button to the right side of the screen.

    ii. Delete the constraint located to the left of the Next button.

    iii. Now, constrain the Next button's top and bottom such that the top is confined to bottom of the TextView and bottom is constrained to bottom of the screen. The button's right side is restricted to the screen's right side.

    Constrict the TextView to the bottom of the screen as well.

    iv. The views may appear to hop around a lot, but this is typical as we add and remove restrictions.

- **Step 7: Gather string resources**

    i. Locate the toast button's text attribute in the fragment_first.xml layout file.

    ```
    <Button
        android:id="@+id/toast_button"
        android:layout_width=
        "wrap_content"
        android:layout_height=
        "wrap_content"
        android:text="Button"
    ```

    ii. Take note that the text "Button" is directly in the layout field, rather than referring to a string resource as the TextView does. This will make translating our application into other languages more difficult.

    iii. To correct this, click the highlighted code. On the left, a light bulb emerges.

iv. Click the lightbulb. Select Extract string resource from the option that appears.

v. In the resulting dialogue box, update the resource name to toast_ button_text and the resource value to Toast, then click OK.

vi. Notice how the android:text property's value has changed to @string/toast_button_text.

```
<Button
    android:id="@+id/button"
    android:layout_width="wrap_content"
    android:layout_height="wrap_content"
    android:text="@string/toast_button_text"
```

vii. Navigate to the file res > values > strings.xml. A new string resource entitled toast button text has been added.

```
<resources>
    .....
    <string name="toast_button_text">Toast</string>
</resources>
```

viii. Run the app to ensure that it displays as expected.

We now understand how to generate new string resources from existing field values. (We may also manually add additional resources to the strings.xml file.) We also understand how to alter the id of a view.

- **Step 8: Update Next button**

The text for the Next button is already in a string resource, but we'll update it to reflect its new role, which is to produce and show a random number.

i. In the Attributes panel, change the Next button's id from button first to random button, just like we did with the Toast button.

ii. If a dialog box appears requesting you to update all button usages, click Yes. Any additional references to the button in the project code will Fix.

iii. Right-click on the next string resource in strings.xml.

iv. Go to Refactor > Rename… and rename the file random button text.

v. To rename our string and exit the window, click Refactor.

vi. Change the string's value from Next to Random.

vii. We may relocate random button text underneath toast button text if we ike.

- **Step 9: Add third button**

  Our final layout will have three buttons that are vertically constrained and evenly separated from one another.

  i. In fragment_first.xml, add another button to the layout and place it below the TextView, between the Toast and Random buttons.

  ii. Use the same vertical constraints as the other two buttons. Constrain the third button's top to the bottom of TextView and the bottom of the screen.

  iii. Apply horizontal restrictions to the other buttons from the third button. Constrain the third button's left side to the right side of the Toast button, and the third button's right side to the left side of the Random button.

  iv. Examine the fragment first.xml XML code.

  When both sides are bound in opposing directions, the "bias" constraints enable us to alter the location of a view to be more on one side than the other. For example, if both top and bottom sides of a view are confined to the top and bottom of the screen, we may apply a vertical bias to shift the view to the top rather than the bottom.

  Here is the completed layout's XML code. Our layout may include varying margins as well as vertical or horizontal bias limits. For our project, the precise values of the properties for the look of the TextView may change.

```
<?xml version="1.0" encoding="utf-8"?>
<androidx.constraintlayout.widget.
ConstraintLayout <?xml version="1.0"
encoding="utf-8"?>
<androidx.constraintlayout.widget.
ConstraintLayout xmlns:android="http://schemas.
android.com/apk/res/android"
    xmlns:app="http://schemas.android.com/apk/
res-auto"
```

```
    xmlns:tools="http://schemas.android.com/
tools"
    android:layout_width="match_parent"
    android:layout_height="match_parent"
    android:background="@color/screenBackground"
    tools:context=".FirstFragment">
    <TextView
        android:id="@+id/textview_first"
        android:layout_width="wrap_content"
        android:layout_height="wrap_content"
        android:background="@color/
colorPrimaryDark"

android:fontFamily="sans-serif-condensed"
        android:text="@string/
hello_first_fragment"
        android:textColor="@android:color/black"
        android:textSize="34sp"
        android:textStyle="bold"

app:layout_constraintBottom_toBottomOf="parent"

app:layout_constraintEnd_toEndOf="parent"

app:layout_constraintStart_toStartOf="parent"
        app:layout_constraintTop_
toTopOf="parent" />
    <Button
        android:id="@+id/random_button"
        android:layout_width="wrap_content"
        android:layout_height="wrap_content"
        android:text="@string/
random_button_text"

app:layout_constraintBottom_toBottomOf="parent"

app:layout_constraintEnd_toEndOf="parent"
        app:layout_constraintTop_
toBottomOf="@+id/textview_first" />
    <Button
        android:id="@+id/toast_button"
        android:layout_width="wrap_content"
        android:layout_height="wrap_content"
```

```
            android:text="@string/toast_button_text"

    app:layout_constraintBottom_toBottomOf="parent"

    app:layout_constraintStart_toStartOf="parent"
            app:layout_constraintTop_
    toBottomOf="@+id/textview_first" />
        <Button
            android:id="@+id/button2"
            android:layout_width="wrap_content"
            android:layout_height="wrap_content"
            android:text="Button"

    app:layout_constraintBottom_toBottomOf="parent"
            app:layout_constraintEnd_
    toStartOf="@+id/random_button"
            app:layout_constraintStart_
    toEndOf="@+id/toast_button"
            app:layout_constraintTop_
    toBottomOf="@+id/textview_first" />
    </androidx.constraintlayout.widget.
    ConstraintLayout>
```

- **Step 10: Get our UI for the next task**

  The following job is to make the buttons perform something when pressed. First, we must prepare the user interface.

  i. Modify the TextView's text to show 0 (the number zero).

  ii. Move the text alignment to the middle.

  iii. In the design editor's Attributes panel, change the id of the last button we inserted, button2, to count_button.

  iv. Extract the string resource to count_button_text in the XML and update the value to Count.

      The following text and ids should now appear on the buttons:

Button	Text	id
Left-button	Toast	@+id/toast_button
Middle-button	Count	@+id/count_button
Right-button	Random	@+id/random_button

  v. Run app.

- **Step 11: Fix errors if necessary**

  The issues arise because the id of the buttons has changed, and these constraints are now referring to non-existent views.

  If we see any of these issues, just update the buttons' id in the restrictions shown in red.

  ```
  app:layout_constraintEnd_toStartOf="@+id/
  random_button"
  app:layout_constraintStart_toEndOf="@+id/
  toast_button"
  ```

CHANGE THE LOOK OF THE BUTTONS AND THE TextView

Our app's layout is nearly complete, but it may be enhanced with a few minor changes.

- **Step 1: Add new color resources**

  i. In colors.xml, set screenBackground to #2196F3, a blue color from the Material Design palette.

  ii. Add a new color to the palette called buttonBackground. Use the color #BBDEFC, which is a paler tone of blue.

  ```
  <color name="buttonBackground">#BBDEFC</color>
  ```

- **Step 2: Change the background color of the buttons**

  Fill in the background color for each of the buttons in the layout. (We may either change the XML in fragment first.xml or utilize the Attributes panel, whichever we want.)

  ```
  android:background="@color/buttonBackground"
  ```

- **Step 3: Modify the left and right button margins**

  Give the Toast button a 24dp left (start) margin and the Random button a 24dp right (end) margin. (Using start and finish rather than left and right, these margins work in all language directions.)

  The Constraint Widget in the Attributes panel is one method to accomplish this. The number on each side represents the margin on that side of the chosen view. Enter the number 24 into the slot and hit Enter.

- **Step 4: Update the TextView appearance**

  i. Remove the TextView's background color by deleting the value in the Attributes panel or removing the android:background property from the XML code.

When the backdrop is removed, the view background becomes translucent.

ii. Increase the TextView's text size to 74sp.

```
android:textSize="74sp"
```

iii. If it isn't already, change the font-family of the TextView to sans-serif.

iv. Add an app:layout constraintVertical bias attribute to the TextView to slightly bias the view's position upward so that it is more uniformly spaced vertically on the screen. We are allowed to change the value of this restriction as we like. (We can see how the arrangement appears in the design view.)

```
app:layout_constraintVertical_bias="0.4"
```

v. We can also use the Constraint Widget to set the vertical bias. Click and drag number 50 that appears on the left side, then slide it upward until it says 30.

BENEFITS OF KOTLIN FOR ANDROID App DEVELOPMENT

Kotlin is becoming a popular programming language among Android developers. Despite Java's overwhelming dominance as the go-to platform for Android app development, Kotlin has emerged as a formidable competitor. Java is still a popular development language for creating Android apps. Nonetheless, Kotlin is making significant inroads into the app development business. Java and Kotlin are now Android's official programming languages.

This section will discuss the most notable advantages of adopting Kotlin over Java for Android app development. The advantages are numerous, from ease of learning to code structure to correctness. Continue reading to learn more.

The Benefits of Kotlin-Based Android App Development

Developers are increasingly choosing Kotlin over Java.

Kotlin compiles the same byte code as Java and may interact with it naturally. Despite Java's familiarity and dependability, an increasing number of Android app developers are switching to Kotlin for its more sophisticated capabilities. Here's a selection of the most eye-catching.

1. **Simplified and shorter code:** Kotlin provides both shorter code and improved readability. Kotlin's official developers have been working hard to keep the language as compact as feasible. Shorter codes offer fewer risks of coding mistake. We may concentrate on the code's quality and logic rather than avoiding lengthy code-related faults.

   Kotlin is statically typed programming language that is simple to understand and write. The brevity and simplicity of the programs also make debugging easier. Katlin's codes can streamline the programming process more effectively than Java. Katlin's smooth integrated development environment makes it feasible.

2. **Java compatibility:** Kotlin is entirely compatible with all Java libraries and development frameworks. This makes it easy for Android app development businesses to transition from Java to Kotlin. If we are an Android developer, you may simply utilize Katlin without making any substantial modifications, such as rewriting a whole app. This is, in fact, one of the most significant benefits in terms of the time and work required to change the present coding language.

   Furthermore, Katlin's simplicity makes it exceedingly simple for developers to understand and code. We'll have no trouble writing code with Katlin if we're comfortable with Java. We may also quickly translate Java code to Katlin. We only need IntelliJ or Android studio to convert Java to Katlin. That's why Katlin is being used for so many Android development projects.

3. **Elimination of null references:** This is the most significant advantages of using Katlin versus Java. Null references, called "the billion-dollar mistake" by computer scientist Sir Tony Hoare, are a serious impediment to high-quality code.

   In Java, null references can cause a null reference exception known as the NullPointerException (NPE). The Kotlin programming language is intended to eliminate NPE from code. NPE might be caused by:

   - A call to throw NullPointerException().

   - Initialization-related data consistency.

   - Among other things, Java interoperation attempts to access a member of the null reference.

4. **Solution for Java's shortcomings:** Kotlin improves and smartens coding for Android app development by solving several typical Java faults. For example, it allows us to avoid the null pointer problem. Kotlin has effectively taken several fantastic aspects from other languages like C# and Scala. These modifications are intended to address some of Java's long-standing faults. Kotlin's coding components, such as parameter lists and variable declarations, make it an ideal tool for coping with Java's problems.

5. **Development of cross-platform apps:** Kotlin's development skills extend beyond Android app development and even mobile apps. Kotlin's support for JavaScript interoperability allows you to move frontend development to Kotlin. Kotlin also allows you to create Gradle code in Kotlin. This also allows mobile app developers to develop iOS apps. As a result, Kotlin-written cross-platform apps offer native-like performance.

Aside from this, Kotlin supports efficient multithreading. It allows us to synchronize many threads while simultaneously changing data. Pure functions and immutable objects can reduce the requirement for continual change.

INTEGRATE in-app REVIEWS

This section will show us how to add in-app reviews into our project using Kotlin.

Set Up Our Development Environment

The Play Core SDK includes the In-App Review API. Follow the instructions in the Kotlin section of the Play Core library documentation to set up our development environment.

Create ReviewManager

The ReviewManager interface allows our app to initiate an in-app review flow. Create an instance of the ReviewManagerFactory to obtain it.

```
val managers = ReviewManagerFactory.create(context)
```

Request ReviewInfo Object

To establish suitable moments in our app's user flow to prompt the user for a review, follow the recommendations on when to seek in-app reviews (e.g., when the user completes a level in a game). When our app reaches one of these stages, create a request task using the ReviewManager object. The API delivers the ReviewInfo object required to begin the in-app review procedure if the request is successful.

```
val request = manager.requestReviewFlow()
request.addOnCompleteListener { task ->
    if (task.isSuccessful) {
        // We got ReviewInfo object
        val reviewInfo = task.result
    } else {
        // There was problem, log or handle error code.
        @ReviewErrorCode val reviewErrorCode = (task.
getException() as TaskException).errorCode
    }
}
```

Launch in-app Review Flow

To launch the in-app review cycle, use the ReviewInfo instance. Wait until the user has finished in-app review flow before continuing with the usual user flow of our app (such as advancing to the next level).

```
Val flow = manager.launchReviewFlow(activity,
reviewInfo)
flow.addOnCompleteListener { _ ->
    // flow has finished.  The API does not indicate
whether user
    // reviewed or not, or even whether review dialog
is shown.
    // Thus, no matter the result, we continue our app
flow.
}
```

In this chapter, we covered Building Android apps in Kotlin, Benefits of Kotlin for Android app development, and Integration with Android Studio.

Appraisal

Kotlin is a popular cross-platform and statically typed programming language. The Java Virtual Machine (JVM) is used for programming implementations in application development. As an alternative to Java programming, Kotlin is increasingly employed in Android app and constructors. Because of its compatibility, low run time, and efficient coding capabilities, Kotlin is a popular programming language.

WHAT EXACTLY IS KOTLIN?

Kotlin is one of the most significant subjects in social media and the new future for software developers; let us go through it in depth. Kotlin is a cross-platform statically typed programming language based on the JVM. The JVM is widely used for developing java computer programs. Now, let's talk about history and development of Kotlin. Jet-brains designed and developed it. The programming language is named Kotlin after the island of the same name near St. Petersburg. The Java computer language was named after the Indonesian island of Java. In the current industry, it might be considered the successor of Java.

HISTORY

The Kotlin language was initially introduced in 2011 by the business JetBrains; if we're unfamiliar with them, they were previously known as the creators of the popular IntelliJ IDEA and are now equally well-known as the inventors of the Kotlin language.

Although their initial release was in 2011, it wasn't until 2016 that Kotlin v1.0 was released, the first official release for which JetBrains would guarantee backward compatibility; the Kotlin release versioning method can be seen here. Kotlin is presently at version 1.5, and the following timelines compare Kotlin's release cycle to JDK's release cycle.

UNDERSTANDING

These may be executed on an open-source platform and are mostly regarded as a Java substitute. It may combine with both Java and Javascript programs and Java libraries. Kotlin has its libraries that may access via the Application programming interface. The program in Java is redundant and repeated in nature, resulting in long code, whereas Kotlin is more simple and current, making it readily accessible by newcomers. It primarily focuses on decreasing functional code while also removing repetitive code. Kotlin protects null points by removing null point exceptions and the semicolons (;) required in Java code but can be ignored. There is no problem if the user uses it by default.

HOW DOES KOTLIN MAKE WORK SO SIMPLE?

Google officially announced it as the programming language used for Android development. Please explain how Kotlin can make our work more accessible and more comfortable. The Kotlin language program is short and gives the programmer greater conveniences through built-in apps. Lengthy Java applications may develop in a short time with the help of Kotlin. That is, it consumes less code while producing the same outputs. Shortcode needs less time to write, which is directly related to financial considerations.

WHAT IS THE IMPORTANCE OF KOTLIN?

Understanding the usage of Kotlin, the successor to Java, would be simpler when learned by comparing Java with Kotlin. This may use both on the source and client sides. It is simple to use on any operating systems, including iOS, macOS, and embedded systems. People utilize it in server-side apps, java scripts, and data science.

Kotlin requires less code and has fewer bugs. It also allows test-driven development, which further minimizes the number of bugs. Even if you make a mistake when coding the code, we can quickly correct it. Because of its shortcode and fewer issues, it is simple to maintain and can thus be handled by a new team. It also supports multiple plugins, making life much easier. With so many applications, any developer prefers this language.

WHAT ARE THE POSSIBILITIES FOR KOTLIN?

In reality, there are several domains where Kotlin may play a major role. It may utilize in practically every situation where Java is used.

Let us look at some examples of how it may utilize:

- In scientific Game creation

- Data examination

- Reusing code from Android apps in iOS

- Systems that are embedded

- Web apps such as Netflix

KOTLIN FOR THE SERVER-SIDE

Kotlin is a fantastic choice for creating server-side apps since it enables us to create expressive and simple code while staying completely interoperable with current Java-based technology stacks and having a short learning curve:

- **Expressivity:** The innovative language features of Kotlin, like type-safe constructors and delegated properties, enable the creation of robust and simple abstractions.

- **Scalability:** Kotlin supports, step-by-step transfer of large Java code-bases to Kotlin. We could start writing new code in Kotlin while keeping current pieces of our system in Java.

- **Tooling:** Via addition to generic IDE support, Kotlin offers framework-specific tooling (e.g., Spring) in the IntelliJ IDEA Ultimate plugin.

- **Learning Curve:** For Java developer, getting started with the Kotlin is pretty straightforward. The automated Java to Kotlin converter in the Kotlin plugin helps in the early stages. Kotlin Koans guide us through the main aspects of the language through a series of interactive games.

WORKING WITH KOTLIN?

It mainly works with:

- Data types, operators, and I/O comments

- Expressions such as if, when, while, for, break, and continue

- Function calls, recursions, and arguments

- Constructors, Classes, Objects, Companions, Extensions, and so on.

WHAT ARE THE BENEFITS OF KOTLIN?

Kotlin was created due to Lead Developer Dmitry Jemerov's search for functionality that he couldn't find in the Java. Scala, another language that runs on the JVM, came close, but compiling took too long.

Jemerov desired a language with all of the characteristics of more recent programming languages, which could operate on the JVM and compile as quickly as Java. As a result, he developed his language, Kotlin.

On the Android operating system, Kotlin was designed to replace Java. In 2019, Google ultimately agreed with Jemerov and most Android developers and proclaimed that Kotlin was the ideal language for Android app development eight years after it was launched.

Here are some of the reasons why developers choose Kotlin over Java:

- Kotlin is succinct, which saves time spent creating boilerplate code in Java.

- A script may use to convert a Java file to a Kotlin file.

- There is no runtime overhead with Kotlin. Adding features to a language can sometimes result in increased overhead, which reduces efficiency. Not the case with Kotlin.

- Kotlin has a large community. If we get stuck, we may obtain support from other developers on coding forums and social networks.

- Kotlin makes asynchronous programming more accessible. Making asynchronous network and database calls in Java is cumbersome and inconvenient. Coroutines in Kotlin make asynchronous programming efficient and straightforward.

- Nulls are handled in Kotlin. If we don't plan for a null in Java, it might cause a program to crash. To avoid these problems, we may add a simple operator to variables null in Kotlin.

- Kotlin can operate on a variety of systems. Kotlin can run everywhere Java can, allowing us to create cross-platform programs.

- It is simple to transition to Kotlin. Because Kotlin is entirely compatible with Java, we do not need to replace all of our code at once. We may gradually move an application to Kotlin.

WHAT IS THE PURPOSE OF KOTLIN?

Kotlin is intended to operate on a JVM and can coexist alongside Java. Although Kotlin began as a language for Android development, its features quickly spread beyond the Java community, and it is now utilized for a wide range of applications.

Android Development

Kotlin is the recommended language for Android development because it allows developers to produce more concise, expressive, and secure code. Android Studio, the official IDE for Android development, fully supports it, so we can receive the same sort of code completion and type checking to assist us to create Kotlin code as we can with Java.

Because more people now access the Internet via mobile phones, most companies must have a mobile presence. Because Android accounts for more than 70% of the mobile phone market, Kotlin developers would be in great demand even if Kotlin was solely used for Android development. It may, however, be used for much more.

Web Development on the Back-End

Back-end web development in Java is common, with popular frameworks such as Spring. However, since it was simpler to work with, Kotlin made inroads into server-side web development.

The language's contemporary capabilities enable Web Developers to create apps that expand fast on commodity hardware. Because Kotlin and Java are compatible, we may gradually migrate an application to use Kotlin one file at a time while the remainder of the program continues to use Java.

Kotlin works with the Spring and other frameworks, so migrating to Kotlin does not need to redesign our existing code completely. Google, Amazon, and many more organizations have already replaced Java in their server-side code with Kotlin.

Full-Stack Web Development

Kotlin makes sense for server-side web development. After all, Java has been around since the beginning. We may still use Kotlin for front-end programming using Kotlin/JS.

Kotlin/JS gives developers type-safe access to a sophisticated browser and online APIs. Full-Stack Developers simply need to be familiar with Kotlin. They can create front-end code in the same language as back-end code, and it will be compiled to JavaScript to execute in the browser.

Data Science

Data Scientists have long used Java to crunch information, discover patterns, and make predictions, so it seems to reason that Kotlin will find a home in the field as well.

Data Scientists can utilize all of the normal Java libraries used in Java projects, but they must develop their code in Kotlin. Jupyter and Zeppelin, two tools that many Data Scientists regularly utilize for data visualization and exploratory study, support Kotlin.

Mobile Development for Multiple Platforms

Kotlin Multi-platform Mobile is a software development kit for building cross-platform mobile applications. This implies that we'll be able to generate apps that operate not only on Android phones but also on iPhones and the Apple Watch from a single Kotlin codebase. This is still in its early stages, but it has a lot of potential.

Features	Java	Kotlin
Primitive Type	In Java, primitive types are not objects.	Objects are primitive types.
Product	It is an Oracle Corporation product.	It is a JetBrains product.
Used For	It is used to create both standalone and enterprise applications.	It is used to create server-side apps as well as Android applications.
Compilation Time	Java's compilation time is relatively short.	Its compilation time is slower than that of Java.
File Extensions	Java employs the following file extensions: .java (for source files), .class (for class files), and .jar (for archived file).	Kotlin utilizes the following file extensions: .kt (for Kotlin source files), .kts (for Kotlin script file), and .ktm (for Kotlin module).
Checked Exceptions	The try-catch block in Java is used to handle the checked exception.	It is not necessary to catch or declare any exceptions.
Concise	In comparison to Kotlin, the code is not as concise.	It decreases the amount of boilerplate code.

(Continued)

Features	Java	Kotlin
Extension Function	If we want to enhance the functionality of an existing class, we must build a new class and inherit from it. As a result, Java does not support the extension function.	Using the extension method, we may add additional functionality to a class.
Widening Conversion	Java enables implicit conversion, which allows us to convert a smaller type to a larger one.	Kotlin does not support implicit conversion. As a result, we cannot transform the smaller type into a larger one.
Code Comparison	The line of code is just doubled in comparison to Kotlin.	It cuts the code line in half.
Community Support	Java has a sizable user community.	Its community is not as large as that of Java.
Casting	In Java, we must identify and execute the casting.	Kotlin enables smart casting, which implies that it automatically detects immutable types and executes implicit casting.
Type Interface	The data type must specify explicitly.	It is not necessary to explicitly indicate the type of variable.
Null Values	We can provide variables with null values, but we can't give objects null values.	We are unable to assign null values to any variables or objects.
Ternary Operator	It's only accessible in Java.	The ternary operator is not supported.
Coroutines Support	Java's multithreading functionality complicates matters since controlling several threads is a demanding process. If we start a long-running demanding task, such as network I/O or CPU activities, Java stops the thread.	We can create many threads (long-running heavy activities) in Kotlin just like we do in Java, but coroutine can stop a thread execution at a certain point without blocking the other threads.
Functional Programming	Java is not a functional programming language.	It is a programming language that combines functional and procedural elements.
Data Classes	If we merely require a class to contain data, we must define getter and setter methods, constructors, and other functions.	In Kotlin, we accomplish the same thing by declaring the class with the keyword Data. The compiler handles the rest of the job, such as constructing constructor, getter, and setter methods for the fields.

IS KOTLIN STILL VALUABLE IN 2022?

Yes, considering the ubiquity of Android and the beginner-friendly nature of Kotlin, it is unquestionably worthwhile to learn in 2022. Learning Kotlin will take us only a few weeks if we are seasoned programmers fluent in Java. Indeed, Kotlin is beginning to outperform several popular languages, including Java. As a result, 2022 is an excellent year to study Kotlin.

The need for mobile developers grows in tandem with the demand for Android apps. Android applications provide a wide range of functions in the digital industry, from data retrieval to security to provide a pleasing user experience.

So, if we want to be a successful Android developer, we need to know Kotlin.

FIVE REASONS WHY WE SHOULD LEARN KOTLIN

We may be wondering why we should learn Kotlin instead of other popular programming languages such as Python, C++, and Java as a programmer. Continue reading to discover the top five reasons Kotlin is worthwhile to learn.

Simple to Understand

Compared to more sophisticated programming languages, Kotlin's grammar is simple to grasp. As a newbie, we will rapidly learn and use it for app development. Kotlin will help us improve our programming abilities if we're seasoned developers. It's straightforward to know if we've worked with Python or Java before.

Ample Resources

If we want to study Kotlin, there are several resources available online. We will have no trouble finding resources to learn Kotlin whether we join in a Bootcamp, sign up for an online course, or self-study through online tutorials.

Community

When it comes to Kotlin, there is a sizable developer community. There are Kotlin communities throughout the world, and these platforms allow professionals of different skill levels to help one another. Furthermore, we will have the opportunity to network with experienced programmers who may give free mentorship.

Prospective Careers

Kotlin developers are in great demand. As Kotlin developers, we will have a wide range of job options accessible to us. We will discover a suitable job opportunity whether we seek work in mobile development, game development, or web development. Furthermore, Kotlin developers may expect to earn between $120,000 and $166,000 per year.

Modern Programming Language

Kotlin is a contemporary programming language that combines object-oriented and functional programming to produce a robust, feature-rich language. Among these benefits include easy syntax, general-purpose application, and cyber security. Furthermore, Kotlin may utilize cross-platform programming.

IS IT WORTHWHILE TO LEARN KOTLIN?

Yes, Kotlin is worth learning, especially if we design mobile apps. Kotlin is an easy-to-learn, flexible programming language that is the leading force in Android app development. Kotlin provides a strong foundation for future potential as Google's preferred programming language. Additionally, Kotlin developers are in great demand.

ADVANTAGES OF KOTLIN FOR MULTIPLATFORM

- **Modular integration:** Kotlin is a SDK rather than a framework is perhaps its most important benefit. This means that teams with existing apps may add a module or relocate a tiny section to explore its possibilities without making a significant commitment. This greatly assists Kotlin in overcoming the most major obstacle to transitioning to a new codebase.

- **Learning curve:** Kotlin is already a popular programming language, and its syntax is strikingly similar to those of other popular languages like Swift and Java. This lowers the barrier to entry and encourages developers to utilize Kotlin as an alternative.

- **A unified codebase for business logic:** By definition, cross-platform development solutions allow us to utilize a single code base across many systems, and Kotlin Multiplatform is no exception. The advantage of adopting Kotlin is that we can share functionality and libraries behind the UI layer. This enables developers to interface with their local environment directly.

- **Native UI experience:** Unlike other cross-platform options like Flutter, Kotlin Multiplatform does not impose a UI on developers. It allows us to use native UI components as if we were creating natively.

- **Improved performance:** By utilizing native components, Kotlin-written apps may perform as well as natively developed apps. This is a widely desired advantage for many developers that want to produce anything more significant than an MVP.

POTENTIAL REASONS TO USE KOTLIN

- **Write Less Code:** Every developer wants to write the least amount of code feasible while still accomplishing the goal. Kotlin lets us write the least amount of code possible, enhancing app speed.

- **Adoption Ease:** It is relatively simple to migrate the existing Android app code to Kotlin.

- **Supports Functional Programming:** Kotlin supports functional programming by allowing developers to simply and swiftly handle tasks.

- **Complete Java Compatibility:** Developers may utilize all Java libraries and frameworks when working in Kotlin.

- **No Runtime Overhead:** There is no runtime overhead since Kotlin has a minimal library, and most of the hard lifting is done during compilation.

- **Multi-Platform Compatibility:** Kotlin is compatible with Android development and with JavaScript and Gradle.

- **Less Error-Prone:** Kotlin is less error-prone because the language itself removes a few frequent coding errors; also, the developer's error risks are lowered when a developer needs to write less code.

HOW COULD KOTLIN BECOME ANDROID'S NEW "PYTHON" FOR MACHINE LEARNING?

If we enjoy programming, creating ML algorithms will sound exciting. First and foremost. Assume you're about to build a Decision Tree Classifier in Python. Why would we do that? We'll most likely use NumPy for array manipulation and Pandas for data processing. Some people may employ scikit-DecisionTreeClassifier. Learn's If we want to build a decision tree from scratch, Python is an excellent choice.

Like other programming languages, Python does not need us to identify a variable's data type explicitly.

It also has many programs available via pip, so save our lives! However, as the number of edge devices around us grows, we will likely have to build ML algorithms for iOS, Android, and Rasberry Pi. Working with arrays on Java might be a pain when it comes to Android. Then there's Kotlin. Android now has a new programming language. It includes simple array manipulation techniques, making it powerful and developer-friendly. Its syntax is also similar to Python's. This section will learn about several fantastic Kotlin functions that can help us in our ML adventure on Android.

1. **Element mapping in an array:** We can utilize Kotlin's map function to do picture categorization or detection on some of our users' photos.

```
// Create File object for images directory
val imageDir = File( "path_to_image_dir" )
.listFiles()
// Map files to the Bitmaps.
val bitmaps = imageDir.map { file ->
BitmapFactory.decodeFile( file.absolutePath ) }
// at once resize them.
val resizedBitmaps = bitmaps.map { image -> Bitmap.
createScaledBitmap( image, 118, 118, false ) }
```

In Java, we'll most likely need to construct a for loop that iterates over the files, converting them to Bitmap one by one.

Various ML methods rely on computing the minimum, maximum, and average of integers contained in an array. We can have the argmax function, as well as the max and min functions in Python, in Kotlin.

```
val p1 = floatArrayOf( 8f, 2f, 2.3f, 0.001f )
// Compute-mean
val mean = p1.average()
// Compute sum of all the elements
val sum = p1.sum()

// Compute-min/max
val max = p1.max()
```

```
val min = p1.min()
// Normalize values
val normalizedValues = p1.map { ai -> ( ai - min )
/ max }
// Index of max element ( useful in classification )
val argmax = p1.indexOf( max )
// Filter elements greater than 2
p1.filter { xi -> xi > 2f }
// Use the map() successively to normalize multi
dim arrays
// An image ( W * H * 3 ) could be an example
val multiDimArray = arrayOf(
    arrayOf(
        floatArrayOf( 1f,   2f,   3f )
    ),
    arrayOf(
        floatArrayOf( 4f,   5f,   6f )
    ),
    arrayOf(
        floatArrayOf( 9f,  10f,   2f )
    )
)
val normalizedMultiDimArray = multiDimArray.map {
        column -> column.map {
        row -> row.map {
        element -> element / 255f
} } }
```

2. **Array filtering:** For example, in a decision tree method, the probability of a certain element in an array is required for computing information gain. Similarly, term frequencies and IDFs must be calculated for TF-IDF. The count and filter methods in Kotlin make it easy to work with probabilities and frequencies of array elements.

```
val labels = arrayOf("Rainy",   "Cloudy",
"Thunder",  "Cloudy",  "Rainy" )
// Compute the probability of "Rainy"
val p1 = labels.count { it == "Rainy" } / labels.
size
// Compute probabilities of all the elements
val p1Labels = labels.map {
```

```
        label -> labels.count { it == label } /
labels.size
}
```

Filtering is also beneficial when preparing data for an NLP model. The filter function might use to do tokenization, stop word removal, and punctuation tasks.

```
// s1 -> The sentence provided by the user
val sentence = s1.trim().toLowerCase()
// Tokenize sentences
var tokens = sentence.split( " " )
// Remove all the punctuation/numbers
tokens = tokens.map { Regex("[^A-Za-z0-9 ]").
replace( it,  "") }
// Remove all the stopwords
tokens = tokens.filterNot { !englishStopWords.
contains( it.trim() ) }
// Filter the empty tokens
tokens = tokens.filter { it.trim().isNotBlank() }
```

An example of creating a (word, frequency) vocabulary and storing it as a HashMap<String,Int>

```
// Build ( word,  frequency ) table given 'words'
fun buildVocabs( words : Array<String> ) :
HashMap<String,Int> {
    val sortedWords = words.toSet()
    val vocabs = HashMap<String,Int>()
    for ( word in sortedWords ){
        vocabs[word] = words.count { it.equals(
word ) }
    }
    return vocabs
}
```

3. **Coroutines in Kotlin:** Kotlin Coroutines can assist us in running ML models on background threads, resulting in a superior user experience. We'll want to execute it asynchronously if we're using a model to improve an image's resolution (super-resolution).

WHY SHOULD WE USE KOTLIN INSTEAD OF JAVA?

It is a compiled language, so we must compile the code before running it. The source code is kept in a file with the extension .kt. Developers prefer Kotlin over Java because it offers less coding risks. The language enables developers to write less code while maintaining project quality.

Kotlin developers are in great demand in the IT industry. Almost every mobile app development business prefers to hire developers to create apps in Kotlin for Android. These businesses strive to capitalize on every available opportunity. The need for Kotlin developers is really strong.

To become a Kotlin developer, we must have the following skills:

- We must be familiar with OOPs principles such as design patterns, extension functions, invariant arrays, etc.

- It is necessary to be familiar with the Android features such as APIs, Android Studio, Flutter, and the NDK.

- It is required to have a basic grasp of XML files, JSON, and online services.

- It is necessary to be familiar with multithreading, navigation components, data binding libraries, cloud services, and automated testing.

- Data structure and algorithm knowledge are also required.

WHY DID GOOGLE SEEK SOMETHING MORE ADVANCED THAN JAVA?

To begin with, Google does not want to eliminate the entire Java ecosystem, though it wishes it could. However, it has always sought better alternatives to the Java programming language for android app development.

It may have started in 2010, when Oracle, the new owner of Sun Microsystems, sued Google for stealing the Java API used to construct the Android operating system. The nine-year-old court struggle has taken many twists and turns. Google's most effective defense in the lawsuit was that the APIs were not copyrighted. On the other hand, Oracle argued that they were not and that Google did not license the Java API before utilizing it.

This does not imply that we will lose Android if Oracle wins the case because Google avoided such a scenario by creating all versions of Android, beginning with Android 7.0 (Nougat) with an open-sourced version of the JDK (Java Development Kit).

Nonetheless, Google has long desired to distance itself from the eco-system. Java is a nearly ubiquitous programming language. But, whether android developers detest it or avoid it, the need for Java persists in some form or another. That is why they needed to discover something that complements rather than replaces Java. A language that is more enjoyable to use than Java and is compatible with it, Kotlin was born.

WHY DID GOOGLE CHOOSE KOTLIN AS THE PREFERRED LANGUAGE FOR DEVELOPING ANDROID APPS?

Kotlin isn't a brand-new language created by Google. It is an open-source language developed in 2011 by JetBrains (a well-known Google development partner). But it didn't get the respect it deserved until Google announced Kotlin, along with Java and C++, as an official language for Android app development at its annual I/O event in 2017.

There has been no turning back for the Kotlin since then. What made the meal even better was that Kotlin received full support from the IDE. This was because JetBrains, the firm responsible for Kotlin, also created the core of Android Studio, namely IntelliJ.

Google and JetBrains' involvement and support for Kotlin guaranteed that Android developers could simply transition from Java to Kotlin. Soon after, Android developers began to recognize the advantages of Kotlin over Java for Android app development, including the following:

• In contrast to the verbosity of Java coding, developers may write succinct yet expressive code.

• The NullPointerException was a big source of contention for Java for Android app development. Kotlin addresses this issue by requiring developers to allow null variables, eliminating any potential difficulties expressly.

• It's difficult for developers to switch to new languages, mainly when writing Android apps in an old language like Java. The Android Studio's Java to Kotlin conversion functionality, allowing developers to transform Java code directly into Kotlin, quickly fixed this issue.

These and other significant features finally led to 50 percent of Professional Android developers switching to Kotlin and embracing the transition. Kotlin is one of today's most popular programming languages, according to the findings.

THE FUTURE OF ANDROID APP DEVELOPMENT USING KOTLIN

Google's intention in releasing Kotlin and pushing its adoption in Android app development is not to replace Java. But it just requires something to accompany the former.

Kotlin runs on the JVM; therefore, the new programming language won't make much of a difference for end-users. As a result, comparing Kotlin to Java, as has recently occurred, is not even fair. Java is Kotlin. We can have our Kotlin code translated to Java, and your Kotlin code will still execute on the JVM.

However, it is undeniable that Kotlin is one of the fastest developing programming languages. Kotlin has risen to the top 50 programming languages in the TIOBE ranking in just six years. This demonstrates Kotlin's promise as a fun, productive programming language for producing Android apps.

Is this increase sustainable, or will another future language surpass Kotlin? For the time being, it appears that such a situation is unlikely. On the other hand, Oracle understands the importance of Java in android app development and beyond. So it shouldn't be too difficult for them to launch Java with a few enhancements in its next version to compete with Kotlin.

To sum, Kotlin became Google's recommended mobile app development language because Google wanted it to! Kotlin was created to be superior to Java. It was intended to be a rung on which android app development firms might climb to move away from Java and onto something purportedly superior.

KOTLIN FEATURES SURVEY 2021 RESULTS

The Most Desired Characteristics

The following are the top three features:

- Types of multicatch and union (45 percent)

- Literals from a collection (32 percent)

- Extension functions and attributes have many recipients (30 percent)

The features in the fourth through ninth positions on the list, on the other hand, received a lot of support from the community. The six features at the bottom of the list garnered much less votes. Some of them, such as Lateinit for nullable and basic types and Overloadable bitwise operators like I and &, ended up in the top three most disliked features.

Because there are other ways to implement the Multicatch and union types functionality, we asked the Kotlin community to vote on which of the two options they preferred:

- Eighty-seven percent voted in favor of union types, which would allow you to write a function that returns one of the available values without introducing a separate ParseResult type at all.

- Because current Java APIs don't exploit exceptions as extensively as they used to, 13 percent proposed that we make no special adjustments for exceptions (and older ones will eventually supersede). They would prefer a succinct enum-like syntax for defining sealed classes, making it easier to build Kotlin-style error-returning methods.

EXAMPLES IN KOTLIN FOR MULTIPLATFORM

Apps for Android and iOS

One of the most common Kotlin Multiplatform use cases is code sharing between mobile platforms. We may use Kotlin Multiplatform Mobile to create cross-platform mobile apps and share common code between Android and iOS, such as business logic and connections.

Full-Stack Web Apps

A linked application where the logic may reuse on both the server and the client-side running in the browser is another example where code sharing may be advantageous. Kotlin Multiplatform also handles this.

Cross-Platform Libraries

Library writers can also benefit from Kotlin Multiplatform. We may build a multiplatform library with shared code and platform-specific implementations for the JVM, JS, and Native platforms. Once released, a multiplatform library can utilize as a dependency in other cross-platform applications.

Mobile and Web Applications Use the Same Code

Sharing same code across Android, iOS, and web apps is another prominent use case for Kotlin Multiplatform. It decreases the amount of business logic coded by frontend developers and aids in effectively implementing products by reducing coding and testing requirements.

Cheat Sheet

IN THIS CHAPTER

➤ Kotlin cheat sheet

➤ Interoperability with Java

In this section, we provide some useful Kotlin code snippets, as well as discuss its interoperability with Java.

BASICS

"Hello, Everyone" program

```
fun main(args: Array<String>) {
 println("Hello, Everyone")
}
```

Declaring function

```
fun sum(x: Int, y: Int): Int {
    return x + y
}
```

Single-expression function

```
fun sum(x: Int, y: Int) = x + y
```

Declaring variables

```
val name = "Mehak" // Can't be changed
var age = 12       // Can be changed
age++
```

DOI: 10.1201/9781003308447-9

Variables with nullable types

```
var name: String? = null
val length: Int
length = name?.length? : 0
// length, or 0 if the name is null
length = name?.length? : return
// length, or return when the name is null
length = name?.length? : throw Error()
// length, or throw error when the name is null
```

CONTROL STRUCTURES

If as an expression

```
fun bigger(x: Int, y: Int) = if (x > y) x else y
```

For loop

```
val list = listOf("X", "Y", "Z")
for (element in list) {
    println(element)
}
```

When expression

```
fun numberTypeName(a: Number) = when(a) { 0 -> "Zero"
// Equality check
in 1..5 -> "Five or less"        // Range check
6, 7, 8 -> "Six to eight"        // Multiple-values
is Byte -> "Byte"                // Type check
  else -> "Some number"
}
```

When expression with predicates

```
fun signAsString(a: Int)= when {
 a < 0 -> "Negative"
    a == 0 -> "Zero"
    else -> "Positive"
}
```

CLASSES

Primary constructor

val declares read-only property, var mutable one

```
class Persons(val names: String, var ages: Int)
// names is read-only, ages is mutable
```

Inheritance

```
open class Persons(val names: String) {
    open fun hello() = "Hello, My name is: $name"
      // Final by default so, we need open
}
class PolishPersons(name: String) : Persons(names) {
    override fun hello() = "Rzeiń robry, kestem $names"
}
```

Properties with assessors

```
class Persons(var names: String, var surnames: String)
{
    var fullName: String
      get() = "$names $surnames" set(values) {
          val (first, rest) = values.split(" ",
limit = 2)
          names = first
          surnames = rest
      }
}
```

Data classes

```
data class Persons(val names: String, var ages: Int)
val mike = Persons("Kiran", 29)
```

Modifier data adds

1. toString that displays all the primary constructor properties

   ```
   print(kiran.toString()) // Person(name=Kiran, age=29)
   ```

2. equals that compares all the primary constructor properties

```
print(kiran == Persons("Kiran", 29)) // True
print(kiran == Persons("Kiran", 24)) // False
```

3. hashCode that is based on all the primary constructor properties

```
val hash = kiran.hashCode()
print(hash == Persons("Kiran", 23).hashCode()) // True
print(hash == Persons("Kiran", 21).hashCode())
// False
```

4. component1, component2 etc. that allows the deconstruction

```
val (names, ages) = kiran print("$names $ages")
// Kiran 29
```

5. copy that returns copy of object with the concrete properties changed

```
val drake = kiran.copy(name = "Drake")
```

COLLECTION LITERALS

```
listOf(1,5,2,4) // List
<Int> mutableListOf(1,5,2,4) // MutableList<Int>

setOf("X", "Y", "Z") // Set<String>
mutableSetOf("X", "Y", "Z") // MutableSet<String>

arrayOf('x', 'y', 'z') // Array<Char>

mapOf(1 to "X", 2 to "Y") // Map<Int, String>
mutableMapOf(1 to "X", 2 to "Y")
// MutableMap<Int, String> sequenceOf(4,6,2,1)
// Sequence<Int>

1 to "X" // Pair<Int, String>

List(4) { it * 2 } // List<Int>
generateSequence(4) { it + 2 } // Sequence<Int>
```

COLLECTION PROCESSING

```
students
    .filter { it.passing && it.averageGrade > 5.0 }
    // Only passing-students
```

```
.sortedByDescending { it.averageGrade }
// Starting from ones with the biggest grades
.take(10) // Take-first 10
.sortedWith(compareBy({ it.surnames }, { it.names }))
// Sort by surnames and then names

generateSequence(0) { it + 1 }
// Infinitive sequence of the next numbers starting on 0
    .filter { it % 2 == 0 } // Keep even only
    .map { it * 3 } // Triple-every one
    .take(100) // Take-first 100
    .average() // Count-average
```

Most important functions for collection processing

```
val l = listOf(11,22,33,44)
filter - returns only the elements matched by
predicate
 l.filter { it % 2 == 0 }
map - returns elements after the transformation l.map
{ it * 2 }
flatMap - returns elements yielded from the results of
trans.
l.flatMap { listOf(it, it + 10) }
fold/reduce - accumulates-elements
l.fold(0.0) { acc, i -> acc + i }
l.reduce { acc, i -> acc * i }
forEach/onEach - performs an action on every element
l.forEach { print(it) }
l.onEach { print(it) }

partition - splits into the pair of lists
val (even, odd) = l.partition { it % 2 == 0 }
print(even)
print(odd)
min/max/minBy/maxBy
l.min()
l.minBy { -it }
l.max()
l.maxBy { -it }
l.first { it % 2 == 0 }
count - count the elements matched by predicate
l.count { it % 2 == 0 }
```

```
sorted/sortedBy - returns the sorted collection
listOf(2,3,1,4).sorted()
l.sortedBy { it % 2 }
groupBy - group elements on the collection by key
l.groupBy { it % 2 }
distinct/distinctBy - returns unique elements only
 listOf(1,1,2,2).distinct()
```

```
Mutable vs immutable collection processing functions
val list = mutableListOf(3,4,2,1)
val sortedResult = list.sorted() // Returns sorted
println(sortedResult)
println(list)
val sortResult = list.sort() // Sorts mutable
collection println(sortResult) // kotlin.Unit
println(list)
```

EXTENSION FUNCTIONS TO ANY OBJECT

```
val dialog = Dialog().apply {
 title = "Dialog-title"
onClick { print("Click") }
 }
```

Returns Reference to Receiver	Receiver	Result of Lambda
it	also	let
this	apply	run/with

FUNCTIONS

Function types

```
( )->Unit - takes no-arguments and returns nothing
(Unit).
(Int, Int)->Int - takes two-arguments of type Int and
returns Int.
(( )->Unit)->Int - takes the another function and
returns Int.
(Int)->( )->Unit - takes the argument of type Int
and returns function.
```

Function literals

```
val add: (Int, Int) -> Int = { x, y -> x + y }
// Simple lambda-expression
  val printAndDouble: (Int) -> Int = {
     println(it)
     // When the single-parameter, we can reference it
using 'it'
     it * 2 // In lambda, last expression is returned
}

// Anonymous function alternative
val printAndDoubleFun: (Int) -> Int = fun(x: Int): Int {
println(x) // Single argument can't be referenced by 'it'
return x * 2 // Needs return like any function
}
val x = printAndDouble(10) // 10
print(x) // 20
```

Extension functions

```
fun Int.isEven() = this % 2 == 0
print(2.isEven()) // true
fun List<Int>.average() = 1.0 * sum()
print(listOf(1, 2, 3, 4).average())
```

DELEGATES

```
Lazy - calculates the value before first usage
val x by lazy { print("init "); 10 }
print(x) // Prints: init 10
print(x) // Prints: 10

notNull - returns the last setted value or throws an
error if no value has been set

observable/vetoable - calls the function every time
value changes. In vetoable function also decides if
the new value should be set.

var name by observable("Unset") { r, old, new ->
 println("${r.name} changed $old -> $new")
 }
```

```
name = "Mehak"
// Prints: name changed Unset -> Mehak

Map/MutableMap - finds the value on map by property
name
val map = mapOf("a" to 10) val a by map
print(a) // Prints: 10
```

VISIBILITY MODIFIERS

Modifier	Class members	Top-level
Public	Visible-everywhere	Visible-everywhere
Private	Visible only in same class	Visible only in same class
Protected	Visible only in same class and subclasses	Not-allowed
Internal	Visible in the same module if the class is accessible	Visible in the same module

VARIANCE MODIFIERS

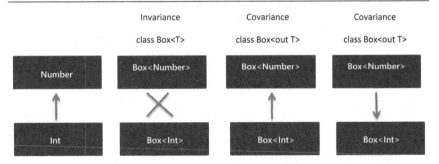

Interoperability of Java

Kotlin code is entirely interchangeable with Java code. Existing Java code can readily call from Kotlin code, and Kotlin code may also call usually from Java code.

Calling Java Code from the Kotlin

Invoking a Java void function from a Kotlin file.

When you call java code from Kotlin, and the return type is void, it will return Unit in the Kotlin file. If you wish to return that value, the Kotlin compiler will allocate it to a Kotlin file and return Unit. As an example:

Kotlin code: (My_Kotlin_File.kt)

```
fun main(args: Array<String>) {
val sum= My_Java_Class.add(15, 20)
println("printing sum inside Kotlin: "+sum)
 }
```

Java code: (My_Java_Class.java)

```
public class My_Java_Class {
    public static void main(String[] args){
    }
    public static void add(int x,int y){
int result = x + y;
System.out.println("printing inside the Java class :
"+result);
    }
}
```

Invoking the Java int Function from a Kotlin Code
When a java code of int or another type (rather than void) is called from
a Kotlin file, the result is returned in the same kinds. Calling an area()
method of a Java class from a Kotlin file, for example, produces an int result.

Kotlin code: (My_Kotlin_File.kt)

```
fun main(args: Array<String>) {
val area: Int = MyJavaClass.area(13, 24)
println("printing area from java insideKotlin file:
"+area)
}
```

Java code: (My_Java_Class.java)

```
public class My_Java_Class {
    public static void main(String[] args){
    }
    public static int area(int l, int a){
int result = l * a;
        return result;
    }
}
```

Kotlin Code Invokes a Java Class Included within the Package
If we want to call Java programs from Kotlin files in separate packages, we must import the package name together with the Java class within the Kotlin file.

For example, a Java class My_Java_Class.java is contained within the package myjavapackage, and a Kotlin file My_Kotlin_File.kt is included within the package mykotlinpackage. In this example, importing myjava-package is required when invoking Java code from a Kotlin file. My_Java_Class is included within a Kotlin file.

Kotlin code: (My_Kotlin_File.kt)

```
package mykotlinpackage
import myjavapackage.My_Java_Class
fun main(args: Array<String>) {
val area: Int = My_Java_Class.area(3, 4)
println("printing area from java inside Kotlin: "+area)
}
```

Java code: (My_Java_Class.java)

```
package myjavapackage;
public class My_Java_Class {
    public static void main(String[] args){
    }
    public static int area(int l, int a){
int result = l * a;
        return result;
    }
}
```

Kotlin Code Access the Java Getter and Setter
We can use Java classes' getter and setter capabilities since Kotlin is totally interoperable with Java (or POJO class). For example, in Java class MyJava.java, add a getter and setter function with the attributes firstNames and lastNames. These attributes are available from the Kotlin file My_Kotlin.kt via the My_Java.java object created in the Kotlin file.

Java code: (My_Java.java)

```
public class My_Java{
    protected String firstNames;
    protected String lastNames;
    public String getfirstNames() {
        return firstNames;
```

```
    }
    public void setfirstNames(String firstNames) {
this.firstNames = firstNames;
    }
    public String getlastNames() {
        return lastNames;
    }
    public void setlastNames(String lastNames) {
this.lastNames = lastNames;
    }
}
```

Kotlin code: (My_Kotlin.kt)

```
fun main(args: Array<String>) {
val myJava = My_Java()

myJava.lastNames = "Sharma"
myJava.setfirstNames("Karan")
println("accessing the value using property: "+myJava.
firstNames)
println("accessing the value using property: "+myJava.
lastNames)
println("accessing the value using method: "+myJava.
getfirstNames())
println("accessing the value using method: "+myJava.
getlastNames())
}
```

Kotlin Code Access Java Array

We may simply invoke a Java class method that accepts an array as an argument from the Kotlin code. Create a method sumValue() in Java class My_Java.java that accepts an array element as an argument, calculates addition, and returns the result. This function is invoked from the Kotlin file My_Kotlin.kt with an array as an argument.

Java code: (My_Java.java)

```
public class MyJava {
    public intsumValues(int[] nums) {
int result = 0;
        for (int x:nums) {
            result+=x;
```

```
        }
        return result;
    }
}
```

Kotlin code: (My_Kotlin.kt)

```
fun main(args: Array<String>){
val myJava = My_Java()
val numArray = intArrayOf(01, 02, 03,04,05)
val sum = myJava.sumValues(numArray)
println(sum)
}
```

Kotlin Code Access Java Varargs

We may give any number of arguments to a method using the Java varargs feature. The ellipsis, i.e., three dots (…) following the data type, is used to specify the varargs argument in Java.

When utilizing the varargs option, keep the following considerations in mind:

- A method has just one varargs parameter.

- Varargs argument must come at the end of the argument.

We must use the spread operator * to pass the array while accessing Java varargs from Kotlin; we must use the spread operator *.

Let's look at an example of a Java function that utilizes an int type vararrgs and is called from a Kotlin file.

Java code: (My_Java.java)

```
public class My_Java {
    public void display(int... values) {
        for (int s1 : values) {
System.out.println(s1);
        }
    }
}
```

Kotlin code: (My_Kotlin.kt)

```
fun main(args: Array<String>){
val myJava = My_Java()
```

```
val array = intArrayOf(0, 1, 2, 3)
myJava.display(*array)
}
```

Let's look at another example that accepts two parameters in a Java function and utilizes them as String and int type varargs called from a Kotlin code.

Java code: (My_Java.java)

```
public class My_Java {
    public void display(String message,int... values)
{
System.out.println("string is " + message);
        for (int s1 : values) {
System.out.println(s1);
        }
    }
}
```

Kotlin code: (My_Kotlin.kt)

```
fun main(args: Array<String>){
val myJava = My_Java()
val array = intArrayOf(0, 1, 2, 3)
myJava.display("Hello",*array)
}
```

Kotlin and Java Mapped Types

Kotlin and Java types are mapped differently, yet they are mapped to the same types. Mapping of these types is only relevant at build time; run time stays unaltered.

Java primitive types are converted to Kotlin types.

Java type	Kotlin type
int	kotlin.Int
Byte	kotlin.Byte
Short	kotlin.Short
Char	kotlin.Char
Double	kotlin.Double
Long	kotlin.Long
Boolean	kotlin.Boolean

Java's non-primitive types are converted to Kotlin types.

Java type	Kotlin type
java.lang.Object	kotlin.Any!
java.lang.Comparable	kotlin.Comparable!
java.lang.Cloneable	kotlin.Cloneable!
java.lang.Enum	kotlin.Enum!
java.lang.Deprecated	kotlin.Deprecated!
java.lang.CharSequence	kotlin.CharSequence!
java.lang.String	kotlin.String!
java.lang.Annotation	kotlin.Annotation!
java.lang.Number	kotlin.Number!
java.lang.Throwable	kotlin.Throwable!

Java's boxed primitive types to their nullable equivalents Types of Kotlin.

Java type	Kotlin type
java.lang.Byte	kotlin.Byte?
java.lang.Integer	kotlin.Int?
java.lang.Long	kotlin.Long?
java.lang.Short	kotlin.Short?
java.lang.Character	kotlin.Char?
java.lang.Float	kotlin.Float?
java.lang.Boolean	kotlin.Boolean?
java.lang.Double	kotlin.Double?

Java collection types are converted to read-only or mutable Kotlin types.

Java type	Kotlin read-only type	Kotlin mutable type
Iterable<T>	Iterable<T>	MutableIterable<T>
Iterator<T>	Iterator<T>	MutableIterator<T>
Collection<T>	Collection<T>	MutableCollection<T>
List<T>	MutableList<T>	MutableList<T>
ListIterator<T>	ListIterator<T>	MutableListIterator<T>
Set<T>	MutableSet<T>	MutableSet<T>
Map<K, V>	Map<K, V>	MutableMap<K, V>
Map.Entry<K, V>	Map.Entry<K, V>	MutableMap.MutableEntry<K, V>

Java Interoperability: Calling Kotlin Code from the Java

Because Kotlin is compatible with the Java programming language; the Java-coded program may readily invoke Kotlin. Similarly, Kotlin code is called from Java code.

Before we get into how to call Kotlin code from Java code, let's look at how a Kotlin file looks inside.

The Internal Representation of a Basic Kotlin Program
In a My_Kotlin.kt file, let's write a basic main function:

```
fun main(args: Array<String>){
//code..
}
fun area(l: Int,a: Int):Int{
    return l*a
}
```

After building the previously mentioned Kotlin file My_Kotlin.kt, which internally looks like:

```
public class My_KotlinKt{
public static void main(String[] args){
                //code..
        }
        public static int area(int l, int a){
                return l*a;
        }
}
```

Internally, the Kotlin compiler inserts a wrapper class with the name My_KotlinKt. The Kotlin file My_Kotlin.kt gets transformed to My_KotlinKt default and made public. The high-level function's default modifier is public, and the process is converted to static by default. Because the return type of My_Kotlin.kt is Unit, it is changed to void in My_KotlinKt.

Calling Kotlin Code from the Java Code
Kotlin code: (My_Kotlin.kt)

```
fun main(args: Array<String>){
//code...
}
fun area(l: Int,a: Int):Int{
    return l*a
}
```

Java code: My_Java.java

```
public class My_Java {
    public static void main(String[] args) {
int area = My_KotlinKt.area(14,25);
System.out.print("printing area inside the Java class
returning from Kotlin file: "+area);
    }
}
```

Java Code Invokes the Kotlin File Included within the Package
If we want to call the Kotlin code from a Java class presents in distinct packages, we must import the package name with the Kotlin file name within the Java class and then call the Kotlin code from the Java class. Another option is to provide the complete path as the package name. KotlinFileKt.methodName().

Kotlin code: (My_Kotlin.kt)

```
package mykotlinpackage
fun main(args: Array<String>) {
}
fun area(l: Int,a: Int):Int{
      return l*a
}
```

Java code: My_Java.java

```
package myjavapackage;
import mykotlinpackage.MyKotlinFileKt;
public class My_JavaClass {
    public static void main(String[] args){
int area = My_KotlinKt.area(4,5);
System.out.println("printing area inside the Java
class returning from Kotlin file: "+area);
    }
}
```

Using the Annotation @JvmName, We May Change the Name of a Kotlin File
The @JvmName annotation may modify the name of a Kotlin file as the wrapper class name.

Kotlin code: (My_Kotlin.kt)

Create a Kotlin program and add the annotation @file: JvmName("My_Kotlin_FileName") at the start. Following the compilation of Kotlin code, the file name is changed to the name (specified _FileName). We must utilize the file name My_Kotlin_FileName when accessing the code of My_Kotlin.kt.

```
@file: JvmName("My_Kotlin_FileName")
package mykotlinpackage
fun main(args: Array<String>) {
}
fun area(l: Int,a: Int):Int{
        return l*a
}
```

Java code: My_Java.java

```
package myjavapackage;
import mykotlinpackage.My_Kotlin_FileName;
public class My_JavaClass {
    public static void main(String[] args){
int area = My_Kotlin_FileName.area(14,25);
System.out.println("printing area inside the Java
class returning from Kotlin file: "+area);
    }
}
```

Using @JvmMultifileClass to Invoke a Method from Many Files That Have the Same Generated Java Class Name

If multiple Kotlin files have the same produced Java file name using the @JvmName annotation, the call from Java file will generally fail. However, the Kotlin compiler outputs a single Java façade class that contains the produced Java file and all declarations from files with the same names. We utilize the @JvmMultifileClass annotation in all files to activate this generation façade.

Kotlin code: (My_Kotlin1.kt)

```
@file: JvmName("My_Kotlin_FileName")
@file:JvmMultifileClass
package mykotlinpackage
```

```
fun main(args: Array<String>) {
}
fun area(l: Int,a: Int):Int{
    return l*a
}
```

Kotlin code: (My_Kotlin2.kt)

```
@file: JvmName("MyKotlinFileName")
@file:JvmMultifileClass
package mykotlinpackage
fun volume(l: Int,b: Int,h: Int):Int{
    return l*b*h
}
```

Java code: (My_Java.java)

```
package myjavapackage;
import mykotlinpackage.My_Kotlin_FileName;
public class My_JavaClass {
    public static void main(String[] args){
int area = My_Kotlin_FileName.area(14,25);
System.out.println("printing area inside the Java
class returning from Kotlin file: "+area);
int vol = My_Kotlin_FileName.volume(14,5,36);
System.out.println("printing volume inside the Java
class returning from Kotlin file: "+vol);
    }
}
```

Property Access in Kotlin Is Access Using the Const Modifier
Kotlin properties tagged with the const modifier at the top level and in classes are translated to static fields in Java. These attributes are accessed as static properties from the Java file. As an example:

Kotlin code: (My_Kotlin2.kt)

```
constval MAX = 189
object Obj {
constval CONST = 1
}
```

```
class D {
    companion object {
constval VERSION = 8
    }
}
```

Java code: (My_Java.java)

```
public class My_Java {
    public static void main(String[] args) {
int c1 = Obj.CONST;
int m1 = My_KotlinKt.MAX;
int v1 = D.VERSION;
System.out.println("const "+c1+"\nmax "+m1+"\nversion
"+v1);
    }
}
```

In this chapter, we learned about Kotlin cheat sheets and Java interoperability.

Bibliography

Agrawal, S. (2020, October 26). *The Nothing Type : Kotlin*. Suneet Agrawal; agrawalsuneet.github.io. https://agrawalsuneet.github.io/blogs/the-nothing-type-kotlin/

Akhin, M., & Belyaev, M. (n.d.). *Kotlin language specification*. Kotlin Language Specification; kotlinlang.org. Retrieved July 11, 2022, from https://kotlinlang .org/spec/introduction.html

Baeldung. (2021, February 8). *Kotlin-Java Interop*. Kotlin Java Interoperability. https://www.baeldung.com/kotlin/java-interoperability

Baeldung. (2022, May 31). *Baeldung Kotlin*. Extension Functions in Kotlin. https:// www.baeldung.com/kotlin/extension-methods

Balauag, T. (2019, May 17). *Idiomatic Kotlin: Local functions | by Tompee Balauag | Familiar Android | Medium*. Medium; medium.com. https://medium.com/ tompee/idiomatic-kotlin-local-functions-4421f86ac864

Basic types | Kotlin. (2022, July 8). Kotlin Help; kotlinlang.org. https://kotlinlang. org/docs/basic-types.html

Build Your First Android App in Kotlin | Android Developers. (n.d.). Android Developers; developer.android.com. Retrieved July 11, 2022, from https:// developer.android.com/codelabs/build-your-first-android-app-kotlin#8

Collections overview | Kotlin. (2022, July 8). Kotlin Help; kotlinlang.org. https:// kotlinlang.org/docs/collections-overview.html#collection-types

Control Flow Statements in Kotlin. (n.d.). CherCherTech; chercher.tech. Retrieved July 11, 2022, from https://chercher.tech/kotlin/control-flow-kotlin

Dehghani, A. (2021, October 25). *Baeldung Kotlin*. Operator Overloading in Kotlin. https://www.baeldung.com/kotlin/operator-overloading

Destructuring Declarations in Kotlin | raywenderlich.com. (n.d.). Destructuring Declarations in Kotlin | Raywenderlich.Com; www.raywenderlich.com. Retrieved July 11, 2022, from https://www.raywenderlich.com/22178807-destructuring-declarations-in-kotlin

Ebel, N. (2021, June 22). *A complete guide to Kotlin lambda expressions – LogRocket Blog*. LogRocket Blog; blog.logrocket.com. https://blog.logrocket. com/a-complete-guide-to-kotlin-lambda-expressions/

EPS Software Corp., Wei-Meng Lee, C. M. (n.d.). *Introduction to Kotlin*. Introduction to Kotlin; www.codemag.com. Retrieved July 11, 2022, from https://www.codemag.com/Article/1907061/Introduction-to-Kotlin

Equality checks in Kotlin (Difference between "==" and "===" Operators). (n.d.). Equality Checks in Kotlin (Difference between "==" and "===" Operators); www.tutorialspoint.com. Retrieved July 11, 2022, from https://www.tutorialspoint.com/equality-checks-in-kotlin-difference-between-and-operators

Equality evaluation in Kotlin – GeeksforGeeks. (2019, August 2). GeeksforGeeks; www.geeksforgeeks.org.https://www.geeksforgeeks.org/equality-evaluation-in-kotlin/#:~:text=The%20referential%20equality%20in%20Kotlin,the%20same%20location%20in%20memory

Exceptions | Kotlin. (2022, July 8). Kotlin Help; kotlinlang.org. https://kotlinlang.org/docs/exceptions.html

Extensions | Kotlin. (2022, July 8). Kotlin Help; kotlinlang.org. https://kotlinlang.org/docs/extensions.html#extensions-are-resolved-statically

Generics & Enums. (2017, June 28). Kotlin Discussions; discuss.kotlinlang.org. https://discuss.kotlinlang.org/t/generics-enums/3538

Get started with Kotlin/Native in IntelliJ IDEA | Kotlin. (2022, July 8). Kotlin Help; kotlinlang.org. https://kotlinlang.org/docs/native-get-started.html

How to develop your first Android app with Kotlin. (n.d.). Educative: Interactive Courses for Software Developers; www.educative.io. Retrieved July 11, 2022, from https://www.educative.io/blog/android-development-app-kotlin

How to use Kotlin for back end development | Quokka Labs. (2021, August 9). Quokka Labs; quokkalabs.com. https://quokkalabs.com/blog/how-to-use-kotlin-for-back-end-development/#:~:text=As%20we%20know%2C%20Kotlin%20is,is%20used%20front%2Dend%20widely

Introduction to Kotlin – GeeksforGeeks. (2019, May 7). GeeksforGeeks; www.geeksforgeeks.org. https://www.geeksforgeeks.org/introduction-to-kotlin/

Introduction to Kotlin Lambdas: Getting Started | raywenderlich.com. (n.d.). Introduction to Kotlin Lambdas: Getting Started | Raywenderlich.Com; www.raywenderlich.com. Retrieved July 11, 2022, from https://www.raywenderlich.com/2268700-introduction-to-kotlin-lambdas-getting-started

Kaseb, K. (2020, March 10). *Software Development.* Https://Medium.Com/Kayvan-Kaseb/Calling-Java-Codes-from-Kotlin-B74890fb4a78. https://medium.com/kayvan-kaseb/calling-java-codes-from-kotlin-b74890fb4a78

Kotlin – Control Flow. (n.d.). Kotlin – Control Flow; www.tutorialspoint.com. Retrieved July 11, 2022, from https://www.tutorialspoint.com/kotlin/kotlin_control_flow.htm#:~:text=Kotlin%20flow%20control%20statements%20determine,do%20are%20flow%20control%20statements

Kotlin – Destructuring Declarations. (n.d.). Kotlin – Destructuring Declarations; www.tutorialspoint.com. Retrieved July 11, 2022, from https://www.tutorialspoint.com/kotlin/kotlin_destructuring_declarations.htm

Kotlin – Exception Handling. (n.d.). Kotlin – Exception Handling; www.tutorialspoint.com. Retrieved July 11, 2022, from https://www.tutorialspoint.com/kotlin/kotlin_exception_handling.htm

Kotlin – Override Method of Super Class. (n.d.). TutorialKart; www.tutorialkart.com. Retrieved July 11, 2022, from https://www.tutorialkart.com/kotlin/kotlin-override-method/

Kotlin Array – javatpoint. (n.d.). Www.Javatpoint.Com; www.javatpoint.com. Retrieved July 11, 2022, from https://www.javatpoint.com/kotlin-array

Kotlin cheatsheet. (n.d.). Devhints.Io Cheatsheets; devhints.io. Retrieved July 11, 2022, from https://devhints.io/kotlin

Kotlin Class and Object – javatpoint. (n.d.). Www.Javatpoint.Com; www.javatpoint.com. Retrieved July 11, 2022, from https://www.javatpoint.com/kotlin-class-and-object

Kotlin Collections – Studytonight. (n.d.). Kotlin Collections – Studytonight; www.studytonight.com. Retrieved July 11, 2022, from https://www.studytonight.com/kotlin/kotlin-collections

Kotlin Control Flow – if else, for loop, while, range – JournalDev. (2018, February 4). JournalDev; www.journaldev.com. https://www.journaldev.com/18483/kotlin-control-flow-if-else-for-while-range

Kotlin Data Types. (n.d.). Kotlin Data Types; www.w3schools.com. Retrieved July 11, 2022, from https://www.w3schools.com/kotlin/kotlin_data_types.php

Kotlin Environment setup in Windows – bbminfo. (n.d.). Kotlin Environment Setup in Windows – Bbminfo; www.bbminfo.com. Retrieved July 11, 2022, from https://www.bbminfo.com/kotlin/kotlin-environment-setup.php

Kotlin Environment setup in Windows – bbminfo. (n.d.). Kotlin Environment Setup in Windows – Bbminfo; www.bbminfo.com. Retrieved July 11, 2022, from https://www.bbminfo.com/kotlin/kotlin-environment-setup.php

Kotlin Exception Handling | try, catch, throw and finally – GeeksforGeeks. (2019, June 25). GeeksforGeeks; www.geeksforgeeks.org. https://www.geeksforgeeks.org/kotlin-exception-handling-try-catch-throw-and-finally/

Kotlin Hello World – You First Kotlin Program. (n.d.). Kotlin Hello World – You First Kotlin Program; www.programiz.com. Retrieved July 11, 2022, from https://www.programiz.com/kotlin-programming/hello-world

Kotlin Higher-Order Functions – GeeksforGeeks. (2019, June 3). GeeksforGeeks; www.geeksforgeeks.org. https://www.geeksforgeeks.org/kotlin-higher-order-functions/#:~:text=Higher%2DOrder%20Function%20%E2%80%93, pass%20anonymous%20function%20or%20lambdas

Kotlin Lambdas – javatpoint. (n.d.). Www.Javatpoint.Com; www.javatpoint.com. Retrieved July 11, 2022, from https://www.javatpoint.com/kotlin-lambdas#:~:text=Lambda%20is%20a%20function%20which,)%20followed%20by%20%2D%3E%20operator

Kotlin Map – javatpoint. (n.d.). Www.Javatpoint.Com; www.javatpoint.com. Retrieved July 11, 2022, from https://www.javatpoint.com/kotlin-map

Kotlin Map : mapOf() – GeeksforGeeks. (2019, August 9). GeeksforGeeks; www.geeksforgeeks.org. https://www.geeksforgeeks.org/kotlin-map-mapof/

Kotlin Null Safety – GeeksforGeeks. (2019, July 3). GeeksforGeeks; www.geeksforgeeks.org. https://www.geeksforgeeks.org/kotlin-null-safety/#:~:text=Nullable%20and%20Non%2DNullable%20Types,variable%2C%20it%20gives%20compiler%20error

Kotlin Null Safety – Studytonight. (n.d.). Kotlin Null Safety – Studytonight; www.studytonight.com. Retrieved July 11, 2022, from https://www.studytonight.com/kotlin/kotlin-null-safety

Kotlin Nullable Non Nullable Safety – javatpoint. (n.d.). Www.Javatpoint.Com; www.javatpoint.com. Retrieved July 11, 2022, from https://www.javatpoint. com/kotlin-nullable-and-non-nullable-types

Kotlin Operator Overloading – GeeksforGeeks. (2019, August 1). GeeksforGeeks; www.geeksforgeeks.org. https://www.geeksforgeeks.org/kotlin-operator-overloading/

Kotlin Operator Overloading (With Examples). (n.d.). Kotlin Operator Overloading (With Examples); www.programiz.com. Retrieved July 11, 2022, from https://www.programiz.com/kotlin-programming/operator-overloading.

Kotlin Operator Overloading (With Examples). (n.d.). Kotlin Operator Overloading (With Examples); www.programiz.com. Retrieved July 11, 2022, from https://www.programiz.com/kotlin-programming/operator-overloading

Kotlin Regular Expression – GeeksforGeeks. (2019, July 9). GeeksforGeeks; www. geeksforgeeks.org. https://www.geeksforgeeks.org/kotlin-regular-expression/

Kotlin String Operations. (n.d.). TutorialKart; www.tutorialkart.com. Retrieved July 11, 2022, from https://www.tutorialkart.com/kotlin/kotlin-string-operations/

Miu, M. (2020, March 16). *Collections in Kotlin. The subject covered in this new post is... | by Magda Miu | ProAndroidDev*. Medium; proandroiddev.com. https://proandroiddev.com/collections-in-kotlin-a2bd8649f697

Nullable Types and Null Safety in Kotlin | CalliCoder. (2018, February 15). CalliCoder; www.callicoder.com. https://www.callicoder.com/kotlin-nullable-types-null-safety/

Operator overloading | Kotlin. (2022, July 8). Kotlin Help; kotlinlang.org. https:// kotlinlang.org/docs/operator-overloading.html

Operator overloading | Kotlin. (2022, July 8). Kotlin Help; kotlinlang.org. https:// kotlinlang.org/docs/operator-overloading.html

PACKT. (2019, January 24). *Interoperability between Java and Kotlin | Codementor*. Interoperability between Java and Kotlin | Codementor; www.codementor .io. https://www.codementor.io/@packt/interoperability-between-java-and-kotlin-rifmhfip0

Placona, M. (2018, June 12). *Local functions in Kotlin | Real Kotlin*. Real Kotlin; realkotlin.com. https://realkotlin.com/tutorials/2018-06-12-local-functions-in-kotlin/

Placona, M. (2018, June 12). *Local functions in Kotlin | Real Kotlin*. Real Kotlin; realkotlin.com. https://realkotlin.com/tutorials/2018-06-12-local-functions-in-kotlin/

Raj, M. (2019, October 30). *Logging in Kotlin—the right way. Let's see how we typically log... | by Muthu Raj | Medium*. Medium; muthuraj57.medium.com. https:// muthuraj57.medium.com/logging-in-kotlin-the-right-way-d7a357bb0343

Singh, C. (2019, March 8). *Kotlin Class and Objects – Object Oriented Programming (OOP)*. BeginnersBook; beginnersbook.com. https://beginnersbook.com/2019/03/kotlin-class-and-objects-oop/

Soroker, T. (2020, December 6). *Best Practices for Logging in Kotlin – Coralogix.* Coralogix; coralogix.com. https://coralogix.com/blog/best-practices-for-logging-in-kotlin/

Technologies, M. (2021, April 22). *Kotlin vs Python | What are the differences?* Mindmajix; mindmajix.com. https://mindmajix.com/kotlin-vs-python

Index

Printed in the United States
by Baker & Taylor Publisher Services